Office of National Marine Sanctuaries
National Oceanic and Atmospheric Administration

NATIONAL MARINE
SANCTUARIES

Florida Keys
National Marine Sanctuary

CONDITION
REPORT 2011

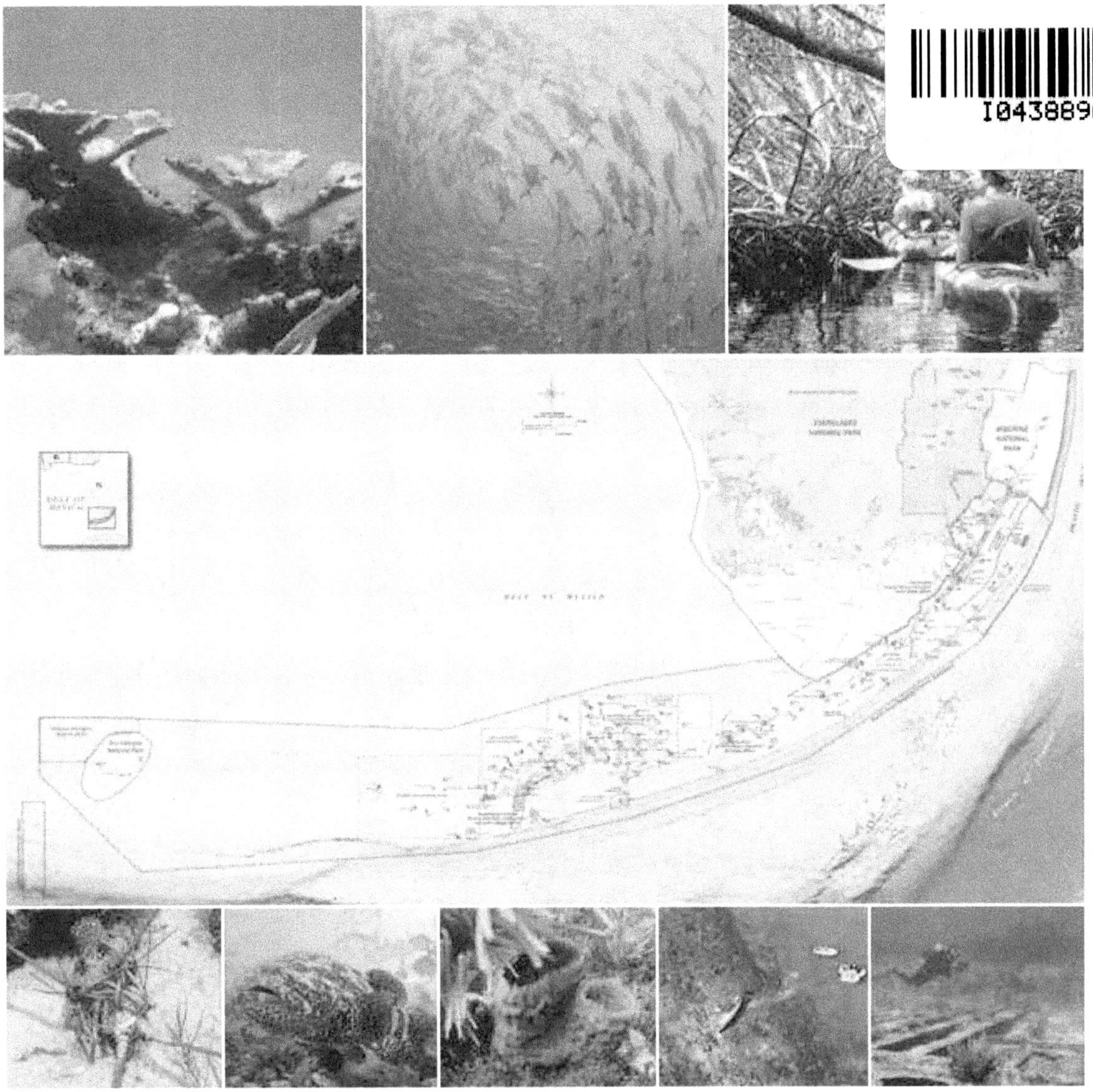

I0438896

September 2011

A Tribute to a Friend and Colleague

This report is dedicated to Dr. Brian Keller, a longtime member of the sanctuary science team. Brian was a sage scientist, patient mentor and committed conservationist, a caring friend and beloved husband who touched countless lives with his science and his humanity over the course of an outstanding 40-year career in the Florida Keys and Caribbean. In the 10 years that Brian worked for NOAA, he was a true leader in the study, management and conservation of the marine ecosystems of the Florida Keys, Gulf of Mexico and Caribbean. In his role as science coordinator with the National Marine Sanctuary System, Brian dedicated himself to finding innovative ways to understand marine ecology and to creating new tools for conserving the ocean world he loved.

Brian came to NOAA in 2000, joining the staff of Florida Keys National Marine Sanctuary as science coordinator after more than two decades of distinguished work in Florida and the Caribbean. During his time with the sanctuary system, he helped lay the foundation for management zones in the Florida Keys and led efforts to measure their effectiveness. He was the architect of the sanctuary's research and monitoring plans, and a report he authored that highlights a decade of success for sanctuary management of the Keys.

Not only was Brian an accomplished scientist and fervent ocean advocate, he was a close friend to many throughout the international science community. He was a man who was knowledgeable and passionate about his work, as well as deeply warm in his personal relationships.

Brian will be greatly missed, and his memory will live on in the hearts and scientific work of his friends and colleagues in the national marine sanctuaries and beyond.

Cover credits:

Map:
Bathymetric Grids provided by Department of Commerce, National Oceanic and Atmospheric Administration, National Ocean Service, Special Projects Office. 1998. Estuarine Bathymetric Digital Elevation Models (30 meter resolution) Derived From Source Hydrographic Survey Soundings Collected by NOAA. Silver Spring, MD. NOAA's Ocean Service, Special Projects (SP)

Photos (from top left, clockwise):
Photo credits (clockwise from top left): Elkhorn coral (Cory Walter, Mote Marine Laboratory), permit fish spawning (Jiangang Luo, Rosenstiel School), kayakers in mangrove forest (NOAA/FKNMS), FKNMS Atlas map (see above credit), diver over Mike's wreck (NOAA/FKNMS), vessel grounding (FWC), Azure Vase Sponge (Geoff Cook), grouper (NOAA/FKNMS), Caribbean spiny lobsters mating (NOAA/FKNMS)

Suggested Citation:

Office of National Marine Sanctuaries. 2011. Florida Keys National Marine Sanctuary Condition Report 2011. U.S. Department of Commerce, National Oceanic and Atmospheric Administration, Office of National Marine Sanctuaries, Silver Spring, MD. 105 pp.

U.S. Department of Commerce
Rebecca M. Blank, Ph.D., Acting Secretary

National Oceanic and Atmospheric Administration
Jane Lubchenco, Ph.D.,
Administrator Under Secretary of
Commerce for Oceans and Atmosphere

National Ocean Service
David M. Kennedy, Assistant Administrator

Office of National Marine Sanctuaries
Daniel J. Basta, Director

National Oceanic and Atmospheric Administration
Office of National Marine Sanctuaries
SSMC4, N/ORM62
1305 East-West Highway
Silver Spring, MD 20910
301-713-3125
http://sanctuaries.noaa.gov

Southeast Atlantic, Gulf of Mexico and Caribbean Region
NOAA Office of National Marine Sanctuaries
33 East Quay Road
Key West, Florida 33040
305-809-4670

Florida Keys National Marine Sanctuary
33 East Quay Rd.
Key West, FL 33040
305-809-4700
http://floridakeys.noaa.gov

Report Preparers:

Florida Keys National Marine Sanctuary:
Scott Donahue, Joanne Delaney, Brenda Altmeier

Southeast Atlantic, Gulf of Mexico, and Caribbean Region:
Billy Causey, Sarah Fangman, Brian D. Keller

Office of National Marine Sanctuaries:
Kathy Broughton, Michelle A. Johnston, Steve Gittings, Vernon R. Leeworthy

Copy Editors: Matt Dozier, Sharon Sirkis

Layout: Matt McIntosh, Jason Lentz

NATIONAL MARINE SANCTUARIES

Table of Contents

Florida Keys National Marine Sanctuary

- *Congressionally designated on Nov. 16, 1990, as a national marine sanctuary*

- *2,896 square nautical miles (9,933 square kilometers)*

- *Surrounds the Florida Keys community of more than 72,000 year-round residents and 3–3.3 million annual visitors. The "functional population" (number of people in the Keys on an average day) ranges from 115,000 to 117,000 during the winter season and 101,000 to 104,000 during the summer season*

- *Utilizes over 900 mooring buoys and boundary buoys to protect corals and seagrass from anchors and guide public use*

- *Approximately 60% of the sanctuary is state of Florida waters, and 40% is federal waters*

- *Shares boundaries with three national parks (Everglades, Biscayne, and Dry Tortugas National Parks)*

- *Overlaps four national wildlife refuges, six state parks, three state aquatic preserves, and two previously designated national marine sanctuaries (Key Largo, designated in 1975, and Looe Key, designated in 1981)*

- *Shares trusteeship of marine resources with the state of Florida, the South Atlantic Fishery Management Council, the Gulf of Mexico Fishery Management Council, and NOAA Fisheries Service*

- *Includes mangrove, seagrass, hardbottom, and coral reef habitats in coastal and oceanic waters*

- *Home to more than 6,000 species of marine life*

- *Approximately 1,700 islands with a combined shoreline length of 1,815 miles (2,920 kilometers)*

- *Marine zones for multiple uses, including 24 highly protected "no-take" areas (6% of the sanctuary)*

- *An "Area to be Avoided" codified into sanctuary regulations prohibits ships larger than 50 meters in length, except in corridors into Key West Harbor*

- *Extensive education and outreach, research, monitoring, and law enforcement programs*

- *Contains an estimated 400 underwater historical sites, 14 of which are listed in the Department of the Interior's National Register of Historic Places*

About this Report

This "condition report" provides a summary of resources in the National Oceanic and Atmospheric Administration's Florida Keys National Marine Sanctuary (sanctuary), pressures on those resources, current conditions and trends, and management responses to the pressures that threaten the integrity of the marine environment. Specifically, the document includes information on the status and trends of water quality, habitat, living resources and maritime archaeological resources, and the human activities that affect them. It presents responses to a set of questions posed to all sanctuaries (Appendix A). Resource status of Florida Keys is rated on a scale from good to poor, and the timelines used for comparison vary from topic to topic. Trends in the status of resources are also reported, and are generally based on observed changes in status over the past five years, unless otherwise specified.

Sanctuary staff consulted with a group of outside experts familiar with the resources and with knowledge of previous and current scientific investigations in the sanctuary. Evaluations of status and trends are based on interpretation of quantitative and, when necessary, non-quantitative assessments, and the observations of scientists, managers and users. The ratings reflect the collective interpretation of the status of local issues of concern among sanctuary program staff and outside experts based on their knowledge and perception of local problems. The final ratings were determined by sanctuary staff. This report has been peer reviewed and complies with the White House Office of Management and Budget's peer review standards as out-

> *Despite a large diversity in habitat types and communities within the Florida Keys sanctuary, a single, sanctuary-wide status and trend rating is given for each question. Although the ratings are generalized for the entire sanctuary, text found in the report section titled "State of Sanctuary Resources" provides a detailed description of the basis for judgment for each question, and may include recognition and description of any conditions that are not consistent with the rating.*

lined in the Final Information Quality Bulletin for Peer Review.

This is the first attempt to describe comprehensively the status, pressures and trends of resources at Florida Keys National Marine Sanctuary. Additionally, the report helps identify gaps in current monitoring efforts, as well as causal factors that may require monitoring and potential remediation in the years to come. The data discussed will enable resource managers and stakeholders to not only acknowledge prior changes in resource status, but will provide guidance for future management challenges.

Summary and Findings

Florida Keys National Marine Sanctuary is one of the largest marine protected areas in the United States, encompassing 2,896 square nautical miles (9,933 square kilometers). It was designated by Congress and exists under federal law, and became effective in state waters with the consent of the state of Florida. Marine zones for multiple uses, including 24 highly protected "no-take" areas (6% of the sanctuary), have been in place since 1997. The sanctuary helps protect more than 6,000 species of marine life, including the nation's only bank-barrier coral reef that lies adjacent to the continent, and one of the largest seagrass communities in this hemisphere. An estimated 400 underwater historical sites also lie within sanctuary waters, 14 of which are listed on the Department of the Interior's National Register of Historic Places.

The Florida Keys and their environs have a long history (>100 years) of exploitation, thus many pressures on sanctuary resources are chronic, and to some degree cumulative. A historical perspective of sanctuary biodiversity suggests that the populations of many higher-trophic-level species, such as marine mammals and predatory fishes, were dramatically reduced by hunting and fishing prior to the sanctuary's designation. Today, pressures on the resources include commercial and recreational fishing, disturbances to wildlife, coastal development, harmful algal blooms, marine debris, vessel groundings, the introduction of non-indigenous species, and vessel traffic. Human-driven factors such as climate change, sea level rise and ocean acidification are large-scale issues that may also affect sanctuary resources.

Generally, the status and trends of the resources protected by Florida Keys National Marine Sanctuary reflect the inherited condition of a system that has been heavily exploited during the past century, more so than the relatively short time frame that these resources have been managed at the current geographic scale. For example, many of the historically abundant species (e.g., green turtles) and biogenic habitats had already been severely altered or reduced when the sanctuary was designated. Thus, resource managers are working to conserve pieces of the former system so that it can be restored to an improved state. However, understanding the degree of change in biodiversity that has occurred over time and how the coral reef ecosystem functioned in a "pre-exploitive" state can help managers and stakeholders identify realistic ecological and socioeconomic targets for maintaining or improving

ecosystem services. For example, there are positive signs that some ecosystem services are responding to recent management actions, most notably in the form of recovering fish spawning aggregations, and increasing sizes and abundances of economically important fisheries species inside the larger ecological reserves.

The current management plan for Florida Keys National Marine Sanctuary was released in December 2007, and it contains a number of management actions that address current issues and concerns. The plan stresses an ecosystem-based approach to management, which requires consideration of ecological interrelationships not only within the sanctuary, but within the larger context of the Gulf of Mexico and South Atlantic ecosystems. The management plan includes 14 action plans that will guide sanctuary management for the next few years.

National Marine Sanctuary System and System-Wide Monitoring

The National Marine Sanctuary System manages marine areas in both nearshore and open ocean waters that range in size from less than one to almost 140,000 square miles (362,598 square kilometers). Each area has its own concerns and requirements for environmental monitoring, but ecosystem structure and function in all these areas have similarities and are influenced by common factors that interact in comparable ways. Furthermore, the human influences that affect the structure and function of these sites are similar in a number of ways. For these reasons, in 2001 the program began to implement System-Wide Monitoring (SWiM). The monitoring framework (NMSP 2004) facilitates the development of effective, ecosystem-based monitoring programs that address management information needs using a design process that can be applied in a consistent way at multiple spatial scales and to multiple resource types. It identifies four primary components common among marine ecosystems: water, habitats, living resources and maritime archaeological resources.

By assuming that a common marine ecosystem framework can be applied to all places, the National Marine Sanctuary System developed a series of questions that are posed to every sanctuary and used as evaluation criteria to assess resource condition and trends. The questions, which are shown on the following page and explained in Appendix A, are derived from both a generalized ecosystem framework and from the National Marine Sanctuary System's mission. They are widely applicable across the system of areas managed by the sanctuary program and provide a tool with which the program can measure its progress toward maintaining and improving resource quality throughout the system.

Similar reports summarizing resource status and trends will be prepared for each marine sanctuary approximately every five years and updated as new information allows. The information in this report is intended to help set the stage for the management plan review process. The report also helps sanctuary staff identify monitoring, characterization and research priorities to address gaps, day-to-day information needs and new threats.

Florida Keys National Marine Sanctuary Condition Summary Table

The following table summarizes the "State of Sanctuary Resources" section of this report. The first two columns list 17 questions used to rate the condition and trends for qualities of water, habitat, living resources, and maritime archaeological resources. The Rating column consists of a color, indicating resource condition, and a symbol, indicating trend (see key for definitions). The Basis for Judgment column provides a short statement or list of criteria used to justify the rating. The Description of Findings column presents the statement that best characterizes resource status, and corresponds to the assigned color rating. The Description of Findings statements are customized for all possible ratings for each question. Please see Appendix A for further clarification of the questions and the Description of Findings statements. The Response column describes current or proposed management responses to pressures impacting sanctuary resources.

Status:

| Good | Good/Fair | Fair | Fair/Poor | Poor | Undet. |

Trends:
Conditions appear to be improving................................. ▲
Conditions do not appear to be changing...................... −
Conditions appear to be declining .... ▼
Undetermined trend.. ?
Question not applicable .... N/A

#	Questions/Resources	Rating	Basis for Judgment	Description of Findings	Sanctuary Response
WATER					
1	Are specific or multiple stressors, including changing oceanographic and atmospheric conditions, affecting water quality and how are they changing?	▼	Large-scale changes in flushing dynamics over many decades have altered many aspects of water quality; nearshore problems related to runoff and other watershed stressors; localized problems related to infrastructure.	Selected conditions may inhibit the development of assemblages and may cause measurable but not severe declines in living resources and habitats.	In conjunction with the Environmental Protection Agency and Florida Department of Environmental Protection, the sanctuary will continue implementation of its Water Quality Protection Program and conduct long-term water quality monitoring and research to understand the effects of water transported from near-field and far-field sources, including Florida Bay on water quality in the sanctuary. New regulations prohibit discharge or deposit of sewage from marine sanitation devices (MSD) within the boundaries of the sanctuary and require MSDs be locked to prevent sewage discharge or deposit while inside sanctuary boundaries. The marine area surrounding the Florida Keys has been designated as a Particularly Sensitive Sea Area by the International Maritime Organization. Florida Department of Health Florida Healthy Beaches Program tests for the presence of fecal coliform and enterococci bacteria in beach water on a weekly basis, at 17 locations throughout the Keys. The MEERA Project, which is designed to provide early detection and assessment of biological events occurring in the Florida Keys and surrounding waters, continues to be supported by the sanctuary. A well-established law enforcement program is in place, including NOAA Fisheries Service, Florida Fish and Wildlife Conservation Commission, and U.S. Coast Guard.
2	What is the eutrophic condition of sanctuary waters and how is it changing?	−	Long-term increase in inputs from land; large, persistent phytoplankton bloom events, many of which originate outside the sanctuary but enter and injure sanctuary resources.	Selected conditions have caused or are likely to cause severe declines in some but not all living resources and habitats.	
3	Do sanctuary waters pose risks to human health and how are they changing?	−	Rating is a general assessment of "all waters" of the sanctuary, knowing that in very specific locations, the rating could be as low as "poor." Increased frequency of HABs and periodic swim advisories.	Selected conditions have resulted in isolated human impacts, but evidence does not justify widespread or persistent concern.	
4	What are the levels of human activities that may influence water quality and how are they changing?	▲	Historically, destructive activities have been widespread throughout the Florida Keys, but many recent management actions are intended to reduce threats to water quality.	Selected activities have caused or are likely to cause severe impacts, and cases to date suggest a pervasive problem.	

Table is continued on the following page.

Florida Keys National Marine Sanctuary Condition Summary Table (Continued)

#	Questions/Resources	Rating	Basis for Judgment	Description of Findings	Sanctuary Response
Habitat					
5	What are the abundance and distribution of major habitat types and how are they changing?	—	In general, mangrove and benthic habitats are still present and their distribution is unchanged, with the exception of the mangrove community, which is about half of what it was historically. The addition of causeways has changed the distribution of nearshore benthic habitats in their vicinity.	Selected habitat loss or alteration has taken place, precluding full development of living resource assemblages, but it is unlikely to cause substantial or persistent degradation in living resources or water quality.	Marine zoning is used in the sanctuary to protect sensitive habitats like shallow coral reefs. Mooring buoys have been installed as a threat-reduction measure. Sanctuary staff and volunteers educate and inform boaters about the unique nature of the coral reef habitat, and organize shoreline clean-up and marine debris removal efforts. Sanctuary staff assess and restore vessel grounding injuries to seagrass and coral habitats, as well as perform coral rescue activities associated with coastal construction. Large vessel avoidance and Racon beacons in lighthouses have resulted in declines in large vessel groundings. An Area To Be Avoided was established to prevent ships larger than 50 meters in overall length from transiting through sensitive areas in the sanctuary. A well established permitting program is in place to issue a variety of permits for activities that are otherwise prohibited by sanctuary regulations. There is also a well-established law enforcement program in place, including NOAA Fisheries Service, the Florida Fish and Wildlife Conservation Commission, and the U.S. Coast Guard. State of Florida's Magrove Trimming and Preservation Act of 1996 (§403.9321-403.9333) regulates how mangroves can be trimmed and altered, and by whom.
6	What is the condition of biologically structured habitats and how is it changing?	▼	Loss of shallow (<10 meters) *Acropora* and *Montastraea* corals has dramatically changed shallow habitats; regional declines in coral cover since the 1970s have led to changes in coral-algal abundance patterns in most habitats; destruction of seagrass by propeller scarring; vessel grounding impacts on benthic environment; alteration of hard-bottom habitat by illegal casitas.	Selected habitat loss or alteration has caused or is likely to cause severe declines in some but not all living resources or water quality.	
7	What are the contaminant concentrations in sanctuary habitats and how are they changing?	?	Few studies, but no synthesis of information.	N/A	
8	What are the levels of human activities that may influence habitat quality and how are they changing?	▼	Coastal development, highway construction, vessel groundings, over-fishing, shoreline hardening, marine debris (including derelict fishing gear), treasure salvaging, increasing number of private boats, and consequences of long-term changes in land cover on nearshore habitats.	Selected activities have caused or are likely to cause severe impacts, and causes to date suggest a pervasive problem.	

Table is continued on the following page.

Florida Keys National Marine Sanctuary Condition Summary Table (Continued)

#	Questions/Resources	Rating	Basis for Judgment	Description of Findings	Sanctuary Response
Living Resources					
9	What is the status of biodiversity and how is it changing?	▼	Relative abundance across a spectrum of species has been substantially altered, with the most significant being large reef-building corals, large-bodied fish, sea turtles, and many invertebrates, including, the long-spined sea urchin. Recovery is questionable.	Selected biodiversity loss has caused or is likely to cause severe declines in some but not all ecosystem components and reduce ecosystem integrity.	Marine zoning assists in the protection of the biological diversity of the marine environment in the Keys. Mooring buoys have been installed in these zones to reduce anchor damage to coral reef biota. The sanctuary's education and outreach team established the "Blue Star" program to help reduce the impact of divers and snorkelers on the coral reef ecosystem. NOAA has also established the Dolphin SMART program encouraging responsible viewing of wild dolphins. Sanctuary staff assesses and restores vessel grounding injuries to seagrass and coral habitats, as well as performs coral rescue activities associated with coastal construction. NOAA Fisheries Service (American Recovery and Reinvestment Act) awarded $3.3 million to support *Acropora* coral recovery and restoration in Florida (including the Keys) and the U.S. Virgin Islands. Other coral nursery efforts are also underway that contribute to coral restoration. Private efforts examining potential of long-spined sea urchin recovery via nursery propagation and rearing are also underway. A well-established permitting program is in place to issue a variety of permits for activities that are otherwise prohibited by sanctuary regulations, including removal of the invasive lionfish from the small no-take zones. The Florida Keys "Bleach Watch" Program utilizes volunteers to provide reports from the reef on the actual condition of corals throughout the bleaching season. The sanctuary also participates in oil spill drills sponsored by the U.S. Coast Guard and is a partner in the Florida Reef Resilience Program. There is a well-established law enforcement program in place.
10	What is the status of environmentally sustainable fishing and how is it changing?	?	Historical effects of recreational and commercial fishing and collection of both targeted and non-targeted species; it is too early to determine ecosystem effects of new fishery regulations and new ecosystem approaches to fishery management.	Extraction has caused or is likely to cause severe declines in some but not all ecosystem components and reduce ecosystem integrity.	
11	What is the status of non-indigenous species and how is it changing	▼	Several species are known to exist; lionfish have already invaded and will likely cause ecosystem level impacts; impacts of other non-indigenous species have not been studied.	Non-indigenous species may inhibit full community development and function, and may cause measurable but not severe degradation of ecosystem integrity.	
12	What is the status of key species and how is it changing?	—	Reduced abundance of selected key species including corals (many species), queen conch, long-spined sea urchin, groupers and sea turtles.	The reduced abundance of selected keystone species has caused or is likely to cause severe declines in ecosystem integrity; or selected key species are at severely reduced levels, and recovery is unlikely.	
13	What is the condition or health of key species and how is it changing?	▼	Hard coral and gorgonian diseases and bleaching frequency and severity have caused substantial declines over the last two decades; long-term changes in seagrass condition; disease in sea turtles; sponge die-offs; low reproduction in queen conch; cyanobacterial blooms; lost fishing gear and other marine debris impacts on marine life.	The comparatively poor condition of selected key resources makes prospects for recovery uncertain.	
14	What are the levels of human activities that may influence living resource quality and how are they changing?	—	Despite the human population decrease and overall reduction in fishing in the Florida Keys since the 1990s, heavy recreational and commercial fishing pressure continues to suppress biodiversity. Vessel groundings occur regularly within the sanctuary. Annual mean number of reported petroleum and chemical spills were around 150 during that time period, with diesel fuel, motor oil, and gasoline representing 49% of these incidents collectively. Over the long term, localized direct impacts may be overwhelmed by the adverse and wide-ranging indirect effects of anthropogenic climate change resulting in sea level rise, abnormal air and water temperatures, and changing ocean chemistry.	Selected activities have caused or are likely to cause severe impacts, and cases to date suggest a pervasive problem.	

Table is continued on the following page.

Florida Keys National Marine Sanctuary Condition Summary Table (Continued)

#	Questions/Resources	Rating	Basis for Judgment	Description of Findings	Sanctuary Response
Maritime Archaeological Resources					
15	What is the integrity of known maritime archaeological resources and how is it changing?	▼	Resources are non-renewable and are subject to deterioration or loss resulting from looting, chemical processes, shifting sediments, marine life, fishing gear entanglement and vessel groundings (the last two are increasing in frequency).	The diminished condition of selected archaeological resources has substantially reduced their historical, scientific, or educational value and it likely to affect their eligibility for listing in the National Register of Historic Places.	Proactive management of submerged archaeological resources in sanctuary waters is occuring in conjunction with the state of Florida and the Advisory Council on Historic Preservation. This partnership is responsible for managing cultural resources in the sanctuary consistent with the Federal Archaeology Program, the Abandoned Shipwreck Act of 1987 and the National Historic Preservation Act. The sanctuary's education team has also developed a historic Shipwreck Trail, which highlights nine historic vessels that sank in sanctuary waters and represents three broad periods of keys maritime history. Sanctuary regulations prohibit alteration of the seafloor, thus commercial salvage in the sanctuary must go through a review process before a permit for salvage is issued. A well-established law enforcement program is in place, including NOAA Fisheries Service, the Florida Fish and Wildlife Conservation Commission, and the U.S. Coast Guard.
16	Do known maritime archaeological resources pose an environmental hazard and is this threat changing?	—	Movement of sunken vessels during storm threatens nearby resources.	Selected maritime archaeological resources may pose isolated or limited environmental threats, but substantial or persistent impacts are not expected.	
17	What are the levels of human activities that may influence maritime archaeological resource quality and how are they changing?	▼	Reports of looting and vessel grounding cases involving potential resources are increasing.	Selected activities have caused or are likely to cause severe impacts, and cases to date suggest a pervasive problem.	

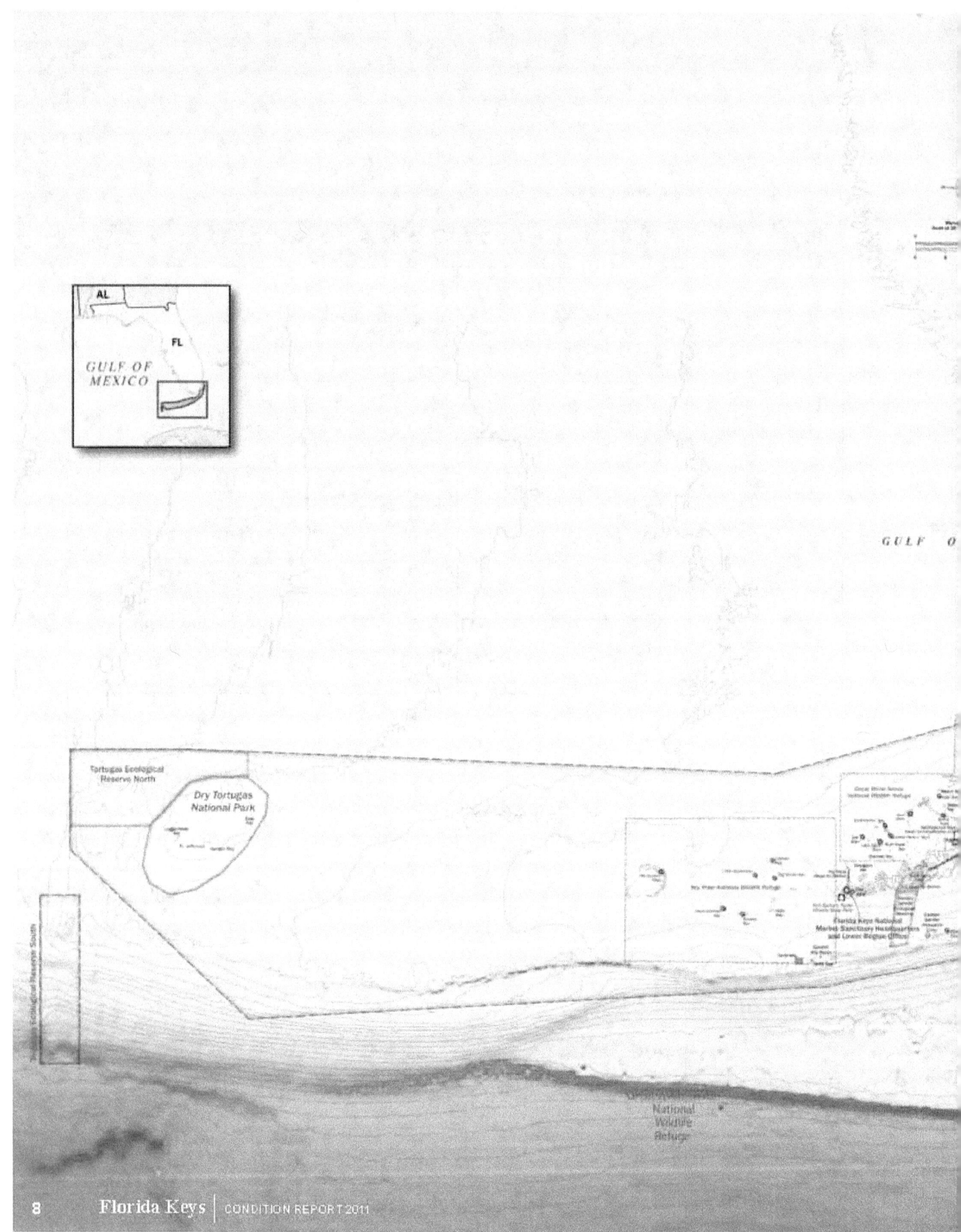

Figure 1. The 2,896 square-nautical-mile (9,844 square kilometer) Florida Keys National Marine Sanctuary surrounds the majority of the Florida Keys archipelago and includes productive waters

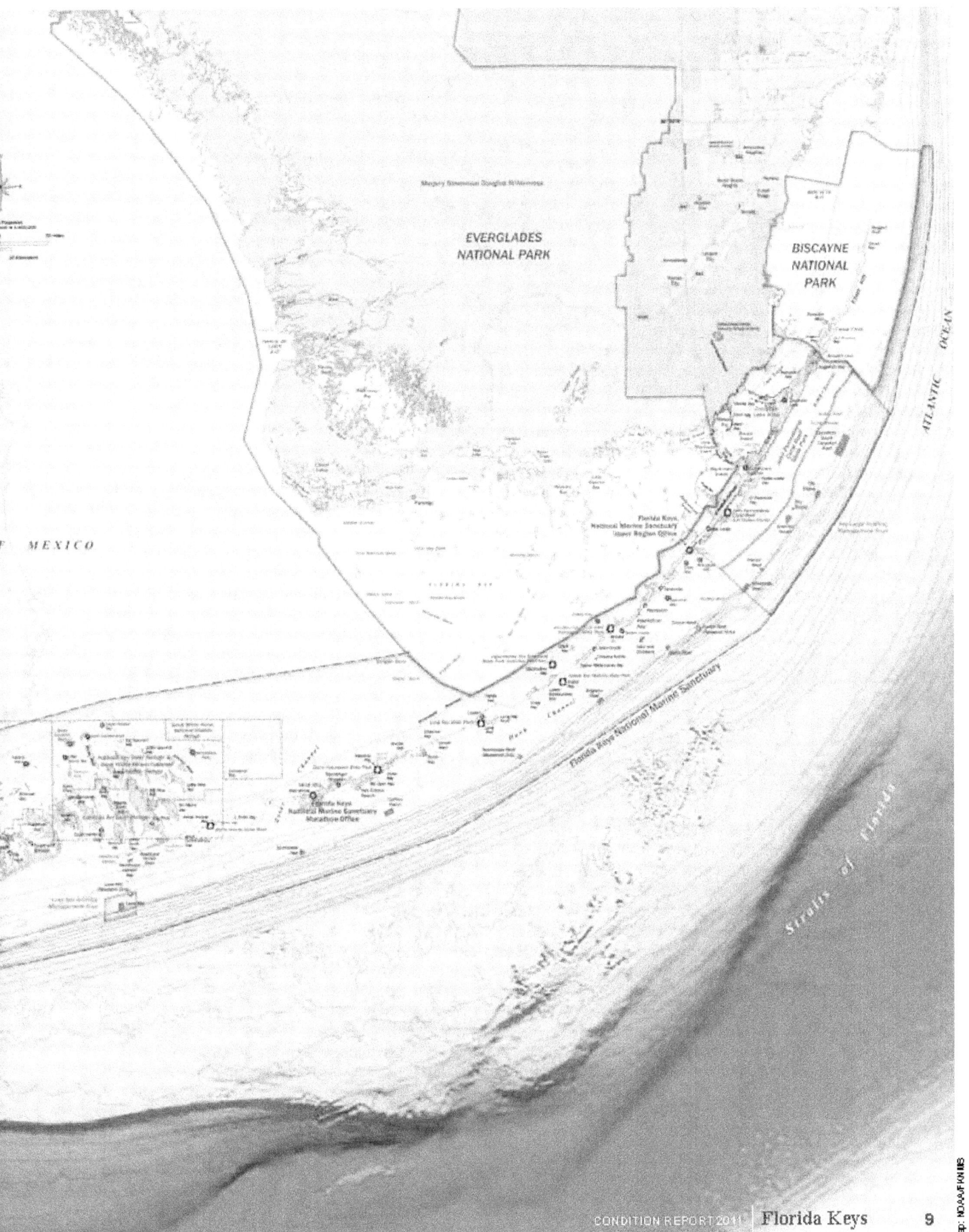

of Florida Bay, the Gulf of Mexico and the Atlantic Ocean.

Map: NOAA/FKNMS

Site History and Resources

Florida Keys National Marine Sanctuary covers 2,896 square nautical miles (9,933 square kilometers) and is one of the largest marine protected areas in the United States. It spans a shallow-water interface between the Gulf of Mexico and the Atlantic Ocean, and is adjacent to most of the relatively shallow estuarine waters of south Florida, including those of Florida Bay and Biscayne Bay. The sanctuary surrounds more than 1,700 islands, which constitute most of the limestone island archipelago of the Florida Keys. This archipelago extends from the Florida peninsula south and westward over 220 miles (354 kilometers), terminating at the islands of Dry Tortugas National Park. Hawk Channel is located "ocean side", between the island chain and the extensive bank reef tract (about 5 miles offshore). The oceanic boundary of the sanctuary is the 300-foot isobath (~100 meter depth), beyond which the Florida Straits separate the Florida Keys from both Cuba and the Bahamas.

The western tip of the Florida Keys sanctuary lies in an area of high diversity due to the presence of both tropical and subtropical species, with an intermingling of a tropical biota characteristic of the greater Caribbean and the warm-temperate biota of the Gulf of Mexico (Figure 1; Pages 8 and 9). Though the sanctuary surrounds much of the Florida Reef Tract, this subtropical region also sustains many other interdependent habitats including fringing mangroves, seagrass meadows, hard-bottom regions, and patch reefs. Together, this diverse set of habitats supports significant commercial and recreational activities including scuba diving, fishing, and other water-based tourism. This marine ecosystem supports more than 6,000 species of plants, fishes, and invertebrates, and also has the largest documented contiguous seagrass community in the northern hemisphere. The coral reefs and associated soft-sediment communities comprise one of the most unique and diverse assemblages of plants and animals in North America.

The sanctuary is also home to maritime heritage resources that encompass a broad historical period from the European Colonial Period to the Modern Era. Because of the Keys' strategic location in early European shipping routes, the area's shipwrecks reflect the history of the entire period of discovery and colonization. The Florida Keys sanctuary has an extensive education and volunteer program focused on the protection of maritime heritage resources. Volunteers on the Submerged Cultural Resources Inventory Team have documented more than 400 underwater historical sites in the sanctuary.

Approximately 1,680 square nautical miles (5,762 square kilometers), or 60%, of sanctuary waters are under Florida state jurisdiction, and numerous state and federal parks and reserves are located within the sanctuary's boundaries (NOAA 1996). The sanctuary is administered by the Department of Commerce's National Oceanic and Atmospheric Administration (NOAA) and is managed by both NOAA and the state of Florida's Board of Trustees of the Internal Improvement Trust Fund through the Florida Department of Environmental Protection (FDEP).

Geology

The Florida Keys are a chain of limestone islands that extends from the southern tip of the Florida mainland southwest to the Dry Tortugas, a distance of approximately 220 miles (354 kilometers). The islands are the fossilized (lithified) remnants of ancient coral reefs and sand bars that flourished during a period of higher sea levels approximately 125,000 to 100,000 years ago during the last interglacial period of the Pleistocene epoch (Hoffmeister and Multer 1968, Shinn 1988, Lidz and Shinn 1991). Today those remnants are known as Key Largo Limestone and Miami Oolite, respectively. During this period of lower sea level, the Florida land mass was much larger than today, and the area now referred to as Florida Bay was forested. As glaciers and polar ice caps started melting 15,000 years ago, sea level rise and flooding of land combined with tidal influence to create the geography of the Keys and their surrounding areas.

Florida Bay formed about 4,000 years ago, during a time when coral communities thrived along the entire seaward edge of the Keys. As sea level continued rising, tidal passes started forming, which facilitated the export of terrestrial material, sediments, and organic matter from both Florida and Biscayne Bays toward the Atlantic Ocean. In the Middle Keys in particular, tidal passes that formed allowed for inimical waters to flow offshore, resulting in conditions less favorable for coral reef development (Ginsburg and Shinn 1964, Shinn et al. 1989, Lidz and Shinn 1991, Shinn et al. 1994, Ogden et al. 1994). This is reflected, for example, in the sparse present-day distribution of patch reefs and offshore bank reefs between Alligator Light and Moser Channel (Seven Mile Bridge) (Marszalek et al. 1977). In the upper and lower Keys, ocean-side habitats were less influenced by these waters due to the size and orientation of the islands, so relatively vigorous coral reef growth continued (Lidz and Shinn 1991, Shinn et al. 1989). Thus, prior to human impacts in south Florida, water exchange between inshore and offshore environments significantly impeded coral reef (and seagrass) development in the same areas.

Today, the Florida Keys outer reefs are a semi-continuous series of offshore bank reefs located at the northern zoogeographic boundary of tropical waters. They began forming between 6,000 to 10,000 years ago during the Holocene sea-level rise and all present-day bank reefs are located on pre-existing topographic highs in the Pleistocene bedrock (Shinn et al. 1977, 1989). Due to its location at the northern limit of coral reef development, Florida Keys reefs regularly experiences natural stresses such as winter temperatures below those normally associated with vigorous coral reef development (Roberts et al. 1982). Also, the reef system experiences higher summer temperature extremes than many other reefs in the Caribbean basin (Vaughn 1918, Kruczynski and McManus 2002).

The Florida Keys sanctuary also includes the Florida Plateau, which extends 223 miles (360 kilometers) from Miami to the Dry Tortugas. This shelf forms part of the Florida-Bahamas carbonate province and is the only area in the continental U.S. where active carbonate deposition is occurring on a large scale (Enos 1977, Shinn et al. 1989). The Florida Plateau is bounded by the Florida Straits to the east and south and by the Gulf of Mexico to the west.

Water Circulation

South Florida is located at the convergence of the subtropical and temperate climate zones. Physical oceanographic processes in the Florida Keys region consist of oceanic currents, tides and wind-driven currents, along with upwelling along the outer reef tract (Enos 1977, Schomer and Drew 1982, Brooks 1990, Leichter et al. 1998, 2003). The physical environment of the Florida Straits is dominated by the Florida Current, a strong surface current originating in the South Atlantic and Caribbean Sea (Figure 2) (Lee et al. 1992, Lee and Smith 2002). The Florida Current is the convergence of the Yucatan Current and Gulf of Mexico Loop Current off peninsular Florida. The Florida Current is renamed the Gulf Stream System off the southeastern U.S. (Lee et al. 1992). The Florida Current transports warm water from the Caribbean and is the major reason for reef development and the occurrence of tropical marine biota in the Florida Keys (Jaap 1984). The Florida Current comes within 9 miles (15 kilometers) of the upper Florida Keys, but runs further offshore, around 50 miles (80 kilometers), off Key West. Differences in the proximity of the Florida Current to the Florida Keys seascape result in complex circulation patterns on the south Florida shelf (Lee et al. 1994). For example, eddies of 31 to 62 miles (50 to 100 kilometers) in diameter frequently form when meanders break free from the main axis of the Loop Current. These eddies move into the Florida Straits and are trapped between the Florida Current to the south and the Dry Tortugas to the north. These "Tortugas gyres" can remain stationary for 50 to 140 days until they are pushed out by the arrival of the next gyre moving along the Loop Current. Once displaced, they are transformed into the smaller "Pourtales Gyre" by their movement downstream and the nar-

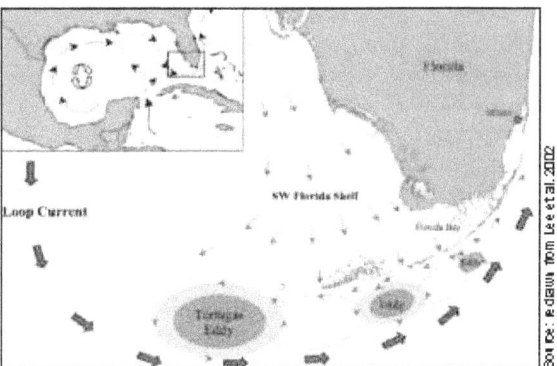

Figure 2. Schematic of general surface circulation of southern and southwestern Florida coastal waters. Subregions include: (1) Keys coastal zone, with Upper, Middle, Lower, and Western Keys localities; (2) Florida Bay; and (3) the Southwest Florida Shelf. Major tidal passages are indicated by the arrows immediately west (Seven-Mile Bridge) and east (Long Key Channel) of Marathon; additional tidal passages lie east of Long Key Channel (Channels 5 and 2) and between some of the lower Keys. Major boundary currents are the Loop and Florida Currents. Depth contours in meters.

rowing of the distance between the Florida Current and the Keys (Lee et al. 1994, Lee and Williams 1999). These gyres potentially contribute to the nutrient and larval transport between the Loop Current and the Florida Keys system, and may also serve to retain coastal-derived larvae that would otherwise be carried away by the Florida Current (Cowen et al. 2006, Sale 2006). On a more localized scale, tides and wind-driven currents are the dominant processes affecting circulation in the Florida Keys and Florida Bay (Schomer and Drew 1982). The Florida Keys and Florida Bay are micro-tidal environments (<3.3 feet or one meter); tidal exchange between Florida Bay and Hawk Channel mostly occurs in the middle Florida Keys, and to a lesser extent in the lower Florida Keys. From November to February, atmospheric cold fronts from the north supplement tidal flow out of Florida Bay (Smith 1994, Smith and Lee 2003).

Nearshore waters of the Florida Keys, defined as from the shoreline to the seaward edge of Hawk Channel, generally experience high variability in temperature, salinity and other factors relative to the reef tract further offshore. Differences in circulation and the physical and chemical characteristics of water in the Florida Keys reflect exchange processes between Florida Bay and the Atlantic Ocean, the influence of the Florida Current, and wind-driven currents in Hawk Channel. Nearshore waters in the upper Florida Keys are generally well-flushed and dominated by seagrasses, large sandy shoals (e.g., White Banks), and large patch reef areas (e.g., Mosquito Bank). They are not as significantly influenced by Florida Bay because of the larger sizes of islands and the absence of larger tidal passes in the northern Keys. The nearshore environment of the middle Florida Keys is characterized by significant exchange of water between Florida Bay and the Atlantic Ocean. The sea bottom in areas adjacent to tidal channels consists of seagrasses, bare sand, low-relief hard-bottom communities, and patch reefs. Nearshore waters in the lower Florida Keys are influenced by exchange of water between the eastern Gulf of Mexico and Atlantic Ocean. Bottom or benthic habitats consist mostly of seagrass and bare sand, low-relief hard bottom, and abundant nearshore and mid-channel patch reefs.

With the exception of nutrient variability from upwelling events, offshore waters of the Florida Keys are relatively stable in terms of some water quality parameters compared to nearshore areas, particularly temperature, salinity, and dissolved oxygen. Distinct gradients can occur in circulation patterns and water residence time from the upper to lower Florida Keys. The offshore environment of the upper Florida Keys is relatively well-circulated, and dominated by Florida Current circulation (Klein and Orlando 1994). The upper Florida Keys area has the most robust reef development, most likely due to the warm-water influence of the Florida Current coupled with the lack of water exchange with Florida Bay. The offshore waters of the middle Florida Keys exchange with Florida Bay via tidal channels, thus reef development is relatively poor. The offshore waters of the lower Florida Keys are influenced by wind-driven circulation in Hawk Channel and offshore gyres (or smaller circular currents) of the Florida Current. The offshore waters of the lower Florida Keys have a significantly longer residence time than other offshore areas. This has considerable implications for nekton, plankton, and larval transport in these areas. In the offshore environment of the lower Florida Keys, there is moderate bank reef development, with several well-developed bank reefs (e.g., Sand Key, Eastern Sambo) and patch reef areas (Jaap 1984).

Early Exploration and Settlement

Indigenous peoples have long resided throughout the Florida peninsula and on the surrounding islands. The southernmost regions of Florida, including the Florida Keys, were dominated by the Tequesta and the Calusa tribes, who arrived in the region about 7,000 years ago, probably from northeast Florida (Carr 1991). These Native Americans depended on the sea for almost everything they needed, subsisting on fish, turtle, crabs, clams, lobster, and mollusks (Tilmant 1989). The bountiful marine resources in the Florida Keys provided a cultural subsistence tradition that remained unchanged for at least 4,000 years, until European contact served to eliminate the Native American population, mostly through disease (Carr 1991).

The first confirmed European contact with the Keys was made in 1513 by Ponce de Leon of Spain, while exploring the Florida Straits (Wells 1991). In 1519, the Spanish established Havana, Cuba, and by the mid-1500s and throughout the 1600s, they colonized Florida. In 1763, the Spanish ceded Florida to the British in a trade for the port of Havana. The treaty was unclear as to the status of the Florida Keys. An agent of the king of Spain claimed that the islands, rich in fish, turtles and mahogany for shipbuilding, were part of Cuba, fearing that the English might build fortresses and dominate the shipping lanes. The British also realized the treaty was ambiguous, but declared that the Keys should be occupied and defended as part of Florida. Although the British claim was never officially contested, ironically, the British gave the islands back to Spain in 1783 in order to keep them from the newly formed United States. In 1821, however, all of Florida, including the Florida Keys, officially became American territory, followed by formal statehood in 1845.

Development of the Florida Keys

The 20th century brought major changes to the Florida Keys in terms of transportation and residential and commercial infrastructure. In the early 1900s, travel between many of these islands was only possible by boat. However, this changed in the 1890s when Henry Flagler, president of the Florida East Coast Railway, brought the Overseas Railroad down Florida's east coast to Miami. The railroad was later extended to Key West in 1912 (Parks 1968). On Labor Day 1935, a hurricane struck the upper Florida Keys and permanently destroyed the railroad. The railroad's right-of-way was then sold and rebuilt into the Overseas Highway, which opened in 1938. This replacement road, which includes more than 40 bridges connecting the islands, eliminated the ferry rides and narrow wooden bridges of the first highway, making the Florida Keys more accessible from the Florida mainland (Marzyck 1991).

Between 1938 and the early 1980s, vehicles traveled down the Keys on a narrow two-lane roadway that was built on top of the old railroad bridges. The narrow Overseas Highway restricted or deterred the movement of wide vehicles to some extent. Large recreational vehicles, camper trailers, and wide boats seldom ventured south of the upper Keys. Several events occurred in the early 1980s that permanently changed the infrastructure and subsequently the economy of the Keys. First was the construction of wider bridges from Key Largo to Key West. Additionally, the roadway was widened to allow passage of supply trucks and the safe transit of recreational vehicles, camper trailers, and wide boats. Along with the bridges came a larger water pipeline that supplied the Keys with fresh water from the well-fields in Florida City and a new electrical line to supply dependable power throughout the islands.

Another benchmark of change came when the Monroe County Tourist Development Council was created in 1982, which is currently funded through a "bed tax." A portion of this bed tax was and remains dedicated to advertising to attract more visitors to the Keys. From 2002 to 2009, the total revenue from the bed tax fluctuated between $14 million and $15.5 million. The peak was 2005 at $15.5 million but declined to $14.1 million in 2009.

Development of the islands outside of Key West began slowly in the 1940s and boomed from the 1950s to 1990s, thus allowing for a

Since 1995, the Florida Keys have lost over 500 camp-sites because those lands were sold to developers to build condominiums. In addition, several hotels have been converted to condominiums. We hypothesize that this change in development pattern will change the goods and services and recreational activities in which people participate. We further hypothesize that the changes will be towards less natural resource-dependent and water-based activities than those chosen by people who stayed in campsites.

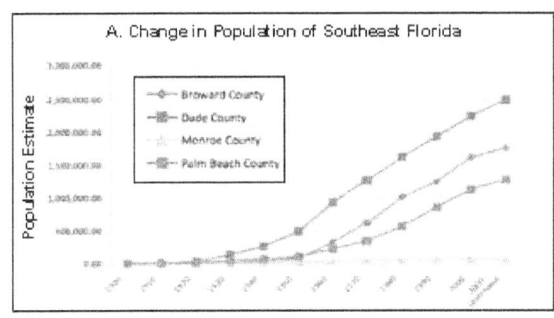

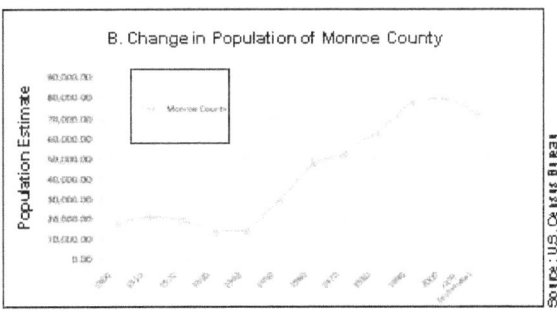

significant growth in population (Figure 3). The population of Monroe County rose from 17,114 in 1900 to 78,024 by 1990. The population increased more slowly between 1990 and 2000 and was 79,589 by 2000. However, the population has been steadily declining in Monroe County since 2000 and as of July 1, 2009, the population is estimated at 73,165 (U.S. Census Bureau 2010).

Population growth in and development of Monroe County have been driven largely by the tourism industry, but also the Florida Keys as a place for retirement, commercial fisheries, the military, and the upper part of the Keys as a "bedroom community"[1] for South Florida. These are referred to by economists as "basic industries" as they bring new dollars into the community, which then have ripple effects on the rest of the economy. These industries are discussed further in the "Commerce" section below.

From 2007 to 2008, there were about 73,300 year-round residents and about 3.3 million visitors to the Florida Keys. This translates into a "functional population"[2] of between 116,000 and 118,000 during the winter season and 102,000 –105,000 during the summer season. The peak functional population was estimated between 150,000 and 152,000 during the winter season (December–May) and 132,000 – 135,000 during the summer season (June–November). (Leeworthy et al. 2010)

Figure 3. (a) The population change in the four counties of southeast Florida from 1920 to 2009. (b) The population change in Monroe County, Florida from 1920 to 2009; note the axis uses a different scale than figure 2(a).

Figure 4. Snorkelers visit the Florida Keys National Marine Sanctuary.

Commerce

Five primary factors influence population growth and land development in Monroe County: 1) the tourism industry; 2) Florida as a retirement destination; 3) the commercial fishing industry; 4) the military; and 5) the "bedroom community" nature, particularly in the upper Keys due to their proximity to Miami-Dade and Broward counties. These factors each bring dollars into the Florida Keys community, which then have multiplier impacts on the rest of the economy.

Florida's coral reefs are located near the four most densely popu-lated counties of the state. The combined population of these counties is over 5.6 million, with 1.2 million in Palm Beach, 1.77 million in Broward, 2.5 million in Miami-Dade, and 73,200 in Monroe (Figure 3; U.S. Census Bureau 2010).

Tourism is the number one industry of the Florida Keys economy. Resident and visitor use includes activities such as guided eco-tours, diving and snorkeling trips (Figure 4), and recreational fishing.

---

[1] Bedroom community refers to the people who live in the Florida Keys/Monroe County but commute to work outside the Florida Keys/Monroe County area.

[2] An important concept for planning for growth management that is a result "basic industry" drivers is the "functional population." The "functional population" is the number of people in the Florida Keys on an average or peak day. This is the relevant population for growth management planning since it is the number of people that require housing, water, sewage, electric, transportation and other infrastructure services. In the Florida Keys the "peak" functional population is also used for planning hurricane evacuation, which is a limiting factor in the growth of the Monroe County population.

Monroe County residents spend significantly more days snorkeling, scuba diving and fishing in comparison to visitors. In addition, reef diving and reef fishing are equally common, while snorkeling is more common than scuba diving (Johns et al. 2003). During 1995 to 1996, 2.54 million visitors spent $1.63 billion (2008 $) in Monroe County, which in turn generated $1.82 billion dollars in sales, $693 million in income, and supported over 21,800 jobs. By 2008, 3 million visitors increased their spending impact by 22% to $1.99 billion in Monroe County, which generated $2.23 billion in sales, $970 million in income, and supported 32,000 jobs (Leeworthy 2010)[3].

The next largest industry is the retirement and "bedroom community" nature of the Florida Keys. Over 50% of the income received by Monroe County residents is not related to work in Monroe County; retirement income in the form of social security and pensions make up most of this income.

The commercial fishery industry also has a significant impact on the Florida Keys economy. The economic impact of this industry is great, representing close to 5% of the Monroe County economy in terms of output and sales and close to 9% of employment. In 1994, the total economic contribution of the commercial fishery industry to the Monroe County economy was estimated (CEMR 1995, Leeworthy 1995), with revenue from fisheries landings in at approximately $56.5 million (1994 $). This revenue can then be converted to total impacts generated through the wholesale, processing, retail, restaurant, and export markets to have a total economic impact in Monroe County of $92.2 million in sales, $58.2 million in income and supported 4,130 jobs (1994).

The military is also a major industry in Monroe County, with the U.S. Navy located in Key West. Until September 2001, the Navy was down-sizing its operations in Key West and giving up properties for other development. For example, the sanctuary's Key West office and Eco-Discovery Center are both located on a small portion of former Navy property (Truman Annex), which was transferred to NOAA during this down-sizing operation. In 1995, the military directly contributed $81.6 million in income to Monroe County and supported 2,028 employees. In 2007, the direct income received by military personnel increased to $147.66 million, but the number of employees declined to 1,670. The military directly accounts for about 7% of Monroe County's income by place of work and in 2007 accounted directly for 2.9% of employment (U.S. Bureau of Economic Analysis 2010).

Designation of the Sanctuary

The lure of the Florida Keys has attracted explorers and visitors for centuries. The clear tropical waters and appealing natural environ-

ment are among the many qualities that attract visitors to the Keys. However, warning signs, including the loss of habitat and living resources, came early, indicating that the Keys' environment and natural resources are fragile, and not infinite. As early as 1957, a group of conservationists and scientists held a conference at Everglades National Park to discuss the demise of the coral reef resources in the Keys. This conference resulted in the creation of John Pennekamp Coral Reef State Park in 1960, the world's first underwater park. However, a little more than a decade following, public outcry sounded that pollution, overfishing, physical impacts, overuse, and user conflicts continued to occur in the Keys. Those concerns were echoed by environmentalists and scientists alike as monitoring of the Florida Keys reefs began in the late 1970s, throughout the 1980s and into the 21st century. As a result, additional management efforts were instituted to protect the Keys' coral reefs. In the upper Keys, Key Largo National Marine Sanctuary was established in 1975 to protect 103 square nautical miles (353 square kilometers) of coral reef habitat from north of Carysfort Lighthouse to south of Molasses Reef. In the lower Keys, the 5.32 square-nautical-mile (18.25 square-kilometer) Looe Key National Marine Sanctuary was established in 1981. (NOAA 2007)

In 1989, mounting threats to the health and ecological future of the coral reef ecosystem in the Florida Keys prompted Congress to take action to further protect this fragile natural resource. The threat of oil drilling off the Florida Keys in the mid-1980s, in combination with reports of deteriorating water quality throughout the region, the die-off of the long-spined sea urchin (*Diadema antillarum*), loss of living coral cover on reefs, a major seagrass die-off, declines in reef fish populations, and the spread of coral diseases, were topics of major scientific concern and the focus of several scientific workshops. While these scientific pursuits were underway, three large ships (M/V *Elpis*, M/V *Alec Owen Maitland* and *Mavro Vetranic*) ran aground on the coral reef tract within an 18-day timeframe in fall 1989. These cumulative events of environmental degradation that prompted Congress to designate the 2,800 square-nautical-mile (9,603 square-kilometer) Florida Keys National Marine Sanctuary on Nov. 16, 1990, in order to expand the scale of resource protection beyond the existing Key Largo and Looe Key national marine sanctuaries; these two smaller sanctuaries then became a type of marine zone (Existing Management Areas) within the larger sanctuary. This was the first national marine sanctuary to completely surround a community.

Beginning in 1998, a public process was initiated to create additional protection for the region surrounding the Dry Tortugas archipelago. This public process included a comprehensive characteriza-

---

[3] As a share of the total Monroe County economy, recreating visitors in 2007 to 2008 accounted for about the same share of output/sales as 1995 to 1996 (60.5% in 1995 to 1996 and 59.9% in 2007 to 2008), a slight increase in income received by place of work (45% in 1995 to 1996 and 46.9% in 2007 to 2008), and a significant increase in employment (46.5% in 1995 to 1996 and 57% in 2007 to 2008).

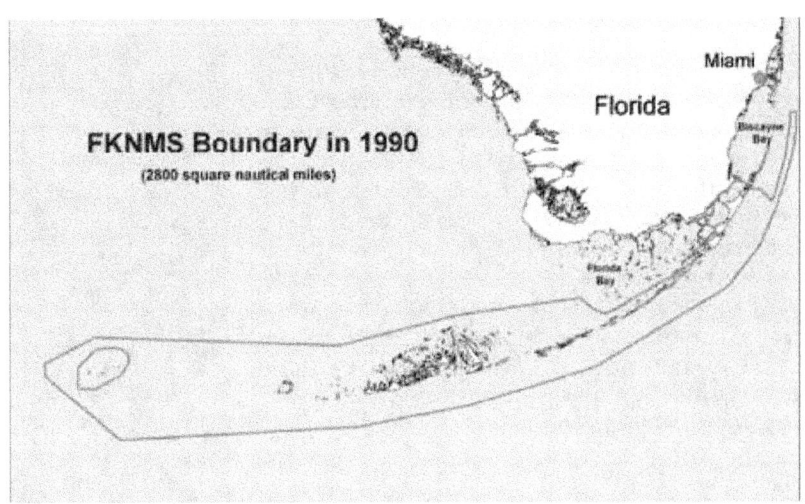

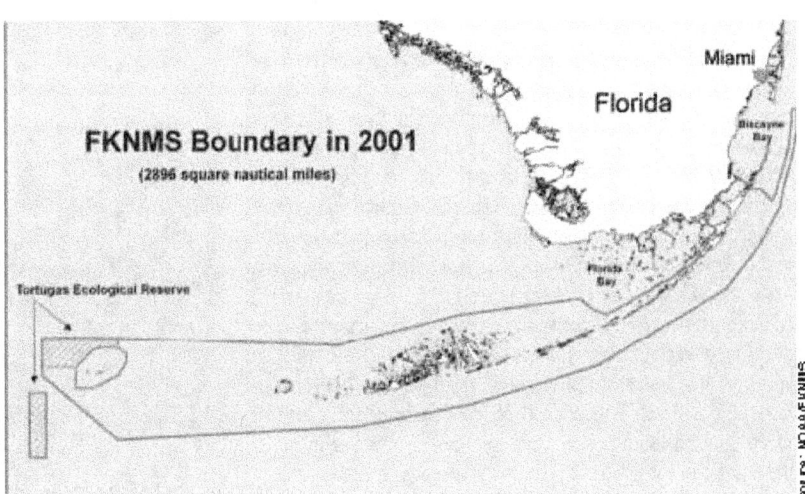

Figure 5. (a) Original boundary of the sanctuary in 1990, (b) and the modified boundary of 2001, which includes the Tortugas Ecological Reserve.

tion of the ecological and socioeconomic importance of the area. On July 1, 2001, the Tortugas Ecological Reserve (TER), a no-take zone, was designated in order to protect the diverse marine life and lush coral reefs of the Tortugas. The TER is divided into two separate sections:

■ *TER North* - adjacent to Dry Tortugas National Park, comprises 90 square nautical miles (309 square kilometers) of ocean habitat, and contains relatively extensive areas of spectacular deeper (>50 feet or 15 meters) coral reef formations in the Florida Keys. TER North incorporated 54 square nautical miles (186 square

kilometers) of existing sanctuary area and added 36 square nautical miles (123 square kilometers) to the original boundary by "squaring off" the northwestern corner.

■ *TER South* - located to the southwest of Dry Tortugas National Park, comprises 60 square nautical miles (205 square kilometers) of ocean and includes the critical fish spawning grounds of Riley's Hump.

The TER expanded the boundary of the sanctuary from 2,800 to 2,896 square nautical miles (9,603 to 9,933 square kilometers) in 2001 (Figure 5).

Habitats

The boundaries of the sanctuary encompass numerous habitats and structural zones (Figure 6). Benthic habitats include unconsolidated sediments (e.g., sand and mud), mangrove, submerged aquatic vegetation (e.g., seagrass and algae), coral reefs and colonized hard-bottom habitats (e.g., spur and groove reefs, individual and aggregated patch reefs, and gorgonian-colonized pavement), and uncolonized hard bottom (e.g., reef rubble). Some of the major habitat types of the Florida Keys are shown in Figure 6, starting with fringing mangrove or sandy shorelines, progressing through nearshore seagrass and hard-bottom habitat, to mid-channel and offshore seagrass beds and patch reefs, and finally to the offshore bank reef system. Typical coral reef structural zones include the back reef, reef flat, reef crest, and fore reef.

Mangroves

Florida's estimated 496,000 acres (200,724 hectares) of mangrove forests contribute to the overall health of the state's southern coastal zone (Figure 7). Red mangrove (*Rhizophora mangle*) trees fringe much of the 1,700 islands and 1,815 miles of shoreline within the sanctuary, and they are a vital component of the Florida Keys ecosystem. In the abiotic realm, mangroves act as important wave attenuation barriers for all points landward, buffering the action of waves and storm surges associated with both frontal and tropical storms. Thus, they provide important shoreline protection services in the Florida Keys, as in all coastal locations where they occur. They also assist in trapping and cycling various organic materials, chemical elements and important nutrients throughout the interconnected reef-seagrass-mangrove system. Mangrove forests play an important role in the carbon cycle by removing CO_2 from the atmosphere and storing it as carbon in plant materials and soils in a process called sequestration. Layers of soil and peat that make up the mangrove substrate have a high carbon content, and when they are disturbed or removed, carbon is released into the atmosphere. In addition, mangrove roots provide attachment surfaces for various marine organisms, especially on their partially submerged prop roots. Many of these attached organisms filter water and, in turn, trap and cycle nutrients.

The relationship between mangroves and their associated marine life cannot be overemphasized. Mangroves provide protected nursery areas for young fishes, crustaceans, shellfish and other invertebrates (Drew and Eggleston 2008). Many of these species are food for a multitude of fish species such as snapper, jack, snook (*Centropomus undecimalis*), tarpon (*Megalops atlanticus*), sheepshead (*Archosargus probatocephalus*), and red drum (*Sciaenops ocellatus*).

Florida's important recreational and commercial fisheries will decline without healthy mangrove forests to support them. Many animals find

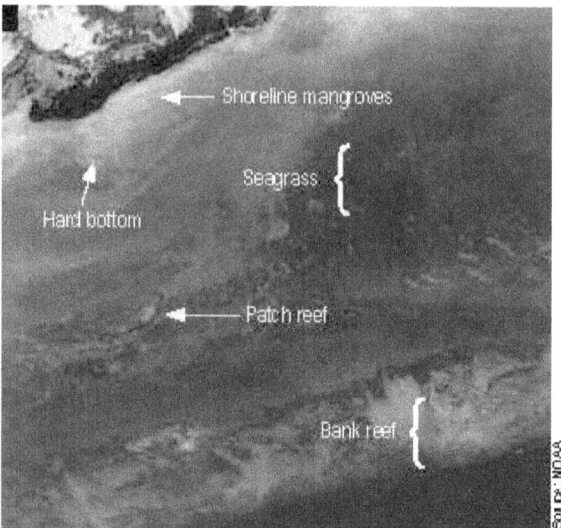

Figure 6. This image shows some of the major habitat types found in the Florida Keys: mangrove, seagrass, patch reef, hard bottom and bank reef.

Figure 7. Mangroves are integral components of the Florida Keys ecosystem. They provide food and serve as nursery grounds for many species, in addition to stabilizing shorelines.

shelter either in the roots or canopies of mangroves. Mangrove tree canopies serve as rookeries, or nesting areas, for coastal birds such as brown pelicans (*Pelecanus occidentalis*) and roseate spoonbills (*Platalea ajaja*).

Figure 8. The Florida Keys ecosystem includes one of the world's largest seagrass beds, which are among the richest, most productive, and most important submerged coastal habitats.

Seagrass Beds

The Florida Keys ecosystem includes one of the world's largest seagrass beds, which are among the richest, most productive, and most important submerged coastal habitats. Seagrasses are flowering plants that live in the ocean (Figure 8). Like land plants, seagrasses utilize carbon dioxide and produce oxygen. Seagrass occurs throughout the soft-bottom, shallow-water areas of the sanctuary wherever water quality is sufficient to allow light penetration to the seafloor to enable photosynthesis. Like mangroves, seagrasses also serve important ecosystem functions, often acting as a kind of "link in the chain" between the reef and mangrove systems, both spatially and in terms of food webs (Valentine et al. 2008). Likewise, seagrass meadows also perform certain coastline services such as stabilizing the bottom with their roots and rhizomes in much the same way that land grasses retard soil erosion, and maintaining water clarity by trapping fine sediments and other particles in their leaves and root system. Like mangroves, seagrasses sequester carbon. They also offer habitat and protection for many fishes and invertebrates, crustaceans (such as lobster and shrimp), and shellfish; provide food for marine animals including green sea turtles (*Chelonia mydas*), West Indian manatee (*Trichechus manatus*), parrotfishes, and sea urchins; and serve as a nursery area for recreationally and commercially important marine life (Rudnick et al. 2005, Acosta et al. 2007).

The Florida Keys ecosystem includes five species of seagrasses, with turtle grass (*Thalassia testudinum*), manatee grass (*Syringodi-um filiforme*), and shoal grass (*Halodule wrightii*) making up most of the coverage of seagrass beds in the sanctuary (NOAA 1996, 2007). Data from the sanctuary's Water Quality Protection Program indicates approximately 4,942 square miles (12,800 square kilometers) of seagrass beds lie within and adjacent to the sanctuary.

Macroalgae

Monitoring of benthic communities by the National Undersea Research Center (NURC) and the University of North Carolina at Wilmington has documented that species of simple plants classified as algae dominate many benthic habitats throughout the sanctuary (NOAA 2007). Due to their ability to grow in the marine environment, fleshy macroalgae are commonly referred to as "seaweeds." Turf algae often form dense, lettuce-like patches on dead coral or other rocky bottoms. There are three basic types depending on the color of the photosynthetic pigments that predominate: green, red, and brown. Like land-based "weeds," seaweeds grow faster when they are fertilized and tend to grow rapidly when they are not grazed by sea urchins or fish, just as land plants in a pasture might grow when they are not grazed by cattle or sheep.

To a major extent, macroalgae compete with coral for living space on the seafloor, but it is important to note that macroalgae are a common and natural component of every coral reef system. Like other plants, it is a food source for a number of reef-dwelling animals, especially sea urchins and certain reef fishes such as surgeonfishes and parrotfishes. Typically, it is only when the ecological balance of a reef is upset (e.g., by widespread coral mortality from bleaching or disease) that it tends to become overgrown by the rapidly growing macroalgae (Maliao et al. 2008).

Coral Reefs and Hard-bottom Habitats

The Florida Reef Tract is the most extensive living coral reef ecosystem in North American waters and the third-largest barrier reef in the world. Coral reefs are created by calcareous marine algae, reef-building corals, and other marine invertebrates that produce skeletons or structures made of calcium carbonate ($CaCO_3$, or limestone). The skeletons of corals and other marine life combine to form a rigid, wave-resistant structure called a reef.

An individual coral animal, called a polyp, resembles a miniature sea anemone just a few millimeters in size. Like anemones, a coral polyp is soft-bodied, tubular, and topped by a ring of tentacles. Unlike an anemone, a reef-building coral polyp builds a hard external skeleton that forms a protective cup, or calice, around its base, creating a corallite. Hundreds to thousands of coral polyps together make up a reef-building coral colony. Each polyp is connected to the next by a thin layer of tissue, creating a living mat over a shared skeleton. Colonies grow by progressively building more and more skeletal mass.

Figure 9. Coral reefs help to protect the shoreline from destructive storms and provide habitat for marine species.

Within the tissue of most reef-building corals live small microscopic algae called zooxanthellae. These algae produce energy and oxygen for the coral as byproducts of photosynthesis. Some coral species are predominantly reliant on this energy source, whereas other species are less reliant on the photosynthetic byproducts and acquire their most of their energy by suspension feeding. Zooxanthellae also aid in calcium carbonate production by the coral colony, promoting the growth of coral skeletons.

Coral reefs generally are restricted to the tropics, where waters are generally warm, clear, low in nutrients like nitrogen and phosphorus, and have stable temperature and salinity. The Florida Reef Tract is one example in which the warm waters of the Florida Current and Gulf Stream expand the range of corals north of the tropics (Figure 9).

Coral reefs create important habitat for various organisms including both sessile and mobile invertebrates, as well as highly diverse reef fish. In turn, many of these animals provide food for predators that often visit reefs, such as sharks, sea turtles and dolphins. Similar to mangroves and seagrasses, corals also perform vital coastal shoreline services. For example, coral reefs can protect a coastline from wave action, storm surges, and even tsunamis (Cochard et al. 2008).

Living Resources

The Florida peninsula and the Florida Keys archipelago serve as a biogeographic transition zone between the warm-temperate waters of the Gulf of Mexico and the adjacent tropical to subtropical waters of the Atlantic Ocean. This division has resulted in a distribution of marine fauna and flora characterized as having both a warm-temperate and tropical Caribbean component (NOAA 1996). The following section contains general descriptions of select taxa, but a complete list of the marine and terrestrial species found in Florida Keys National Marine Sanctuary can be found at http://floridakeys.noaa.gov/scipublications/speciesList.pdf (Levy et al. 1996).

Invertebrates

Invertebrates in the sanctuary are highly diverse. Resident phyla include, but are not limited to, Cnidaria (corals, sea anemones, jellyfish), Platyhelminthes (flatworms), Porifera (sponges), Annelida (segmented worms), Arthropoda (crustaceans), Ectoprocta (bryozoans), Mollusca (bivalves and snails), Echinodermata (sea stars, sea urchins and sea cucumbers). With the exception of a few "fishery" crustaceans (e.g., shrimp, lobster, stone crab), the ecological roles of many of these invertebrates are not well understood and continue to be studied (Levy et al. 1996).

Porifera (sponges) are important components of coral reef ecosystems, and some species grow quite large, often more than three feet (one meter) in height. Besides filtering large amounts of water, sponges in nearshore hard-bottom habitat are critical shelter habitat for a myriad of obligate and opportunistic invertebrates and fish such as crabs, shrimps and brittle stars (McMurray et al. 2008). In the Keys, there is even a certain genus of sponge (*Cliona*) that serves as an aggressive coral bioeroder, thus providing a key process in a reef's carbonate budget. This genus has been on the increase in recent years, and several of its members are now among the dominant sponge species in the Florida Keys (Keller and Donahue 2006, Chiappone et al. 2007).

Caribbean spiny lobsters (*Panulirus argus*) are one of the Florida Keys' most economically important commercial fisheries, and the Florida Keys stock is heavily exploited by both the commercial fishery and by recreational divers and snorkelers. Between the two fisheries, a large percentage of the available adult population is removed each year (Cox and Hunt 2005).

Sea urchins, more specifically the long-spined sea urchin (*Diadema antillarum*), were historically one of the most important invertebrate grazers on coral reefs in the Florida Keys, helping control the abundance of algae. Though in some parts of the Caribbean the long-spined sea urchin played a major role in controlling algal biomass (Levitan 1988), the roles of both piscine herbivores and sea urchins in controlling algal dominance on coral reefs are still being discovered (Furman and Heck 2008).

Fish

Because of the Florida Keys' connection to adjacent aquatic environments, a variety of different fish assemblages rely on sanctuary resources for all, or part of, their life history. Whether fishes are estuarine, demersal, or pelagic, their species richness is correlated with temporal and seasonal influences. Historic long-term studies, using both visual and consumptive sampling techniques, yielded between 389 and 440 total fish species (Longley and Hildebrand 1941, Starck 1968).

Birds

The Florida Keys host more than 285 species of birds, many of which are seabird or shorebird species. Birds most frequently encountered in and around the water include terns, gulls, plovers, cormorants,

Figure 10. National Association of Black Scuba Divers (NABS) conducting an archeological survey of the shipwreck *City of Washington* in the Florida Keys.

PHOTO: NOAA/FKNMS

pelicans, herons, egrets, osprey (*Pandion haliaetus*) and the Magnificent Frigatebird (*Fregata magnificens*). The Florida Keys are also an important stop-over point for other migratory birds and waterfowl.

Turtles

Five of the seven extant sea turtles frequent the waters of the sanctuary, and some species including the green, loggerhead (*Caretta caretta*) and leatherback (*Dermochelys coriacia*) sea turtles nest along the Florida coastline. All marine turtles are either threatened or endangered and thus protected by the Endangered Species Act in U.S. territorial waters (ESA; see following subsection). The highest densities of sea turtles in the Gulf of Mexico region are observed in waters surrounding the Florida Keys (McDaniel et al. 2000).

Marine Mammals

The Florida Keys and the sanctuary are within the seasonal geographic range of a variety of marine mammals. Thirteen species of whales, seven species of dolphins and the West Indian manatee either reside in or travel through the sanctuary at some point in their lifetimes.

Endangered and Threatened Species

A variety of plants, invertebrates, fishes, reptiles, birds, and mammals that use or contribute to sanctuary resources in the Florida Keys are protected at the federal or state level. Each of these species is a valuable natural resource that contributes to the ecological balance of the sanctuary. Animal species at risk are dependent on the sanctuary's diverse habitats, including mangroves, beaches (below high water mark), seagrass beds, and coral reefs. State and federally threatened and endangered marine and aquatic fauna include, but are not limited to, elkhorn coral (*Acropora palmata*), staghorn coral (*A. cervicornis*), pillar coral (*Dendrogyra cylindrus*), all five species of sea turtles found in the western Atlantic —loggerhead, green, hawksbill (*Eretmochelys imbricata*), Kemp's Ridley (*Lepidochelys kempii*), and leatherback — the American alligator (*Alligator mississippiensis*), American crocodile (*Crocodylus acutus*), smalltooth sawfish (*Pristis pectinata*), Roseate Tern (*Sterna dougallii*), Least Tern (*Sterna antillarum*), and the West Indian manatee. The sanctuary is also in the migratory range of three species of whales: humpback (*Megaptera novaeangliae*), fin (*Balaenoptera physalus*), and North Atlantic right (*Eubalaena glacialis*).

Maritime Archaeological Resources

Florida Keys National Marine Sanctuary is the trustee for maritime heritage resources located within its boundaries (Figure 10). Maritime heritage resources are defined as those possessing historical, cultural, archaeological, or paleontological significance. The sanctuary's maritime archaeological resources are unique, non-renewable remnants of the area's colorful maritime and submerged prehistoric past and include hundreds of documented shipwreck sites and artifacts, cultural remains of early peoples and historical activities, railroad remnants, and historical offshore structures. The sanctuary's maritime archaeological resources encompass a broad historical range from the European Colonial Period to the Modern Era. Because of its unique geographical position on the European and American trade routes, shipwrecks in the Keys contain a record of the 500-year history of the Americas. An estimated 2,000 shipwrecks are thought to have occurred in the Florida Keys since European exploration of the Western Hemisphere. Approximately 669 historic artificial reefs have been documented to date (Halas 1988). Currently, 14 shipwrecks and two lighthouses within the sanctuary are listed in the National Register of Historic Places.

Key West has been the crossroads of the Caribbean since the colonial era, and the sea has remained the common thread through the region's culture and history. The importance of the region's maritime heritage resources is great, and the possibility exists for discovering some of the earliest archaeological sites in North America. A detailed description of the cultural and historical resources of the Florida Keys is contained in the "Description of the Affected Environment," of the Environmental Impact Statement (NOAA 1996).

Pressures on the Sanctuary

N umerous human activities and natural events and processes affect the condition of natural and maritime heritage (archaeological) resources in marine sanctuaries. This section describes the nature and extent of the most prominent pressures in Florida Keys National Marine Sanctuary, many of which originate outside its boundaries.

Pressures on Water Quality

Water quality is a key element that unites all sanctuary resources and is essential to maintaining the richness and diversity of its varied environments. Water quality is both a spatial and temporal phenomenon and can be affected by both natural and anthropogenic influences. Under certain conditions, external sources adjacent to the sanctuary (e.g., Gulf of Mexico Loop Current and Florida Current, land based activities, and atmospheric inputs) can dominate water quality patterns. Pressures on water quality in the sanctuary are described below.

Point Sources of Pollution and Contamination

Point source pollution results when a pollutant is discharged directly into surface waters from a definite location, such as the pipes of industrial waste facilities or domestic sewage treatment plants. Pollutants can be natural substances, like nutrients, that are present in unusually high quantities due to human influence. Contaminants are typically chemicals not found normally in the environment such as industrial chemicals, pesticides, PCBs, and other toxicants. Point source pollution can also include discharge resulting from urban stormwater runoff if coming from a drainage pipe. The effects of point source effluents on receiving surface waters may include the introduction of additional flow, increased microbial abundance, suspended sediments, nutrients (e.g., nitrogen and phosphorus), metals, and organic compounds. In the Florida Keys, wastewater and stormwater treatment and solid-waste disposal facilities were highly inadequate, directly affecting nearshore water quality (Kruczynski and McManus 2002).

When the sanctuary was designated in 1990, there were 19 facilities actively discharging effluent directly into nearshore waters, including water treatment plants, power plants, a desalination plant, and other industrial facilities (NOAA 1996). Today, Monroe County and local municipalities are undergoing extensive upgrades in wastewater infrastructure that provide advanced wastewater treatment, significantly reducing wastewater impacts and pressures in the area (Figure 11).

Nonpoint Sources of Pollution

Unlike point source pollution, nonpoint source pollution comes from many diffuse sources. Nonpoint source water pollution is usu-

Figure 11. Sewer pipes are being placed in the ground throughout the Florida Keys to carry wastewater to advanced wastewater treatment plants being constructed throughout the keys.

ally due to rainfall moving over and through the ground and carrying various chemicals. As the runoff moves, it picks up and carries away pollutants, finally depositing them into surface and subsurface (groundwater) waters. Pollutants and contaminants include excess fertilizers, herbicides, and insecticides from agricultural lands and residential areas; oil, grease, and toxic chemicals from urban runoff and energy production; sediment from improperly managed construction sites and dredging operations; bacteria and nutrients from birds and other wildlife; pet wastes; and faulty septic systems. Eutrophication (an outcome of excess nutrients in the water, such as fertilizers) of nearshore waters has been an ongoing, documented problem in the nearshore waters of the Florida Keys. The process of eutrophication has the potential to shift primary productivity from the slower-growing flora (e.g., seagrasses) to faster-growing species (e.g., macroalgae and microalgae). In time, eutrophication may result in a shift from one type of biological community to one that is adapted to the higher-nutrient conditions (Fourqurean et al. 2003, Wagner et al. 2008).

Because they are generally more soluble than toxicants such as oil and lipid-soluble contaminants, nutrient and organic inputs may affect the environment over a greater spatial area. In addition, while toxicants affect localized environments such as marinas, canals, and areas surrounding industry, nutrients are more susceptible to transport and represent a greater threat to seagrass and coral reef communities (NOAA 1996). Residential canals in the Florida Keys were often dug too deep, and the length and complexity of the residential canal systems also limit flushing with nearshore waters of the sanctuary. They frequently experience microalgal blooms and have anaerobic sediments containing accumulated chemicals and organic matter. While some studies have been conducted, the exact extent to which residential canals affect sanctuary waters has not been fully studied at this time (Chesher 1974, Lapointe and Clark 1990 and 1992).

Domestic wastewater from illegal cesspits and outdated septic systems has been contributing to nonpoint source pollution in the Keys, but is expected to decline due to improvements being made in wastewater treatment, which involves decommissioning the septic systems and cesspits. Other sources of nonpoint source pollution include abandoned landfills, marinas and live-aboard vessels (collectively), and stormwater runoff (NOAA 1996).

Swimming Advisories

Runoff and spills have periodically resulted in high levels of fecal coliform and enterococci bacteria in the Florida Keys, resulting in swimming advisories for nearshore waters and beaches (Figure 12). Enterococci bacteria and fecal coliform bacteria are often used as indicator organisms in nearshore water quality monitoring, and while they may not cause diseases in humans, their presence can indicate that water may be contaminated with organisms that cause human health impacts such as fever, flu-like symptoms, ear infection, respiratory illness, rashes, gastroenteritis, cryptosporidiosis, and hepatitis. Sources of polluted and contaminated water include runoff from urban, suburban and rural areas, aging sewer infrastructure systems pressed to meet increasing demands, and contaminated flows from other upland sources. Contributing factors that generate these sources include illicit storm drain connections, improper disposal of materials or maintenance that clog pipes and cause overflows, cracked or damaged pipes, overflow of sewer systems during storm events, septic system leaching, and various domestic and wildlife sources.

External Input

External sources of pollutants and contaminants also affect the sanctuary's water quality. Examples of this input could include Florida Bay, Biscayne Bay and canal structures operated by the local water management district. Additionally, the sanctuary is considered downstream of currents in the region, like the Loop and Florida currents that transport much of the water from the western coast of Florida, Mississippi River outfall, contributions from Central America and northern South America (Orinoco Flow), and various islands of the Caribbean. Lastly, eddies that form along boundary currents parallel-

Figure 12. The Florida Department of Health posts swimming advisories at beaches throughout the Florida Keys. This sign indicates if it is advisable or not to swim due to water quality issues such as fecal coliform levels.

ing the shore line can cause periodic upwelling of cold, nutrient-rich waters (e.g., Tortugas and Pourtales gyres) (NOAA 1996, Szmant and Forrester 1996, Leichter et al. 2003).

Harmful Algal Blooms

A harmful algal bloom (HAB) can occur when certain types of microscopic algae grow quickly in water, forming visible patches that may harm the health of the environment, plants, or animals. HABs are attributed to two primary factors: natural processes such as warm water and poor water circulation and flow, and anthropogenic causes such as nutrient loading leading to eutrophication. These processes can result in large amounts of certain types of macroalgae or phytoplankton (e.g., dinoflagellates) accumulating in the water. Aggregations of these organisms can discolor the water, giving rise to red, mahogany, brown, or green tides. Red tides occur every year off Florida and are known to deplete the available oxygen supply and block sunlight. In addition, some HAB-causing algae (e.g.,

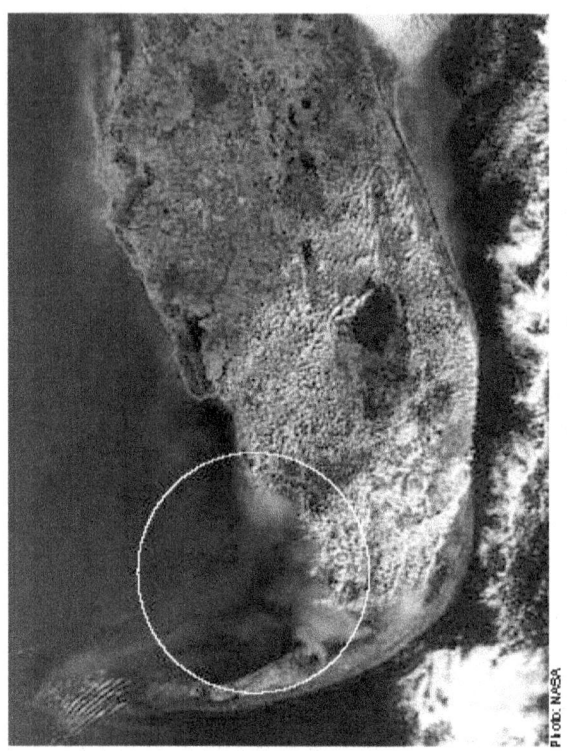

Figure 13. 2002 satellite image of a "black water" event north of the lower Florida Keys.

Figure 14. Boating is a popular activity in the Florida Keys National Marine Sanctuary, however boating activities can have impacts to sanctuary resources.

dinophytes) can release toxins into the water that adversely impact aquatic organisms and humans. Impacts include fish kills, coral stress and mortality, and skin and respiratory problems in humans. HABs have occurred in the waters of almost every U.S. coastal state. Over the last several decades, HABs have caused more than $1 billion in economic losses in the U.S. due to closures of shellfish beds and coastal fisheries, detrimental impacts on tourism and service industry revenues, and public illnesses (Abbott et al. 2009a). Data suggests that HABs are increasing in frequency within the last couple of decades (Harvell et al. 1999).

Of significance, the sanctuary had high concentrations of the microscopic alga that causes red tide (*Karenia brevis*) at the offshore reefs during the 2009 and 2010 annual red tide 'seasons.' Although the first red tide was officially recorded in Florida in 1844, these recent occurrences of *K. brevis* on the reef-line are the first on record. *Karenia brevis* kills fish by producing a powerful toxin (brevetoxin) that affects the central nervous system of fishes. In addition, brevetoxins can become concentrated in the tissues of shellfish that feed on *K. brevis*. People who eat these shellfish may suffer from neu-

rotoxic shellfish poisoning, a food poisoning that can cause severe gastrointestinal and neurologic symptoms, such as tingling fingers or toes. It can also affect birds, mammals, and other marine animals higher up the food chain.

In early 2002, a patch of "black water" more than 60 miles (100 kilometers) in diameter formed off southwestern Florida (Figure 13). Currents carried the black water to the ocean side of the Florida Keys, where it resulted in severe coral reef stress and death (Keller and Causey 2005). Microscopic organisms and toxins contained in the dark water stressed the coral reef system resulting in a 70% decrease in stony coral cover, a 40% reduction of coral species, and a near-elimination of clionid sponge colonies at two reef sites after the dark water passed (Hu et al. 2003). Though a similar black water event was blamed for declines in Acroporid species in the Dry Tortugas in 1878, its origin and composition were never discovered (Jaap et al. 1989).

Marinas and Boats

Water pollution from activities associated with marinas and boating within the sanctuary is also a threat to sanctuary resources (Figure 14). Boater-generated impacts on water quality generally fall into four categories: toxic metals primarily from anti-fouling paints, hydrocarbons from motor operations and maintenance procedures, solid waste and marine debris from overboard disposal, and bacteria and nutrients from boat sewage.

Cruise Ships

A few cruise ships started visiting the Port of Key West infrequently in the late 1980s, by 2010 between five and 13 cruise ships visit Key West weekly. Each ship can carry more than 3,000 people and arguably provide local businesses with positive economic benefits. For example, from 1995 to 1996 approximately 350,000 cruise ship passengers arrived at the Port of Key West, 90% of which departed the ships to participate in recreational activities in Key West (Leeworthy and Wiley 1996). By 2008, numbers nearly doubled and 740,000 passengers visited Key West on the 346 cruise ships that ported that year (Leeworthy et al. 2010). In 2003, cruise ship passengers reached a peak of over 1 million passengers (City of Key West, Finance Department 2005).

Concerns exist about environmental impacts of cruise ships, including discharges impairing water quality and sediment erosion. Cruise ships are floating cities that are capable of carrying as many as 3,000 passengers and crew members, and thus need to provide many of the same services as their land-based equivalent. The main pollutants generated by cruise ships include bilge water (water that collects in the lowest part of the ship's hull that may contain oil, grease, and other contaminants), blackwater (sewage), graywater (waste from showers, sinks, laundries, and kitchens), ballast water (water taken onboard or discharged from a vessel to maintain its stability), and solid waste (food waste and garbage). Ocean currents have the potential to transport these pollutants into sanctuary waters. Although cruise ships are capable of generating volumes of waste comparable to a small city (though many incinerate large portions of their wastes), they are not subject to the same environmental regulations and monitoring requirements as a land-based equivalent. Cruise ships also have the potential to cause benthic disturbances with each porting. Wakes generated by vessels and propeller turbulence re-suspends sediment and transports it elsewhere.

Petroleum (hydrocarbons) and Other Chemical Spills

Petroleum (oil, gasoline, other hydrocarbons) and chemical spills in the sanctuary can potentially range from small, localized spills to large events that span hundreds of miles of coastline. The most common and chronic form of spill is from small boat engine operations and usually involves small discharges of fuel, oil, or hydraulic fluid. Other small spills tend to be associated with oil and fuel discharges due to small vessel (<65 feet or 20 meters) groundings or sinkings and plane crashes. Effects of small spills have not been adequately documented. A larger oil or chemical spill may result from offshore shipping traffic, a cruise ship disaster, or offshore oil and gas drilling and production operations (e.g., upstream Gulf of Mexico sources and potential Cuban sources). A large spill could have a major impact on sanctuary biota including coral reefs, foraging birds, marine mammals, fishes, and fringing mangrove habitat. Tourism and the coastal economy would be also negatively affected by this type of spill.

Live-aboard Vessels

Disposal of wastewater from live-aboard vessels has historically been a significant localized problem because of the low level of treatment, the tendency for live-aboard vessels to congregate in certain marinas or anchorages, and the potential adverse health effects of discharging untreated wastewater. Many live-aboard vessels are

Figure 15. Numerous live-aboard vessels are anchored around the Florida Keys.

Figure 16. Fly-fishing is a popular way to fish for bonefish in the Florida Keys.

permanently anchored and mobile pump-out facilities are required to service those vessels (Figure 15).

Mosquito Control

Application of insecticides to control mosquito-borne pathogens like West Nile virus, Dengue fever, and viral encephalitis affect nearshore waters of the sanctuary. Waters are vulnerable to insecticide runoff and overspraying, while toxic effects may affect non-target organisms, such as the queen conch (*Strombus gigas*) (McIntyre et al. 2006, Glazer et al. 2008).

Commercial and Recreational Fishing

Fishing is the most widespread exploitative activity in coastal ecosystems and poses significant threats to the biodiversity and condition of marine ecosystems (Ault et al. 2005a, Chiappone et al. 2005). Threats are in the form of direct take, by-catch, indirect effects, and habitat damage from the use and loss of fishing gear

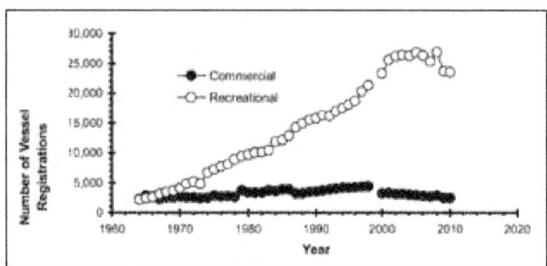

Figure 17. Recreational vessel registrations in Monroe County increased more than 1,000% from 1964 to 2010. Commercial vessel registrations increased by about 100% from 1964 to 1998, but have since decreased by 37%.

Source: Florida Statistical Abstracts and Florida Department of Highway Safety and Motor Vehicles; Ault et al. 2005b

(Figure 16). For example, the removal of targeted species and coincident mortality of non-target species (by-catch) may result in cascading ecological effects (Frank et al. 2005). Because fishing is also size-selective, concerns exist about ecosystem disruption by removal of ecologically important key species such as top predators (e.g., groupers, snappers, sharks, and jacks) and their prey (e.g., shrimps and baitfish).

Both commercial and recreational fishing are economically important to the Florida Keys. In terms of volume of seafood landed, the Florida Keys is the most important area in the state of Florida for landings, dockside value, and numbers of commercial fishing vessels, most of which target the highly valued invertebrate fisheries (Adams 1992). Although fishing pressure (i.e., number of trips, traps, angler days, etc.) from both the commercial and recreational fisheries declined from 1995 to 2008, it is uncertain if these trends will continue. For example, information from socioeconomic surveys in 1995-96 showed over 572,000 visitors and residents did over 2.8 million days of recreational fishing in the Florida Keys (Leeworthy and Wiley 1996, Leeworthy 1996, Leeworthy and Wiley 1997). Similar surveys in 2007 and 2008 showed almost 416,000 visitors and residents did almost 2.1 million days of fishing in the Florida Keys and Key West (Leeworthy and et al. 2010 and Leeworthy and Morris 2010). This represents a 25% decline in recreational fishing effort over the 12-year period. However, this decrease in pressure has an offsetting trend in that the growth in average fishing power (the proportion of stock removed per unit of fishing effort) may have quadrupled in recent decades. This increase results from technological advances in fishing tackle, hydroacoustics (depth finders and fish finders), navigation (charts and global positioning systems), communications, and vessel propulsion (Bohnsack and Ault 1996, Mace 1997). Because of this, there remains a significant but largely undocumented effect of

tens of thousands of recreational fishers who target hundreds of species using mostly hook-and-line and spear guns (Figure 17; Bohnsack et al. 1994a). Reef damage may also occur from anglers anchoring on reefs (Davis 1977), as well as gear impacts from lost fishing gear.

Marine debris in the form of derelict fishing gear can destroy benthic organisms, entangle both benthic and mobile fauna (Donohue et al. 2001), and reduce the structural complexity of habitats (Chiappone et al. 2002a). For example, commercial fisheries targeting lobsters and stone crabs utilize traps that are deployed in habitats adjacent to reefs. Currents associated with strong storms can move traps onto reefs, where corals and other benthic organisms are damaged or killed (e.g., Sheridan et al. 2005). In 2005, it was estimated that approximately 300,000 lobster traps were lost during a series of hurricanes and strong storms (Clark 2006). The ecological impacts caused by fishing gear that is lost when cut or broken after snagging on the bottom is a growing concern to managers and scientists (Chiappone et al. 2005).

Bleaching Events and Climate Change

Seasonal and yearly seawater temperature extremes, increasing UV penetration in the water column, and atmospheric changes all affect the Florida Keys ecosystem. These impacts are most evident in coral disease and bleaching events, which have increased in frequency, duration and range, coinciding with the 10 warmest years on record (1999 to 2009). However, additional human-induced stresses are likely affecting the ability of these organisms to adequately recover from climate fluctuations (Wagner et al. 2010).

During the 20th century, the global mean near-surface air temperature over land and mean sea surface temperature (SST) increased $0.6 \pm 0.2°C$, with the 1990s constituting the warmest decade in the instrumental record and 1998 the warmest year since instrumental records began in 1861 (IPCC 2001). Additionally, so far in the 21st century, mean monthly global ocean temperature anomalies have been 0.45°C above the 20th century mean (NOAA NCDC data). These increasing temperatures have the potential to increase the frequency and intensity of both coral bleaching events and summertime tropical weather disturbances. Coral diseases and hurricane damage have been identified as the main source of mortality of two important reef-building corals in the Caribbean region: elkhorn coral and staghorn coral. These coral species have undergone such a drastic decline in abundance that the NOAA Fisheries Service listed these corals as 'threatened' species under the U.S. Endangered Species Act in 2005.

Elevated water temperatures cause corals and other reef organisms such as sponges and gorgonians to bleach, a process characterized by the loss of zooxanthellae (a symbiotic microalgae)

Figure 18. Bleached and moribund Elkhorn coral (*Acropora palmata*).

from coral tissues (Figure 18). High ultraviolet irradiance, typically from unusually calm, clear waters, may exacerbate the impact of increased temperatures (Lesser and Lewis 1996). Although corals may recover from brief episodes of bleaching, if ocean temperatures warm too much or remain high for an extended period, bleached corals will often die. Several correlative field studies show a close association between warmer-than-normal conditions (at least 1°C higher than the annual maximum) and the incidence of bleaching (Hoegh-Guldberg 1999). In 1997 and 1998, an estimated 16% of the world's coral reefs were seriously damaged in one of the most geographically extensive and severe bleaching events in recorded history (Wilkinson et al. 1999), which caused significant mortality worldwide (Baird and Marshall 2000). The stress for many of these coral reef systems was associated with high sea surface temperature over a 12-week period that was apparently enhanced by an extreme El Niño Southern Oscillation event (Wilkinson et al. 1999). A U.S. Department of State report to the U.S. Coral Reef Task Force (Pomerance et al. 1999) concluded that the severity and extent of the 1998 event cannot be explained by El Niño alone, and that the "...geographic extent, increasing frequency, and regional severity of mass bleaching events are likely a consequence of a steadily rising baseline of marine temperatures...". There is some debate whether or not coral bleaching is a disease, but we know it is a physiological response to stressors. While records show that coral bleaching events have been occurring for many years in the Florida Keys (Jaap 1979, 1984), indications are that the frequency, duration, and severity has steadily increased over the past 20 years (Waddell and Clark 2008). Large-scale coral bleaching was first recorded in the lower Keys in 1979 along the outer reef tract, where shallow fore-reef habitats were the most affected areas (Jaap 1979). Bleaching expanded and intensi-

fied with events in 1987 and 1990, and culminated with mass coral bleaching events in 1997 and 1998 that impacted nearshore and offshore reefs throughout the Florida Keys. Coral bleaching and the secondary impact of coral disease is likely responsible for some of the dramatic declines in stony coral cover observed sanctuary-wide in the last two decades (Causey 2008).

Sponges are also susceptible to bleaching events. The Caribbean barrel sponge (*Xestospongia muta*) is a large and common member of coral reef communities at depths greater than 10 meters, and has been called the "redwood of the reef" (McMurray et al. 2008). Like reef corals, this sponge is subject to bleaching in which it expels the symbiotic microorganisms living within its tissues, often resulting in death. Tissues of *X. muta* contain very primitive cyanobacterial symbionts belonging to the *Synechococcus-Prochlorococcus* clade (Gómez et al. 2004, Steindler et al. 2005) that impart the reddish-brown to brown-gray coloration of the sponge. The first report of a massive die-off of *X. muta* in the Florida Keys was in 1979 (Causey 2008). Hundreds of *X. muta* were observed dying in a one-month time frame on the reef tract, south of Bahia Honda Pass. Other reports of bleaching of *X. muta*, along with other symbiont-containing sponges, began to appear along with reports of coral bleaching events over a decade ago (Vincente 1990). In some cases, bleached sponges deteriorated and disintegrated. Moreover, bleached *X. muta* were more susceptible to predation by parrotfishes and generalist predators (Dunlap and Pawlik 1998). Bleaching and subsequent mortality of sponges has since been observed throughout the Caribbean (Nagelkerken et al. 2000).

Coral communities are also susceptible to cold water. For example, in January 1977, an extreme cold "front" passed through southern Florida, causing water temperatures to drop to 14 – 16°C. Following this thermal stress event there was extensive mortality of branching scleractinia corals. Major mortality of Staghorn coral (*Acropora cervicornis*) was observed, with over a 90% loss from 1976 numbers. In addition, there was also a significant loss of Elkhorn coral (*A. palmata*), with over two-thirds being killed by the cold water. (Davis 1982)

Along with extreme temperature fluctuations from a changing climate, ocean acidification may also affect coral reefs in the Florida Keys as atmospheric carbon dioxide levels continue to increase. The ocean takes up around 25% of atmospheric CO_2 produced by humans through land use changes and the burning of fossil fuels, which then dissolves in seawater to form carbonic acid. Since humans have contributed to greater amounts of CO_2 into the atmosphere over the past century, the ocean has absorbed CO_2 at an increasingly rapid rate, changing the ocean's chemistry and leading to ocean acidification. The acidity of seawater has increased by 30% since the beginning of the Industrial Revolution over 250 years ago, lowering the ocean's natural basic (alkaline) status to an acidic imbalance (Ocean Acidification Reference User Group 2009).

Due to the increased acidity of seawater, many of the animals and plants in the ocean that have calcium carbonate skeletons or shells, such as corals, may experience reduced growth or ability to generate hard shells. For example, in Australia's Great Barrier Reef, corals have already reduced their calcification rates, most likely in response to elevated water temperature and ocean acidification impacts (De'Ath et al. 2009). In a study by Hoegh-Guldberg et al. (2007), it is predicted that if atmospheric CO_2 levels continue to increase, the structure and function of coral reef ecosystems around the world will be compromised and some coral species will become extinct. Ocean acidification could prompt a chain reaction of impacts through the marine food web, beginning with larval fish, shellfish, and corals, cutting valuable ecosystem services provided by coral reefs such as food security, tourism, shoreline protection, and biodiversity (Ocean Acidification Reference User Group 2009).

Weather Disturbances

Climatic events play an important role in the ecosystem dynamics of the sanctuary. South Florida experiences more tropical depressions and hurricanes than any other area in the United States (Schomer and Drew 1982). Tropical storms typically occur between June and November, peaking in late September and early October. Winter storms are also common (Roberts et al. 1982). Tropical storms, which include hurricanes, can cause major damage to the marine environment, affecting the abundance and condition of benthic organisms including corals. Large blocks of coral can be broken from reefs and moved great distances, and sediments can abrade organisms or bury them completely. Damage patterns to coral reefs are commonly influenced by the strength, path and duration of each storm event, storm frequency, and prior disturbance history (Witman 1992, Harmelin-Vivien 1994, Lirman and Fong 1997a, b, Lirman 2000). Recovery of coral colonies is often influenced by colony morphology of corals (Gardner et al. 2005), and may, in some cases, take several decades. The topography of the Florida Keys contributes to their vulnerability to such storms — 96% of the area's land mass is less than 6.5 feet (2 meters) above sea level (Cross 1980).

The record breaking 2005 Atlantic Hurricane Season produced a total of 28 named tropical storms, 15 of which attained hurricane strength throughout the Atlantic, Caribbean Sea, and Gulf of Mexico. Five tropical cyclones (Arlene, Dennis, Katrina, Rita, and Wilma) directly impacted the Florida coastline and sanctuary resources. Hurricane Wilma (Figure 19) produced a six- to eight-foot storm surge throughout the middle and lower Keys.

Diseases of Marine Organisms

Mass die-offs of marine life due to disease outbreaks have increased in frequency and intensity in the past two decades, affecting numerous

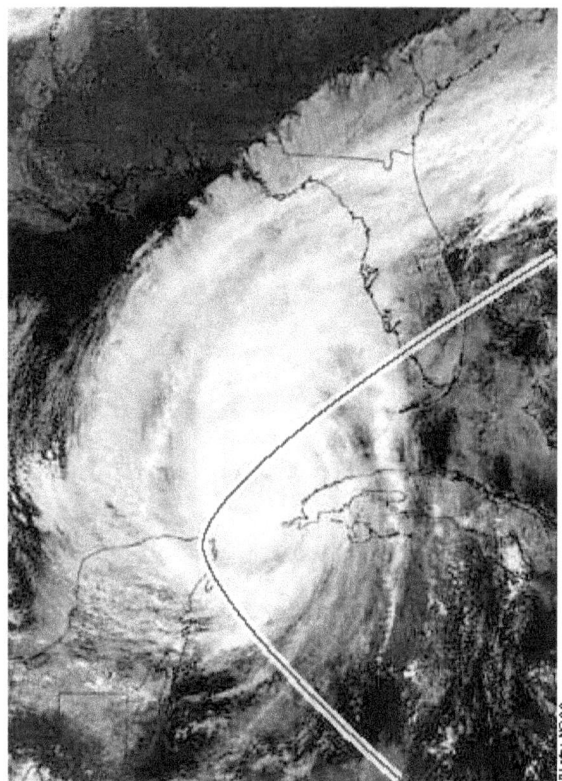

Figure 19. Hurricane Wilma was the 13th hurricane in 2005. It reached 882 mbar pressure in a span of 24 hours, making it the fastest pressure drop of any storm in the Atlantic Basin. At its peak intensity, the eye of Wilma was about 3 miles (5 kilometers) in diameter, the smallest known eye of an Atlantic hurricane. The blue line shows the approximate trajectory of the hurricane.

taxa in the oceans (Harvell et al. 1999). For many marine organisms, including corals and marine mammals, reports of the frequency of epidemics and the number of new diseases is increasing. Recently, the Caribbean basin has emerged as a disease "hot spot" (Harvell et al. 1999, Weil 2004). Mass mortalities of plants, invertebrates, and vertebrates can result in dramatic shifts in community structure. Additionally, diseases affecting benthic marine species such as corals and seagrasses can have disproportionate impacts on the ecosystem because of the changes in habitat and ecosystem function that can result. Despite these impacts the causative agents and the factors contributing disease outbreaks are poorly understood due to lack of information on normal disease levels in the ocean. However, it is believed that factors such as long-term warming trends and human activities, including habitat degradation and pollutant inputs, may play important roles in the transport and spread of diseases (Harvell et al. 1999).

The first documented epizootic event in the Caribbean was the mass mortality of commercial sponges in the northern Caribbean. In December 1938, a blight resulting from a fungus-like filament struck sponge beds in the Bahamas, causing their skeletons to disintegrate (Witzell 1998, McClenachan 2008). The blight quickly reached epidemic proportions, leaving the ocean floor covered with thousands of bleached and rotten sponges, and by February 1939 all sponge-bearing banks were affected (McClenachan 2008). In March, signs of the disease appeared in Key West, and by May sponges showed considerable damage from blight. By the end of 1939, yellow and vase sponges had suffered nearly 100% mortality, while 70% of the commercially valuable sheepswool sponges had been eliminated from the Florida Keys altogether. The disease eventually spread northward and caused extensive mortality to sponges as deep as 70 feet (20 meters). By the end of 1940, the sponge fishery was nonexistent in Florida due to the devastating effects of disease on sponge populations (Shubow 1969).

Another well-studied marine epidemic was the virtual eradication of the long-spined sea urchin. This Caribbean-wide event in 1983 – 1984 spread rapidly in about one year and was caused by an unidentified pathogen which appeared in the Florida Keys in July 1983 (Lessios et al. 1984, Miller et al. 2009). The pathogen was circulated widely throughout the Caribbean by surface currents that connect the southwestern Caribbean with the Florida Keys. In many Caribbean locations, loss of this keystone herbivore contributed to phase shifts from coral- to macroalgae-dominated reefs, especially noticeable in areas where herbivory was nearly solely dependent upon sea urchin grazing because of overfishing (Hughes 1994). Due apparently to low larval supply, recovery of the long-spined sea urchin has generally been slow and incomplete in the Florida Keys since the 1983 and 1991 mortality events (Miller et al. 2009).

Coral diseases have been identified as a significant contributor to coral mortality (Weil 2004, Voss 2006). Although little is known regarding the factors that drive coral disease distributions and dynamics, monitoring of coral diseases in the Florida Keys indicates that there has been an increase in the number of new diseases (Goreau et al. 1998). Coral diseases were first described in the Caribbean in the early-to-mid-1970s (Antonius 1973, Weil 2004). The white plague was the first epizootic event occurring in 1975 and resulted in significant coral mortality. In the 1980s, a white-band disease epizootic event significantly reduced populations of acroporid corals (*A. palmata* and *A. cervicornis*), leading to a reduction in habitat and refuge space and biodiversity (Santavy et al. 2001). The loss of coral cover was correlated with significant increases in algal cover and lack of herbivory, thus changing the community structure and dynamics of shallow coral reef habitats. The first widespread outbreak of black-band disease in the Florida Keys occurred in May 1986 from Looe

Key Reef to Western Dry Rocks (Causey 2008). Prior to this outbreak, only scattered, isolated outbreaks had been reported (Antonius 1973, 1981, Dustan 1977). Following the 1986 massive outbreak, black-band disease became one of the more common coral diseases observed in the 1990s and 2000s. In the 1990s, several new coral diseases were reported, including red-band disease, white-band type II, white plague type II, yellow blotch, dark spots, and white-pox disease. As of 2010, causative agents have only been identified for black-band disease (Bruckner 2000), white-band (Ritchie and Smith 1998), white plague II (Denner et al. 2003), and white pox disease (Patterson et al. 2002). Tumors, as well as lesions associated with parasites, ciliates, bacteria, and fungi, have also been found on a number of coral species. Gorgonians such as sea fans have also been affected by increased disease incidence since 1981 (Nagelkerken et al. 1997), primarily due to exposure to a terrestrial fungus (*Aspergillus sydowii*) (Geiser et al. 1998). Increasing anthropogenic impacts and increasing ocean temperatures may contribute to disease occurrence.

Fibropapillomatosis (FP) is a viral disease specific to sea turtles, although it most commonly affects juvenile green turtles in nearshore habitats around the world (Herbst 1994, Ene et al. 2005). In some localities, such as the Indian River Lagoon, Florida Bay, and the Florida Keys, 50 to 70% of the green turtles are affected (Ene et al. 2005). FP is a debilitating neoplastic disease that can result in benign cauliflower-like tumors on the soft and hard tissues of turtles, both internally and externally. These tumors can disrupt locomotion, feeding, respiration, and vision. While external tumors can be surgically removed, internal tumors cannot and are nearly always fatal. Since the early 1980s, the percentage of green turtles stranded in Florida with FP has been escalating at a rate of 1.2% per year, and based on research from the Florida Sea Turtle Stranding and Salvage Network database, 22% of dead or debilitated green turtles (sample size = 6,027) found in Florida between 1980 and 2005 had tumors (Foley et al. 2005). Although the cause of FP is still not fully understood, recent research has strongly indicated a viral origin. The virus may be spread through biological vectors and specific biotoxins may increase the prevalence of tumors (Foley et al. 2005). Turtles affected by FP are often found in shallow water with poor water circulation, leading to the speculation that environmental factors may play a role in the distribution or prevalence of the disease (Foley et al. 2005).

Panulirus argus virus 1 (PaV1), a lethal herpes-like virus, infects juvenile Caribbean spiny lobster (Behringer et al. 2006). It is transmitted among lobsters via inoculation, prolonged contact with infected lobsters, ingestion of infected tissue, and over short distances in the water (Butler et al. 2008). Because Caribbean spiny lobsters are social and share communal dens, the virus can spread quickly with devastating consequences. PaV1 is the first naturally occurring, pathogenic virus known to infect the Caribbean spiny lobster (Behringer et al. 2008, Butler et al. 2008) affects as many as 16% of the juvenile Caribbean spiny lobster populations sampled from the mid- to lower Florida Keys (ICES 2003). The virus attacks haemocytes, blood cells that are part of the animal's immune system, causing the blood to become milky white, and appears to affect juveniles only. The virus is highly lethal in experimental conditions. Given its virulence, PaV1 represents a serious threat to both commercial and recreational fisheries (Butler et al. 2008).

Cleaner fishes and shrimp in tropical marine habitats assist in keeping the levels of most pathogens and parasites quite low in wild fish populations (Peters 1997). However, injured or weakened reef fish species may become infected with marine bacteria, fungi, protozoans or parasites resulting in lesions, tumors or mortality. In 1980, 1993 and 1994, mass mortality of tropical reef fishes occurred in coastal regions of southeastern Florida and the Florida Keys (Burns 1981, Landsberg 1995, Causey 2001). The affected fish were adult herbivores and omnivores such as angelfishes, parrotfishes, surgeonfishes, and butterflyfishes. Some piscivores and cleanerfishes were also affected. Fishes were observed to have lesions and ulcerated body sores, fin and tail rot, and a heavy mucus coating on the body surface (Landsberg 1995). Causey (2001) noted the close association of these fish mortalities with elevated temperatures that also caused widespread coral bleaching. Landsberg (1995) detected parasites and bacterial infestations in preserved tissues of these fishes, but suggests that ingesting toxins from macroalgae or dinoflagellates may have compromised their health, and the infestations resulted from the fishes' weakened state caused by these toxins.

Vessel Use

A significant threat to the protection and health of sanctuary resources is the impacts from vessels including oil pollution, vessel groundings, noise pollution, and dredged material resulting from maintenance of shipping channels. The Florida Straits have historically been the access route for all commercial vessels entering the Gulf of Mexico from the north and east and, consequently, these waters are some of the most heavily trafficked in the world. It is estimated that 40% of the world's commerce passes within 1.5 days sailing time of Key West (U.S. Department of the Navy 1990). In addition, oil tankers transit the coast daily, including very large and ultra-large crude carriers.

Large commercial vessels are of particular concern because of the potential for oil spills. These vessels often travel close to shore and can carry upwards of 1 million gallons of bunker fuel, a heavy, viscous fuel similar to crude oil that is used to power the ships. As described earlier in this report, a large spill could have a major impact on foraging birds, marine mammals and fishes, as well as important habitats like sandy beaches, mangroves and other intertidal habitats,

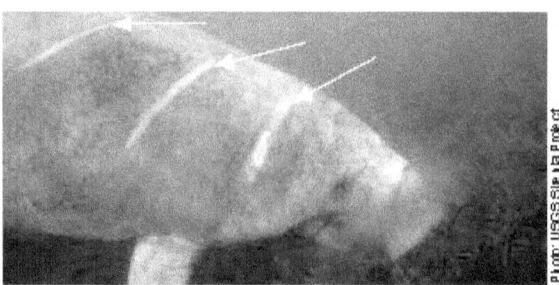

Figure 20. West Indian manatee with old boat propeller scars (as identified with arrows) that biologists use to identify this individual.

seagrass beds, and coral reefs, and therefore could have serious consequences for tourism and the coastal economy.

In addition to the threat of oil spills, more than 300 vessel groundings (vessels 50 feet or less; FKNMS unpub. data) are reported annually within the sanctuary, causing physical damage to sanctuary resources such as seagrass, hard-bottom, and coral reef habitats. There are also many grounding incidents that damage resources but are not reported (NOAA 2007). Although large vessel groundings often result in highly visible, immediate resource devastation with long-term impacts, the vast majority of grounding incidents are caused by smaller recreational vessels. Even so, the cumulative detrimental effect of smaller groundings can also have long-lasting impacts. Vessel groundings from large tankers play a role in the history of the sanctuary. Within a three-week period in 1989, the M/V *Elpis* and the M/V *Alec Owen Maitland* ran aground on two different shallow bank reefs, and a third vessel, the *Mavro Vetranic*, ran aground in Dry Tortugas National Park, killing and displacing corals, gorgonians, and other benthic organisms, in addition to destroying the physical structure of the underlying reef. These three large vessel groundings were important factors in the congressional designation of Florida Keys National Marine Sanctuary and led to the creation of an "Area to be Avoided," which, through sanctuary regulations, prohibits ships greater than 50 meters in length from entering certain areas of the Florida Keys.

Because coral reefs and seagrass beds are found predominantly in shallow water, they are susceptible to a variety of direct impacts from smaller commercial and recreational vessels that may not result in actual groundings. These impacts include damage from the propeller, hull, engine, and keel of these types of vessels. Physical impacts can also result from anchors, anchor chains and cables, unmanned barges, dredge lines, dredge cutter heads, and cables used to tow barges and dredges. Anchor damage, propeller scarring, and other vessel impacts occur frequently and may cause enough damage that impacted reefs and seagrass beds cannot recover. Vessel "strikes" also impact motile fauna such as sea turtles and marine mammals (e.g., dolphins and the West Indian manatee) (Figure 20).

Large commercial shipping traffic and recreational and commercial vessels can also affect noise levels in the marine environment. Certain anthropogenic noise is thought to mask sounds used by marine mammals for mating, feeding, and avoiding predators. Responses vary depending on the acoustic frequency, decibel level, proximity to the source and other species-specific sensitivity factors. Long-term cumulative impacts are uncertain and range from minimal impacts in some situations, to possible physical damage to hearing structures, to stranding events.

Most of these impacts from vessel use correlate with the ever-increasing number of vessels transiting within and around the sanctuary. Recreational vessel registrations in Monroe County increased more than 1,000% from 1964 to 2006, whereas commercial vessel registrations increased by about 100% from 1964 to 1998, but have since decreased by 37% (Figure 17; see page 24). There were 25,370 pleasure and 2,653 commercial vessels registered in Monroe County in 2007 (Federal Register Vol. 74 No 219). These statistics are also reflected in the number of derelict and abandoned vessels located in the Florida Keys in any given year. Monroe County typically has the highest number of derelict or abandoned vessels in the state of Florida, and like marine debris these vessels pose threat to the marine environment, human health, and navigation. From a criminal viewpoint, derelict and abandoned vessels have the potential to be locations for illegal activity, illegal housing, and opportunities for theft and vandalism.

Combined with transits around the sanctuary each year by large shipping vessels (greater than 300 gross tons), cruise ships, and military ships, vessel traffic affecting the sanctuary is continuing on an upward trend. For example, from 2000 to 2005, cruise ships based out of Miami ferried approximately 24.5 million passengers to various locations throughout the greater Caribbean region, including Key West. Additionally, the potential for extremely large vessels traveling the Florida Straits exists when the Panama Canal expansion project is completed over the next few years. Expansion of the Port of Miami is underway to accommodate larger ships en route from the Pacific Ocean.

Coastal Development

Changes to Hydrologic Patterns Associated with Important Nearby Estuaries

South Florida has experienced drastic changes to its freshwater wetlands of the Everglades, and such changes threaten its estuaries (especially Florida Bay), which ultimately could affect the entire sanctuary. During the past century, the pattern (timing, volume, and quality) and intensity of freshwater flows to these estuaries has been significantly altered and reduced due to intense municipal and agricultural activities plus the construction of the Central and Southern Florida Project for Flood Control and Other Purposes (commonly known as

the Project). The Project is a surface-water management facility designed by the U.S. Army Corps of Engineers in the 1950s to drain land, provide flood protection, and regulate South Florida's water supply. Through the Project, enormous volumes of fresh water originally destined for the Everglades and its estuaries have been drained, diverted, or stored in "water conservation areas." The resulting alteration of the natural freshwater cycle has interrupted the distribution, flow, timing, and quality of freshwater delivery through South Florida's wetlands.

Altered flows and drainage canals have also reduced the natural recharge of fresh water to the Biscayne aquifer, the water-bearing limestone beneath southeast Florida and the Everglades. The aquifer is the source of drinking water for all of southern Florida and the Florida Keys via an aqueduct. This long-term reduction in groundwater recharge has gradually allowed salt water to intrude inland from the coast and has reduced freshwater wetlands. A recharged aquifer serves to prevent saltwater intrusion and helps sustain wetlands in times of drought. Reduced freshwater flows over a long period of time and pulses of large amounts of fresh water during heavy rains for flood control have had significant ecological impacts on the two main estuaries adjacent to the sanctuary: Florida Bay and southern Biscayne Bay. Card and Barnes Sounds, which are part of the southern Biscayne Bay system, lie within sanctuary boundaries and have also been affected by reduced freshwater input (USACE 1999). These once-productive estuarine systems have become more marine in species composition over time; negatively affecting their function as a nursery for certain key species like pink shrimp. The impact of this loss of estuary function is not fully known, but restoration projects on the mainland are expected to begin improving flow conditions to both bays in the future.

Nearshore Construction

In addition to altered water flows, shallow, nearshore habitats of the Florida Keys continue to be affected by coastal construction. Rate of growth ordinances for several incorporated Keys communities and Monroe County prevent rapid and uncontrolled development and associated impacts, but some new construction does continue to occur. The small land mass comprised by the individual islands of the Keys, along with the desire by most homeowners to have easy water access, have directed most development to the land-water interface. As such, existing structures such as residential docks, seawalls, and other shoreline protection features are abundant throughout the Florida Keys and are in constant need of repair. Commercial fish houses and similar businesses may be re-purposed for high-end private marinas, often necessitating expansion into nearby coastal habitats. Public infrastructure projects, including bridge and utility line repairs, may encroach into sanctuary waters.

New construction, repairs, or rehabilitation of existing structures in the coastal zone can result in impacts to mangroves, seagrass beds, submerged aquatic algae, nearshore hard-bottom habitat, and coral reefs. While regulations on mangrove destruction and limits on trimming have been in place for many years by the FDEP (Chapter 403 Florida Statutes), protections to less visible, or what may be perceived as "less valuable," species are not consistent among resource agencies. Specific jurisdictions of various agencies and the natural resources they protect may vary, and exemptions to permitting rules for small projects may inadvertently result in impacts to nearshore resources. For example, several ubiquitous stony coral species will recruit to artificial structures such as concrete seawalls and bridge pilings, and may be injured or destroyed during the course of permitted repairs. The manner by which these nearshore corals contribute to the health of the marine ecosystem is an under-studied topic.

Interestingly, some research indicates that corals found in nearshore habitats have higher growth rates and lower partial mortality, despite living in an environment of seemingly poorer water quality (Lirman and Fong 2007). Continued observation of these "hardy" nearshore corals has prompted inquiries about connectivity to their offshore counterparts. While impacts to corals and other species during coastal construction projects may be found to be individually insignificant, this could represent a cumulative threat over space or time to species and habitats, many with unidentified ecosystem worth.

Dredging

As noted in the "Vessel Use section, an increasing number of boats are operating within the sanctuary every year. Dredging activities in the Keys are usually limited to small, private projects, many associated with dock or seawall construction discussed above. Dredging is also occasionally required for maintaining canals or expanding dockage of a local marina. In 2007, the U.S. Navy finished maintenance dredging on the main shipping channel into Key West in preparation for increased fleet presence. The sediment removed from this operation was disposed of at both an upland and offshore disposal site, the latter of which was outside sanctuary boundaries and permitted by the EPA, U.S. Army Corps of Engineers and FDEP. Dredging impacts seafloor communities both at the dredging site and at the disposal site. The physical disturbance of dredging damages or removes organisms living in or on the seafloor and can resuspend buried chemical contaminants. The disposal of dredge material can smother organisms and introduce chemical contaminants at the disposal location. Pipelines or barge routes necessary for upland disposal may impact natural habitats, as can discharges from dredge spoil containment areas. In addition, dredging to deepen channels in harbors can alter water flow dynamics and future sediment deposition rates in the harbor and adjacent habitats.

Beach Nourishment

Sandy beaches are not a prevalent shoreline habitat type in the Florida Keys in comparison to many other counties in the state of Florida.

Florida boasts 825 miles of sandy beach, but just 26 of those miles (42 kilometers) are located within Monroe County. However, several active hurricane seasons, most notably in 2005 and 2006, exacerbated beach erosion and led to the need to supplement local beaches with imported sand. A 2010 report by the Florida DEP Bureau of Beaches and Coastal Systems categorized around 10 miles (16 kilometers) of beach in Monroe County as "critically eroded." The economic benefits of lush sandy beaches in a tourism community are well recognized. However, replenishing beaches with sand may result in direct impacts such as burial of natural, functional nearshore habitats (seagrasses, algae, and hard bottom), especially if unsuitable sediment is used (Wanless and Maier 2007). Indirect impacts may include localized turbidity and increased sedimentation at both the beach and borrow sites (Jordan et al. 2010), as well as a decrease in resident fish assemblages when habitat is lost (Lindeman and Snyder 1999). Sand placement may also change beach attributes, such as burying sea turtle nests, if it is conducted during the active nesting season due to nest burial or changes in beach attributes.

Non-Indigenous Species

Non-indigenous species are recognized worldwide as a major threat to ecosystem integrity when they become invasive. Non-indigenous species in the marine environment can alter community composition, reduce the abundance and diversity of native marine species (Olden et al. 2004), interfere with ecosystem function, alter habitats, disrupt commercial and recreational activities, and in some instances cause extinctions of indigenous plants and animals (Clavero and Garcia-Berthou 2005). They can cause local extinction of native species either by preying on them directly or by out-competing them for food or space. Once established, non-indigenous species can be difficult, if not impossible, to eradicate.

Invasions by non-indigenous aquatic species (e.g., lionfish, orange cup coral, Red-tipped Sea Goddess) are increasingly common worldwide in coastal habitats due to shipping traffic, world travel, and intentional or accidental releases by individuals. Though the most significant global mechanism for the introduction of aquatic species is ship ballast water, it can occur via other mechanisms such as improper disposal of household aquarium pets, commercial aquaculture operations, and research activities.

Wildlife Disturbance

The sanctuary provides many opportunities for wildlife observation, thus the 3 million annual visitors to the region results in a high level of visitation that can have significant direct and indirect effects on the ecosystem. Both motorized (e.g., party boats, jet skis and other personal watercraft) and non-motorized vessels (e.g., kayaks and canoes) are used throughout the sanctuary, often for viewing marine mammals and seabirds. With the multitude of opportunities for observation come the potential for wildlife disturbance including flushing birds from their nests or roosts and harassing marine mammals. Other tourism activities such as diving and snorkeling can also impact resources. The former Key Largo and Looe Key National Marine Sanctuaries included prohibitions on damaging coral in response to increasing threats by recreational visitors.

In addition to physical impacts, some wildlife species are undergo behavioral changes after they are fed by well-intentioned humans. Sharks, manatees, and numerous bird species (most notably pelicans and herons) are routinely fed fish, fish carcasses, lettuce, fresh water, and other items for the purposes of attraction and viewing, or inadvertently though improper disposal. These species may develop unnatural behavioral patterns leading to unsafe interaction with humans or vessels (e.g., sharks and manatees). Wild birds often suffer from punctured gizzards or other internal organs from digesting fish carcasses at marinas and docks where fish are cleaned and carcasses are discarded.

Figure 21. Sanctuary staff and volunteers conduct regular marine debris cleanup efforts in the sanctuary.

Artificial Reefs

A number of artificial reefs (primarily intentionally sunken ships) have been placed in the sanctuary. General agreement exists in the scientific community that artificial reefs can be effective fish attractants; however, most published research addresses the building of artificial reefs or descriptive studies detailing successional changes in fish species composition (Bohnsack and Sutherland 1985, Kruer and Causey 1992). The effects of artificial reefs on fish and invertebrate populations and habitats, and the longevity of these structures, are not fully known. Whether artificial reefs attract fish from nearby natural habitats or serve as a "production" point where new fish can settle remains a debate among the scientific community, but likely depends on multiple factors (Bohnsack et al. 1994b, Osenberg et al. 2002, Powers et al. 2003). Research in nearby Miami-Dade County found that fish assemblages on an artificial reef are more variable than those on nearby natural reefs, leading to additional questions about whether artificial structures can replace lost reef function (Thanner et al. 2006). As such, thorough research is needed on these topics to determine whether the placement of artificial reefs is consistent with the goals and objectives of the sanctuary.

The sanctuary has experienced first-hand that stability of artificial reefs can be variable despite the best attempts to ensure proper deployment. In 1998, the passing of Hurricane Georges caused the *Ea-*

gle, a Dutch freighter sunk in 1985 six miles (nine kilometers) off Lower Matecumbe Key, to break in half. The USS *Spiegel Grove*, scuttled in 2002 as an artificial reef off Key Largo, landed upside down upon sinking. An unplanned, unfunded salvage effort successfully moved the ship onto its starboard side, and the force of Hurricane Dennis in July 2005 righted the ship to its originally intended position. Federal and state permit requirements for artificial reefs typically include thorough stability analyses and the ability for the structure to withstand 100-year storm events. However, it is not until after deployment that these parameters can be tested in the environment and in the face of unforeseen natural events. Logically, the NOAA administration supports a precautionary approach when considering the deployment of artificial reefs, and notes that "NOAA will continue to emphasize the protection, restoration, and enhancement of natural habitats, as opposed to constructing artificial habitats" (J. Dunnigan, pers. comm. NOAA, Dec. 8, 2009).

Some socioeconomic research on the human-use patterns of artificial reefs on nearby natural reefs has been completed for the USS *Spiegel Grove* off Key Largo. The results indicated that visitation declined by 13.7% on the surrounding natural reefs, lead to a 160.5% increase in artificial reef use, and a net increase in total artificial and natural reef use of 9.3% (Leeworthy et al. 2006). While the recreational use of the surrounding natural reefs decreased, the local dive charter business increased, and the local economy grew in terms of both income and employment (Leeworthy et al. 2006). This represents a positive increase to total business, while reducing pressure on the natural reefs. Similar research is underway for the USS *Vandenberg* sunk off Key West.

Marine Debris

Marine debris is defined as any persistent, manufactured, or processed solid material that is directly or indirectly, intentionally or unintentionally, disposed of or abandoned into the marine environment (NOAA 2008). Marine debris includes a wide variety of objects (e.g., derelict fishing gear, lost vessel cargo, plastics, etc.) that pose a threat to the marine environment, human health, and/or navigation. Various types of debris, including fishing gear, plastic bags, foamed polystyrene, balloons, and other consumer goods, are known to have adverse effects on marine species, and increasing levels of debris in both the ocean and at the land-sea interface are of growing concern to sanctuary managers (Figure 21). Ingestion and entanglement are two of the many problems associated with marine debris, and may lead to death in sea turtles, marine mammals, and benthic organisms. Plastics in the marine environment may never fully degrade, and recent studies found that various types of plastic are consumed by organisms at all levels in marine food webs (Derraik 2002).

While the effects of fishing on marine ecosystems are a continuing concern for resource management, the wide-ranging effects of lost or discarded (derelict) fishing gear on organisms and ecological processes is still largely unknown in many coastal areas. Marine debris, in the form of derelict fishing gear, can reduce the structural complexity of habitats and devastate benthic organisms. Derelict gear can also smother and entangle both benthic and mobile fauna, including endangered species (Donohue et al. 2001, Chiappone et al. 2002a).

Derelict gear can also create long-term entrapment mechanisms that continuously kill mobile fauna (e.g., fish, lobsters, sea turtles) for several years. Because net materials are constructed to be strong and resilient, they can persist in the environment for decades and prevent the escape of entangled wildlife. Angling is the predominant form of recreational fishing in the Florida Keys and most of the environmental impact to the benthos from derelict gear results from lost monofilament line, fishing wire, leaders, lead sinkers, and hooks; however, a large percentage of impacts also stem from lost stone crab and lobster traps (DiDomenico 2001, Chiappone et al. 2002a). Lost cage traps catch prey on a continuing cycle as predators enter the traps to feed on previously entrapped organisms that are dead or dying. Nets and traps, when combined with high wave energy, can also physically scrape organisms such as sponges and corals or sweep immobile invertebrates from sandy areas (Chiappone et al. 2002a, Miller et al. 2010).

In a recent study by Miller et al. (2010) of 145 hard-bottom and coral reef sites from northern Key Largo to Key West, surveys of 480 belt transects comprising 77,500 square feet (7,200 square meters) of hard bottom and coral reef habitat yielded a total of 218 marine debris items, comprising 28 different items or combinations of items. Of these 28 diverse debris types, 10 were hook-and-line angling gear and five were lost lobster and crab trap gear. Debris was encountered on the seabed at 85% of the surveyed reef and hard-bottom sites, indicating the pervasive pattern of debris entangled in benthic habitats.

Military Use

Military use of the sanctuary includes surface and underwater activities. Under normal circumstances, pressures to sanctuary resources are related to conflicts and disturbances with marine life or benthic habitat, and disturbance of seabird roosting areas by aircraft. In the worst case, military pressures to sanctuary resources can include the direct and indirect effects of military aircraft crashes, possible grounding of military ships, jet fuel pipeline ruptures caused by storms, maintenance dredging of shipping channels or harbors,

and habitat loss due to facility improvements or expansion. Military presence in the Florida Keys is detailed in the following paragraphs.

The U.S. Department of Defense (DOD) has played an important role in Monroe County (Florida Keys) since the early 1800s, when the federal government established a small naval operation in Key West to control piracy in nearby waters. The DOD currently maintains several sites in the Keys, including the largest unencumbered airspace available for training on the East Coast. Although all of the military departments are represented in the region, the Navy's presence is the most significant.

The Navy's location in the Keys has international significance, as it maintains the closest military installation in the continental United States to Cuba, Central and South America, and the Caribbean. All of the Navy's facilities are in the lower Keys, with the majority in Key West. The largest is the Naval Air Station Key West (NAS Key West) on Boca Chica Key (Monroe County Board of County Commissioners 1986). Key West harbor, including piers at Trumbo Point Annex and the Truman Annex, is also the site of the only active Navy facility within the sanctuary, where Navy vessels conducting operations in the area are berthed, and where naval acoustic research vessels conduct operations. Fuel deliveries and other logistical actions are also conducted to support training and operations. The Navy recently needed to restore to original capability as well as modernize and update its infrastructure and facilities to provide both improved and additional capabilities essential to support aircraft squadrons and ships visiting at NAS Key West. The modernization was completed by 2006 and required maintenance dredging of the main shipping channel into Key West and Truman Harbor, and refurbishing seawalls and mole piers.

NAS Key West's fuel supplies come by sea by way of Key West's main shipping channel. One Military Sealift Command (MSC) tanker every eight to 12 weeks delivers aviation fuel. Diesel is delivered solely via tanker truck to U.S. Coast Guard Sector Key West two to three times per year. The Key West Pipeline Company owns three tender tanks for receipt and storage of aviation fuel and a pipeline that runs between Trumbo Point Annex and Boca Chica Field. The pipeline is four inches in diameter and approximately seven miles of it runs underwater in the sanctuary.

The U.S. Army operates the U.S. Army Special Forces Combat Divers School in Key West. They parachute into the sanctuary at Shark and Sand Key Drop Zones, and occasionally into other areas of the Gulf.

The Coast Guard (Department of Homeland Security) also maintains a significant presence in the region. It has five primary missions: search and rescue, law enforcement, marine safety, marine environmental protection, and the operation and maintenance of navigational aids (e.g., channel markers, navigational lights, and lighthouses). Because of these responsibilities and the vast expanse of waters along the Keys, the Coast Guard provides an important public function in the sanctuary. It is responsible for more than 560 miles (900 kilometers) of coastline and 34,170 square miles (88,500 square kilometers) of ocean area, and typically has several vessels and over 600 personnel located at three stations (Islamorada, Marathon, and Key West) in the area. The largest vessels operate out of Trumbo Annex in Key West.

The U.S. Air Force operates a Tethered Aerostat Radar System (TARS) at Cudjoe Key for aerial surveillance radar. The system is designed to detect low-altitude aircraft, providing detection and monitoring capability in the Florida Straits and a portion of the Caribbean. The TARS surveillance data are used to support customs and border protection.

Pressures to Maritime Archaeological Resources

As modern underwater technology such as scuba gear, metal detectors and remote-sensing devices are developed, both professional and amateur treasure hunters are able to improve their search for lost and submerged maritime archaeological resources (Gerard 1992). For the purposes of this report, three general types of treasure salvors were categorized, each assumed to exert different (but unquantified) levels of pressure on these resources: 1) souvenir collectors/hobbyists who combine the search for treasure with their recreational diving activities; 2) paraprofessionals who hunt for treasure on a regular part-time basis, but for whom treasure salvage is not their primary source of income or full-time job; and 3) professional treasure hunters whose search, recovery, sale and display of recovered items is a full-time endeavor and primary source of income. While not a common practice, the development of propeller-wash deflection devices (e.g., "mailboxes") have enabled professional treasure hunters to excavate crater-like holes in the seafloor, allowing the discovery of shipwreck materials more than 20 feet (6 meters) below the surface on the seabed. Indiscriminate use of mailboxes can cause significant damage to natural resources as well as cultural resources, including reducing the quality and amount of contextual information. In addition, recreational wreck divers may illegally remove resources from a deepwater shipwreck to keep as a souvenir. Although the degree to which looting occurs is not quantified, the cumulative impacts of this activity can affect the condition of wrecks.

State of Sanctuary Resources

This section provides summaries of the conditions and trends within four resource areas: water, habitat, living resources, and maritime archaeological resources. For each, sanctuary staff and selected outside experts considered a series of questions about each resource area. The set of questions is derived from the Office of National Marine Sanctuaries' mission, and a system-wide monitoring framework (NMSP 2004) developed to ensure the timely flow of data and information to those responsible for managing and protecting resources in the ocean and coastal zone, and to those that use, depend on, and study the ecosystems encompassed by the sanctuaries. The questions address information needs that are common to nearly all sanctuaries throughout the sanctuary system. Appendix A (Rating Scheme for System-Wide Monitoring Questions) clarifies the set of questions and presents statements that were used to judge the status and assign a corresponding color code on a scale from "good" to "poor." These statements are customized for each question. In addition, the following options are available for all questions: "N/A" – the question does not apply; and "undetermined" – resource status is undetermined. In addition, symbols are used to indicate trends: " ▲ " – conditions appear to be improving; "—" – conditions do not appear to be changing; " ▼ " – conditions appear to be declining; and "?" – the trend is undetermined.

This section of the report provides answers to the set of questions. Despite a large diversity in habitat types and communities within the Florida Keys sanctuary, a single, sanctuary-wide status and trend rating is given for each question. Although the ratings are generalized for the entire sanctuary, text found in the following section provides a detailed description of the basis for judgment for each question, and may include recognition and description of any conditions that are not consistent with the rating. Answers are supported by specific examples of data, investigations, monitoring and observations, and the basis for judgment is provided in the text and summarized in the table for each resource area. Where published or additional information exists, the reader is provided with appropriate references and Web links.

Judging an ecosystem as having "integrity" implies the relative wholeness of ecosystem structure and function, along with the spatial and temporal variability inherent in these characteristics, as determined by the ecosystem's natural evolutionary history. Ecosystem integrity is reflected in the system's ability to produce and maintain adaptive biotic elements. Fluctuations of a system's natural characteristics, including abiotic drivers, biotic composition, complex relationships, and functional processes and redundancies are unaltered and are either likely to persist or be regained following natural disturbance.

Water

The following information provides an assessment by sanctuary staff and experts in the field of the status and trends pertaining to the current state of water quality in Florida Keys National Marine Sanctuary:

1. *Are specific or multiple stressors, including changing oceanographic and atmospheric conditions, affecting water quality and how are they changing?*

An increasing number of stressors to water quality over the last several decades may cause measurable but not severe declines in living resources and habitats. For this reason, the rating for this question is "fair." The trend is rated as "declining" because stressors affecting water quality in the sanctuary have been increasing since its establishment, and the predicted effects of global climate change are likely to exacerbate conditions via changes in storm frequency and intensity, upwelling frequency and duration, changing variability of seawater temperature (Figure 22), sea level rise (Figure 23), and other changes to oceanographic patterns and ocean chemistry.

Climate and weather affect water quality through winds and storms, precipitation, evaporation, surface water input, sea level and tides, and "boundary" currents (e.g., Loop and Florida Currents), all of which play an important role in the ecosystem dynamics of Florida Bay and the sanctuary. During the last half-century, regional water management practices have evolved to temper the way climate and weather affect human health and well-being. However, water management during this time has also had direct and indirect impacts on nearshore water quality within the sanctuary. In the latter third of the 20th century, it was recognized that flood control modifications to the drainage of fresh water in the south Florida region resulted in serious environmental effects due to altered water delivery into the surrounding estuarine system, specifically Florida Bay. Although some freshwater flow is currently being restored (via the Comprehensive Everglades Restoration Plan, as approved and amended in the Water Resources Development Act of 2000), it can never be restored to its native state due to the needs of the surrounding human population.

Depending on the geographic scale at which water quality within the sanctuary is considered, monitoring results show

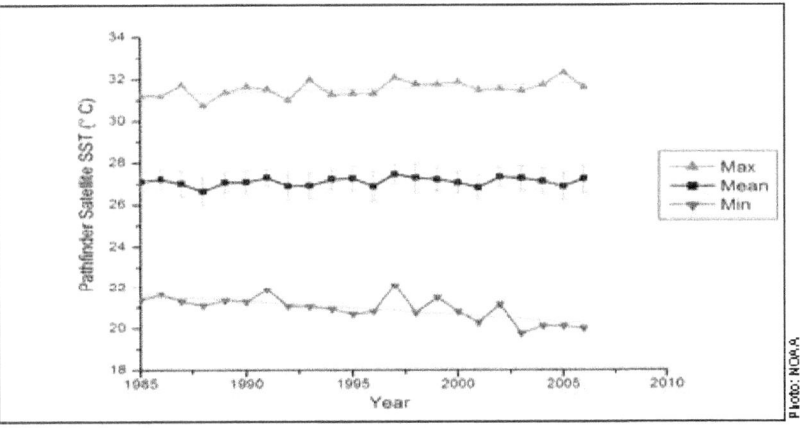

Figure 22. Annual Pathfinder satellite sea surface temperature from eleven 31 mile (50 kilometer) pixels in Florida Bay and around the Florida Keys from 1985 - 2006. Annual maximum SST has a slope = +0.29 °C/decade (p=0.014). Annual mean SST shows no trend. Mean minimum SST has a slope = -0.66 °C/decade (p<0.001).

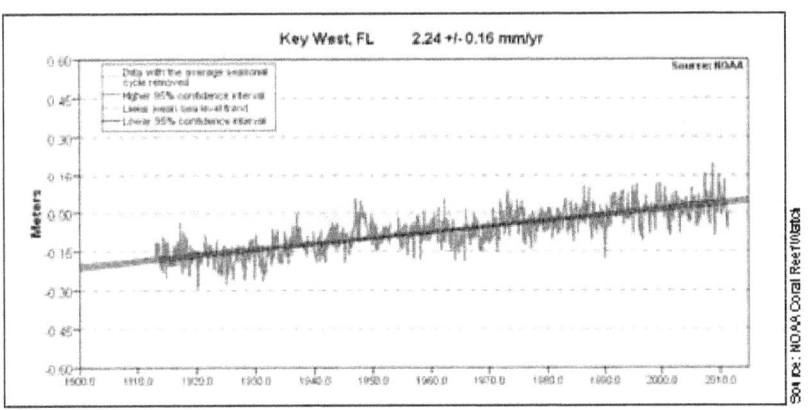

Figure 23. Mean tide measurements from tide station KYWF1 -8724580 at Key West harbor. The mean sea level trend is +2.24 millimeters/year with a 95% confidence interval of +/-0.16 mm/yr based on monthly mean sea level data from 1913 to 2006 which is equivalent to a change of 0.73 feet in 100 years.

there are distinct regional and smaller-scale patterns in water chemistry, some of which are addressed in Question 2. However, in response to this question, we describe and qualify the state of water quality stressors in the sanctuary as a whole, as opposed to separating the various geographic and hydrographic areas of the Florida Keys and their individual states. Detailed water quality information for specific areas of the sanctuary can be found in several references (MACTEC 2003, Hunt and Nuttle 2007, Boyer and Briceño 2009). Generally, we know that the individual "state" of residential canal water tends to have low dissolved oxygen levels, high hydrogen sulfide content, and higher potential for nutrient loading in comparison to the adjacent nearshore waters that have better flushing and flow regimes. In turn, areas of nearshore waters may have eutrophic signals that attenuate further offshore where regional water flows have more substantial influences. The sanctuary is directly influenced by the Florida Current, the Gulf of Mexico Loop Current, inshore currents of the Southwest Florida Shelf (Shelf), discharge from the Everglades through the Shark River Slough, and by tidal exchange with both Florida Bay and Biscayne Bay (Lee et al. 1994, Lee et al. 2002). Thus, not all influences on water quality originate from sources within the Florida Keys. Likewise, Boyer and Briceño (2009) point out that trends observed at smaller (local) scales may also occur across the whole region but at more damped amplitudes. This spatial autocorrelation in water quality is an inherent property of highly interconnected systems such as coastal and estuarine ecosystems driven by similar hydrological and climatological forcings. There have been large changes in the sanctuary's water quality over time, and some sustained monotonic trends have been observed over the last 15 years. However, trend analysis is limited to the window of observation; trends may change, or even reverse, with additional data collection (Wagner et al. 2008, Boyer and Briceño 2009).

Finally, during the last 100 years, the Florida Keys island chain has been physically altered to accommodate passenger trains and vehicles by filling in island passes to create highways and railroad beds. This alteration has permanently affected the flushing dynamics (e.g., oceanographic processes) between the four prominent water bodies adjacent to the sanctuary. With the exception of new bridge construction in upper Key Largo, where flow between water bodies is being enhanced, most altered flow in the Keys is unlikely to change in the immediate future.

2. *What is the eutrophic condition of sanctuary waters and how is it changing?* Water quality in the sanctuary is influenced by waters emanating from freshwater and estuarine habitats near the Florida Everglades, shallow nearshore areas,

and deeper (>100 m) offshore areas. Distinguishing internal from external sources of nutrients in the sanctuary is a difficult task, and the finer discrimination of internal sources from external natural and anthropogenic inputs is even more difficult. Regardless of the source(s), enough evidence exists to rate this question as "fair/poor" because selected conditions have caused or are likely to cause severe declines in some but not all living resources and habitats. The trend is rated as "not changing" because results of the sanctuary's long-term water quality monitoring program do not suggest eutrophic conditions are changing at large spatial scales at this time (Boyer and Briceño 2009).

A large-scale water quality monitoring program was established in the sanctuary in 1995 and provides quarterly sampling of a suite of 18 variables at 155 stations in the sanctuary, extending from the southern boundary of Biscayne National Park to the Dry Tortugas. Several important results have been obtained from this project. First, elevated nitrate has been documented in the inshore waters of the Florida Keys (Figure 24) since the first sampling event in 1995 and continues to be a characteristic of the ecosystem. Interestingly, this nitrate gradient was not observed in a comparison transect from the Dry Tortugas (where there is minimal human impact), thus the nitrate distribution implies a localized, land-based source, which is diluted by lower-nutrient waters of the Atlantic Ocean. Sampling studies also show that there is a similar gradient in total organic carbon as well as a decrease in the variability of salinity moving offshore, further supporting the theory that the source is localized and land-based. There have been no reported trends in either total phosphorous or chlorophyll-a with distance from land. Second, the highest chlorophyll-a concentrations, which are indicative of phytoplankton in the water column, are present on

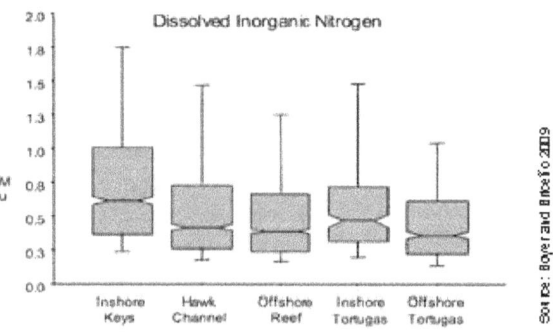

Figure 24. Fifteen year cumulative dissolved inorganic nitrogen (DIN) concentrations in the Florida Keys. Box plots show data distribution and median (line).

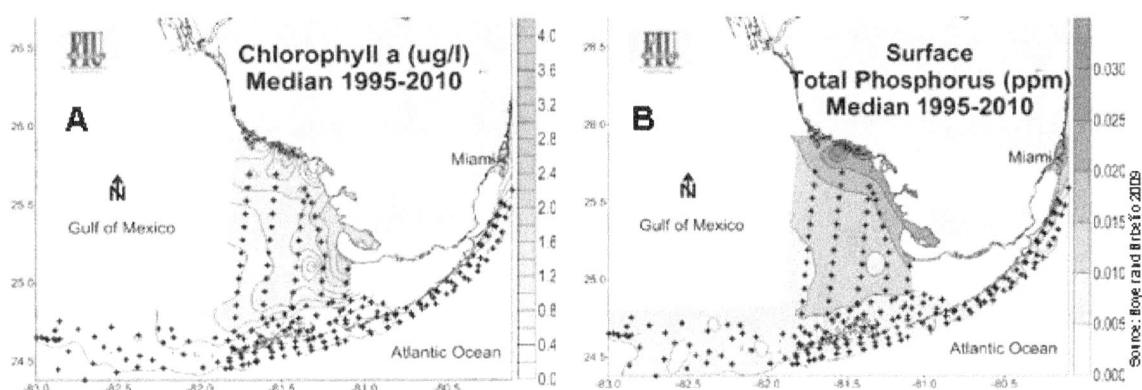

Figure 25. Fifteen-year medians of chlorophyll-a (A) and total phosphorus median concentrations (B) in the Florida Keys and the west Florida shelf.

the southwest Florida Shelf and diminish gradually towards the Marquesas and Dry Tortugas (Figure 25). Water with higher total phosphorus concentrations from the shelf is carried south along the southwest coast of Florida, where it fuels the phytoplankton blooms in the region (Boyer and Briceño 2009).

Generally, trends in most measured nutrient variables since 1995 show relative consistency from year to year, with some exhibiting seasonal variations. Overall, Boyer and Briceño (2009) found that there were statistically significant decreases in dissolved inorganic carbon, total organic nitrogen (except for increases in the Tortugas), total phosphorus, total organic carbon, and dissolved oxygen throughout the region. This is contrary to some of the trend analyses reported in previous years. Most of the important local anthropogenic inputs are regulated and controlled by management activities; other studies have shown that nutrients from shallow sewage injection wells may be leaking into nearshore surface waters (Corbett et al. 2000). There have been large changes in sanctuary water quality over time, and some sustained monotonic trends have been observed; however, trend analysis is limited to the window of observation, and trends may change, or even reverse, with additional data collection. Thus, when looking at what are perceived to be local trends it also seems to occur across the whole region but at more damped amplitudes (Boyer and Briceño 2009).

Large, persistent cyanobacterial blooms originating in Florida Bay have been associated with sponge die-offs (as well as seagrass die-offs) and the associated community dependent upon them (Butler et al. 1995, Fourqurean and Robblee 1999, Hunt and Nuttle 2007). These blooms are not necessarily triggered or sustained by a single change in nutrient load, but rather reflect a combination of multiple biotic and abiotic factors that contribute to their intensity and duration. Unfortunately, we do

not have sufficient data at this time to predict cyanobacterial bloom initiation or longevity, thus there is a need to integrate existing biological, climatological, and oceanographic research efforts so that predictive models can be further developed and refined to support management decisions for control efforts.

It is clear that trends observed within the sanctuary are influenced by regional conditions outside the sanctuary boundaries (Boyer and Briceño 2009). Nutrients originating north of the sanctuary on the Gulf side of Florida may have increased the size and persistence of various harmful algal blooms (ranging from red tides to black-water events). As these phenomena have been correlated with fish kills and seagrass die-offs, their increasing geographic influence could put resources at risk that have not been so previously (including those on the ocean side of the Florida Keys).

3. *Do sanctuary waters pose risks to human health and how are they changing?* Harmful algal blooms (e.g., red tides), fecal coliform and enterococci bacteria, and ciguatera fish poisoning have the potential to affect human health in the sanctuary, thus the rating for this question is "fair" because selected conditions have resulted in isolated human impacts, but evidence does not justify widespread or persistent concern in addition, the trend is rated as "not changing" because there is no evidence to suggest conditions are changing at this time.

Depending on the geographic scale considered, some small patterns in human health emerge. However, for the purposes of this question, we describe and qualify the state of sanctuary waters on human health as a "whole," as opposed to separating the various geographic/hydrographic areas of the Florida Keys and their individual status. As outlined in Question 1, water quality in most residential canals is poor (small-scale, local) when com-

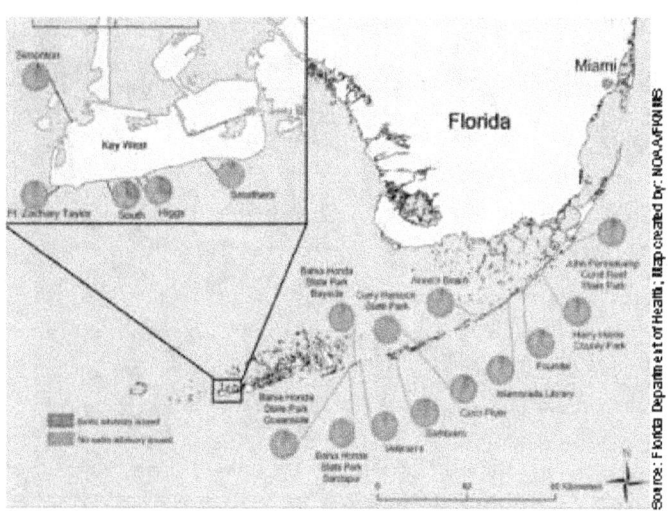

Figure 26. Swim advisories issued in southern Florida. Pie charts represent the mean annual proportion of time per condition per beach from 2003 to 2009. Red indicated swim advisory was issued and green indicated no swim advisory issued.

Periodic swim advisories and warnings are issued by the Florida Department of Health due to the presence of pathogen indicators (enterococci and fecal coliform bacteria). High concentrations of these bacteria and viruses may indicate the presence of microorganisms that could cause gastrointestinal distress, disease, infections, or rashes in people swimming in nearshore waters (Nobles et al. 2000). Advisories and warnings are common at some locations in Monroe County, specifically at South and Higgs Beaches in Key West, which have the highest frequencies of warnings issued per beach since weekly testing began in 2003 (Figure 26). Swim advisories and warnings pertain to very specific areas and the nearshore waters adjacent to them. Therefore, the advisories reflect water quality conditions in specific areas and do not reflect risks to human health throughout the entire sanctuary.

Ciguatera fish poisoning (CFP) occurs throughout the tropical Pacific and the Caribbean. CFP is a reportable disease in Florida (Chapter 64D-3, Florida Administrative Code) (Abbott et al. 2009b). Reported CFP cases in Monroe County are rare, with the most recent case in 2006. However, it is well documented that certain fishes such as grouper, moray eel, jacks, kingfish, snapper, hogfish (*Lachnolaimus maximus*) and barracuda (*Sphyraena barracuda*) are more prone to be ciguatoxic due to their position in the food chain and large adult size (de Sylva 1994, Abbott et al. 2009a). While CFP is an issue regionally and has been reported locally in the Florida Keys, there is no evidence that the incidence of ciguatera is increasing in the sanctuary.

pared to nearshore and oceanic waters (large-scale, regional). Thus swimming in residential canal water may pose risks to human health (e.g., result in gastroenteritis). The same is true for swimming in areas of residential canal outflows. In addition, during the "Swim Around Key West" event in 1999, 30% of swimmers reported at least one symptom of a waterborne disease and 20% reported two or more symptoms (Nobles et al. 2000). However, nearshore and offshore waters are not considered to pose risks to human health.

As described in the "Pressures" section of this document, harmful algal blooms (HABs) have increased in frequency within the last few decades (Harvell et al. 1999). Though no cases of human illness have been documented in association with the consumption of fish during Florida red tide blooms (Abbott et al. 2009b), fishes exposed to red tides can concentrate brevetoxin in their viscera, but levels in the muscle tissue do not suggest a health risk to humans. Notably, sanctuary waters had high concentrations of the microscopic alga that causes red tide on offshore reefs during the 2009 and 2010 red tide "seasons" (MEERA[*]), which is the first documented occurrence of this phenomenon.

4. *What are the levels of human activities that may influence water quality and how are they changing?* Water quality within the boundary of the sanctuary is affected by a combination of regional oceanographic patterns, climatology, and regional and localized anthropogenic influences. As discussed in the "Site History" and "Pressures" sections of this document, during the last century destructive activities (e.g., dredge and fill, untreated storm water, discharge of poorly treated sewage) have been widespread throughout the region, thus the rating for this question is "fair/poor" because many human activities have caused or are likely to cause severe impacts, and cases to date suggest a perva-

---

[*]A joint venture between the Mote Marine Laboratory and the Florida Keys National Marine Sanctuary, the Marine Ecosystem Event Response and Assessment Project (MEERA) is designed to provide early detection and assessment of biological events occurring in the Florida Keys and surrounding waters. The goal of the project is to help the scientific community better understand the nature and causes of marine events that adversely affect marine organisms, and assist ongoing research efforts to assess and monitor events as they develop. Understanding these events will help scientists and managers determine whether such events are natural or linked to human activities (www.mote.org/MEERA).

sive problem. However, the trend is rated as "improving" because management responses are addressing the widespread, pervasive problems, leaving issues that are more localized.

As stated previously, the degree to which human activities influence water quality depends on the scale under consideration. At smaller, localized scales, water quality in the Keys has been affected by the dredging of dead-end residential canals. Most of these canals have poor flushing because of the way they were constructed. Depending on wind and currents, these residential canals accumulate seagrass "wrack" which depletes dissolved oxygen during decomposition and increases the level of nutrients and hydrogen sulfide gas in the water. Hydrogen sulfide gas is toxic and residences near heavily polluted canals may be at risk. Furthermore, residential canals receive additional nutrient and chemical loading via stormwater runoff. At larger, regional scales, island passes that were filled in to create highways and railroad beds have permanently altered the flushing dynamics (e.g., oceanographic processes) between the four prominent water bodies adjacent to the sanctuary.

In addition to the human activities stated in Question 1 (e.g., flood control modifications, runoff, highway/railroad construction), another that affects water quality is mosquito control. The Florida Keys are subtropical in climate and subject to mosquito-borne pathogens like West Nile virus, Dengue fever and viral encephalitis. Successful application of insecticides from both airborne platforms and vehicles is subject to climatological conditions. In the past, the Florida Keys Mosquito Control District used thermal fogging to apply pesticides (specifically adulticides). The pesticide was diluted with diesel oil and either passed through the engine of the plane or through a blower applicator mounted in the back of a truck. This delivery process produced a thick cloud of smoke easily observed by residents. It also produced a certain level of pollution due to the fumes of the diesel oil. Now the district uses ultra-low volume applications, in which a very small amount of pesticide is used to achieve the same results while eliminating pollution caused by the diesel oil carrier.

Nevertheless, though most insecticides are successfully delivered to their target, nearshore waters of the sanctuary are still susceptible to over-spraying, insecticide runoff, and sublethal and lethal effects on non-target organisms (i.e., other invertebrates that are harmed by the poisons used). The Florida

Keys Mosquito Control District has a research program focused on basic and applied aspects of mosquito biology and control; however the impacts of mosquito spraying on non-target marine organisms need further research. The Fish and Wildlife Research Institute has conducted research that demonstrates that mosquito control pesticides are detrimental to queen conch (McIntyre et al. 2006, Glazer et al. 2008).

Water Quality Status & Trends

#	Issue	Rating	Basis for Judgment	Description of Findings
1	Stressors	▼	Large-scale changes in flushing dynamics over many decades have altered many aspects of water quality; nearshore problems related to runoff and other watershed stressors; localized problems related to infrastructure.	Selected conditions may inhibit the development of assemblages and may cause measurable but not severe declines in living resources and habitats.
2	Eutrophic Condition	—	Long-term increase in inputs from land; large, persistent phytoplankton bloom events, many of which originate outside the sanctuary but enter and injure sanctuary resources.	Selected conditions have caused or are likely to cause severe declines in some but not all living resources and habitats.
3	Human Health	—	Rating is a general assessment of "all waters" of the sanctuary, knowing that in very specific locations, the rating could be as low as "poor." Increased frequency of HABs and periodic swim advisories.	Selected conditions have resulted in isolated human impacts, but evidence does not justify widespread or persistent concern.
4	Human Activities	▲	Historically, destructive activities have been widespread throughout the Florida Keys, but many recent management actions are intended to reduce threats to water quality.	Selected activities have caused or are likely to cause severe impacts, and cases to date suggest a pervasive problem.

Status: Good Good/Fair Fair Fair/Poor Poor Undet.

Trends: Improving (▲), Not Changing (—), Declining (▼), Undetermined Trend (?), Question not applicable (N/A)

Habitat

The following information provides an assessment by sanctuary staff and experts in the field of the status and trends pertaining to the current state of marine habitats in Florida Keys National Marine Sanctuary:

5. *What are the abundance and distribution of major habitat types and how are they changing?* Generally, at larger spatial scales, nearshore habitats are still present in the geographic areas they occupied through the history of the sanctuary, which suggests the abundance and distribution of the coral, seagrass, and hard-bottom habitat types in the sanctuary have changed little over the last 20 years. With the exception of the water column realm, the major habitat types in the sanctuary are benthic and biogenic in nature and are defined by dominant fauna or flora: coral reefs, seagrass meadows, hard-bottom communities (a mix of hard corals, gorgonians and sponges), and mangrove habitats. In order to answer this question, the absolute "number" and the "geographic extent" of the major habitat types found in the sanctuary were examined. Questions 6, 9, 12, and 13 of this report will address the "health and condition" of these biogenic habitats. With this in mind, the response to this question is rated "good/fair" because selected habitat loss or alteration has taken place (principally due to nearshore development), precluding full development of living resource assemblages, but it is unlikely to cause substantial or persistent degradation in living resources or water quality. The trend is rated as "not changing" because there is no evidence to suggest that the conditions that affect the abundance and distribution of all habitat types are changing significantly.

During the 20th century, nearshore habitat alteration in the Florida Keys was extensive, with much of the physical alteration occurring from the 1950s through the 1970s to support the growing human population. During that period, many acres of tropical hardwood hammocks were cleared to provide land for housing and commercial development. The attractiveness of waterfront development prompted the creation of "fastland" through dredging and filling of mangrove forests and seagrass beds to construct networks of finger-fill residential canals. Approximately 50% of the historic mangrove habitat has been eliminated. More than 200 canals and access channels were dredged during that period (FDER 1987, Kruczynski and McManus 2002). Turbidity from the dredging and filling operations smothered adjacent areas of hard-bottom and seagrass habitats (MACTEC 2003).

The sanctuary encompasses over 2,800 square nautical miles and encompasses a majority of the archipelago of the Florida Keys. Recently, efforts have been made to accurately map the abundance and distribution of habitat types at a finer scale. In 1998, NOAA and the FWC's Fish and Wildlife Research

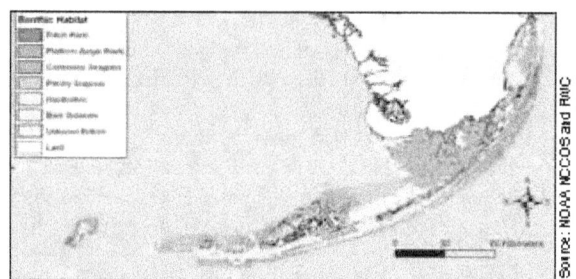

Figure 27. Nearshore habitat types in the sanctuary were mapped based on visual interpretation of aerial photography and hyperspectral imagery.

Institute released habitat maps for the Florida Keys (Figure 27), representing the first large-scale effort to accurately map coral ecosystem habitats in the Florida Reef Tract, from Biscayne Bay to the Dry Tortugas (http://flkeysbenthicmaps.noaa.gov). The 1998 NOAA and FWC effort was a duplication of a 1970s effort to map the basic habitat of the Keys (Marszalek et al. 1977), but utilized more advanced technology. Habitats were delineated based on visual interpretation of 450 aerial photographs collected in 1991 to 1992 (FFWCC et al. 1998). The atlas was revised in 2000, but because it has large areas of unmapped seafloor, a new mapping effort is underway to address this shortcoming.

The sanctuary has also benefited from highly detailed bathymetric maps of portions of the Florida Reef Tract produced by partnerships between USGS, NASA, and the NPS (using Li-DAR technology; http://ngom.usgs.gov/dsp/pubs/ofr/index.html) and from multi-beam sonar surveys performed by the NOAA ship *Nancy Foster*. In spite of these combined efforts, more than 50% of the sanctuary remains to be adequately mapped. As of 2009, a higher proportion of nearshore areas (< 150 feet in depth) were mapped in comparison to deeper areas, thus limiting the ability to quantitatively estimate the abundance and distribution of sanctuary.

6. *What is the condition of biologically structured habitats and how is it changing?* Marine life depends on the integrity of its habitats, and that integrity is largely determined by the condition of particular living organisms. Coral reefs may be the best known examples of such biologically structured habitats. Not only is the substrate itself biogenic, but the diverse assemblages residing within and on the reefs depend on and interact with each other in tightly linked food webs. Based on results from multiple long-term monitoring programs within the sanctuary and separate, focused research projects, this question is rated as "fair/poor" because selected habitat loss or alteration has caused

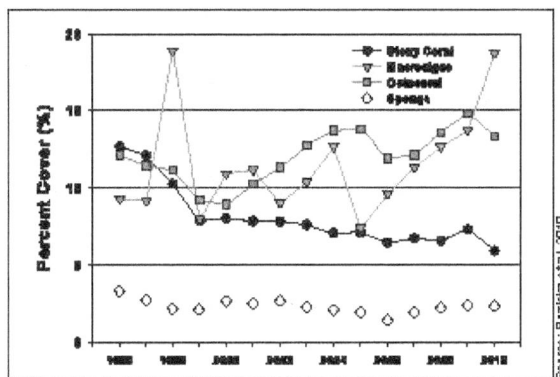

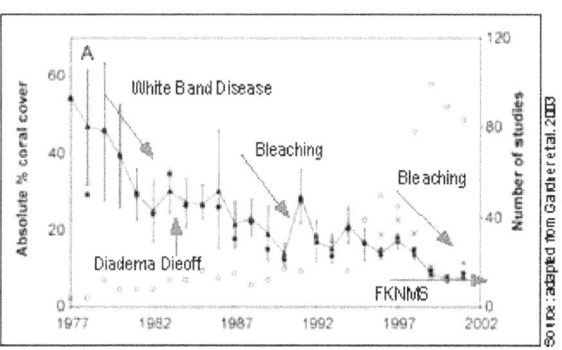

Figure 28. Mean annual percent cover for the four major benthic taxa recorded in CREMP image analysis. Mean percent cover is pooled from 97 stations in the Florida Keys excluding the Dry Tortugas stations. A mixed model regression indicates a decreasing trend for stony corals and sponges (p<0.001), an increasing trend for octocorals (p<0.001), and no trend for macroalgae (p>0.05).

Figure 29. Change in percent coral cover across the Caribbean basin during the past three decades. By the time the Water Quality Protection Program began in 1995, there was already extensive decline in coral cover throughout the region, principally due to coral and urchin diseases, bleaching events, and storms. Annual coral cover estimates (triangles) are weighted means with 95% bootstrap confidence intervals. Also shown are unweighted mean coral cover estimates for each year (solid circles), the unweighted mean coral cover with the Florida Keys Water Quality Protection Program's Coral Monitoring Project (1996–2001) omitted (x), and the sample size (number of studies) for each year (o).

or is likely to cause severe declines in some but not all living resources or water quality. In addition, evidence suggests conditions appear to be "declining."

Coral habitats throughout the sanctuary have been in decline since the late 1970s, principally due to white-band disease and several bleaching events (Dustan and Halas 1987, Jaap 1988, Porter and Meier 1992). Prior to Caribbean-wide coral decline, many reef areas displayed a zonation pattern dominated by three scleractinian coral species: elkhorn coral, staghorn coral, and boulder corals of the genus *Montastraea* (Jackson 1992). Populations of elkhorn and staghorn coral underwent a region-wide decline during the 1980s and 1990s, with losses of 95% or more in some areas, principally due to white-band disease and locally due to storm damage (Figure 28; Gladfelter 1991, Bythell et al. 1993, Aronson and Precht 2001, Gardner et al. 2003). Some scientists have suggested that the loss of these species may have led to increases in algae, reduced rates of reef accretion, and erosion of the reef framework (Aronson and Precht 2001).

In 1995, the Florida Keys Coral Reef Evaluation and Monitoring Project (CREMP) was initiated to provide data on status and trends of hard-bottom and coral reef habitat in the Florida Keys. This long-term monitoring of nearshore coral habitats indicates both a decline in coral species richness and coral cover at the stations surveyed. Since the first monitoring event in 1996, mean species richness has declined sanctuary-wide, with an average loss of two species per survey station. This loss is at-

tributed to a significant decline in the presence of 13 of the 46 species reported for the sanctuary, perhaps most importantly boulder coral (*Montastraea* spp.). Similarly, the percent of stony coral cover declined from 12.7% to 6.6% sanctuary-wide (Figure 29), most precipitously from 1996 to 1999 (falling from 12.7 % to 7.9%). Between 1996 and 2008, coral cover reached its lowest level in 2006 (6.4%) and has remained relatively similar since. For example coral cover was 6.6% in 2008 (Ruzicka et al. 2010). However, it is noted that these data have an inherent bias in that the study sites do not encompass all the diverse hard-bottom and coral reef habitats that vary in topographic complexity, depth, cross-shelf position, geological development and ecological history within the sanctuary.

For example, a complementary sanctuary-wide monitoring program conducted by University of North Carolina, Wilmington since 1998 corroborates some of the findings presented in the previous two paragraphs, with the following notable exceptions. Many areas, especially patch reefs and the deeper fore-reef environment, continue to exhibit relatively high cover (>25%) by reef-building corals. Low-relief, hard-bottom areas, which tend to be dominated by turf algae, sponges and gorgonians, have exhibited little change in over 10 years of surveys. Although declines in the number of corals are apparent for certain habitats, this is not a universal pattern (see Table 3 in Rutten et al. 2009), indicative of the high degree of spatial and temporal variability of hard-bottom and coral reef habitats in the Florida Keys (Miller et al. 2002, Rutten et al. 2009).

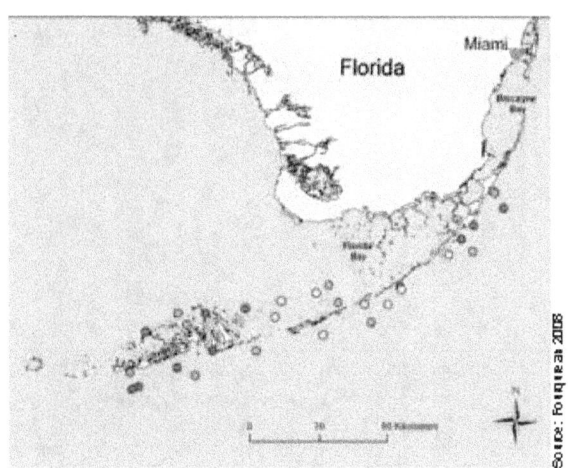

Figure 30. Map of permanent, long-term seagrass monitoring stations depicting where *Thalassia testudinum* is decreasing (red) in relative importance (showing signs of increasing nutrification), where it is becoming more dense (showing initial signs of increasing nutrification) shown in yellow, and where there has been no change (green).

The seagrass beds that carpet most of the south Florida shelf, including the sanctuary, are part of the largest documented contiguous seagrass beds on Earth (Fourqurean et al. 2002). Seagrass habitats have been monitored as part of the Water Quality Protection Program since 1995. These extensive meadows are vital for the ecological health of the sanctuary and the marine ecosystems of all of south Florida. This seagrass monitoring program has yielded evidence showing more widespread, long-term changes in the seagrass communities at stations that are annually surveyed. These changes are consistent with model predictions of nutrient-induced changes of these systems. Although no significant overall loss of seagrass coverage in the sanctuary has occurred since monitoring began, there have been significant changes in the species composition of seagrass communities. For example, 13 of the 30 permanent monitoring stations exhibited shifts in the dominant species of seagrass, which points to increasing nutrient availability at those sites. In other words, slower-growing species (i.e., turtle grass, *Thalassia testudinum*) are being replaced by faster-growing species (i.e., shoal grass, *Halodule wrightii*) (Figure 30). Three of the 30 permanent monitoring stations were buried by sand and have remained so since Hurricane Georges in 1998. The spatial pattern of changes and the agreement of the changes with models of the system suggest that there is regional-scale change in nutrient availability that is causing changes in seagrass beds over a wide portion of the sanctuary (Fourqurean 2009).

From 1987 to 1991, a significant seagrass die-off occurred in Florida Bay (Robblee et al. 1991, Zieman et al. 1999). It is not completely understood what caused this event, however salinity, nutrient conditions, and light levels are thought to be potential causes. Following the seagrass die-off, an algae bloom occurred, followed by sponge die-off (Butler et al. 1995, Hunt and Nuttle 2007).

Injuries to seagrass caused by small boats are also a chronic problem. Monroe County has approximately 30,000 acres of significantly scarred seagrass beds, more than any other county in Florida. Most propeller scarring is due to the actions of inexperienced or careless boaters. Propeller damage not only destroys the seagrasses, but also results in a change in the hydrology of the bed from the altered movement of water through the channel within the scar. Propeller scars may take anywhere from two to 26 years to recover (censu Hammerstrom et al. 2007). If the prop scar is deep enough, it will require filling to allow rhizomes to grow across the un-vegetated gap (Kenworthy et al. 2002).

Many acres of coastal mangrove habitat have been lost from the Florida Keys due to historic and continuing shoreline development. Many canal communities were created by dredging areas dominated by mangroves and filling areas adjacent to the canal cuts to create land for development. Loss of mangrove habitat has severely reduced the ecosystem's ability to filter runoff, thus causing an increase in nutrient export to adjacent waters. A healthy mangrove community is critical to stabilizing shorelines, sustaining economically important fisheries by providing nursery habitat, providing nesting and roosting sites for birds, and maintaining the character and beauty of the Florida Keys. Mangrove resources are vast and the trusteeship for these important communities is shared between the sanctuary and the FDEP. NOAA Fisheries Service also plays an important role in protecting mangrove habitat, which serves as essential fish habitat for managed fish species. Because there have been no comprehensive time-series studies of mangrove abundance and distribution throughout the Florida Keys (but see Strong and Bancroft 1994), sanctuary staff have identified this need in the Florida Keys National Marine Sanctuary Comprehensive Science Plan (2002), specifically to assess historic shoreline conditions using aerial photography and evaluate these data and develop priority restoration plans for mangroves in the sanctuary.

Coastal habitats are often drastically altered or compromised by the effects of hurricanes and associated strong winds, storm surges, flooding, and high-energy waves. For example, increases in hydrodynamic activity can compromise the structural integrity of reef zones by fracturing or dislodging corals. Sediment is often shifted and subsequently can bury corals or seagrasses. Storm surge and winds can uproot mangroves and modify beaches. Increased runoff resulting from heavy rains and wind can result in increased pollution (e.g., raw sewage, bacteria, pesticides, fertilizers, oil and gas spills, toxic chemicals, etc.) entering the system, thus making it difficult for corals and other habitat-forming biota to regenerate. Hurricanes can also increase the rate of erosion or result in land subsidence. To date, such effects of hurricanes in the sanctuary are estimated and anecdotal because only a few biological studies have been completed (see Fong and Lirman 1994, Fong and Lirman 1995, Lirman and Fong 1997a, b).

Fishing gear and associated marine debris can have a detrimental effect on the condition of biologically structured habitats. For example, in 2010 500,000 lobster traps and 315,000 (commercial) stone crab traps licensed by the Florida Fish and Wildlife Conservation Commission (FWC) in the Florida Keys. Although routine trap placement and retrieval causes few, small injuries to sessile flora and fauna, only 34% of those injuries recover (Matthews et al. 2004). Furthermore, the FWC estimates that upwards of 20% of trap gear is "lost" annually (up to 100,000 traps), with even higher losses (>75%, such as during 2005) during active storm years. Because of their high number, long-term placement, and potential to move during storms, lost traps may have a chronic effect on sessile flora and fauna (Matthews et al. 2004).

The placement of illegal casitas (lobster attraction structures) and the subsequent lobster capture is common in the backcountry area north of the lower Keys. Casitas are usually constructed from materials such as concrete cinder blocks, tin roofing material and modified trash dumpsters. There is concern among wildlife management agencies that there could be detrimental effects to natural habitat and lobster population dynamics as a result of this type of debris. Placement of these structures on the seafloor violates sanctuary regulations and alters sanctuary habitats, and when disrupted by storms have the potential to damage marine resources.

Furthermore, in a typical year, approximately 100 boats are abandoned in the Florida Keys. In addition to this number, the 2004 and 2005 hurricane seasons caused more boats to be moved into sensitive habitats like seagrass beds and mangrove islands. After the 2005 hurricane season, Monroe County initially surveyed 355 vessels aground, but cleanup operations ultimately removed nearly 500 vessels from the water. A concerted effort to document the spatial extent, amount and impacts of marine debris in 2008 indicated derelict angling and trap gear is ubiquitous in the sanctuary, even within no-take zones. The sheer amount of debris recovered annually is testament to an increasingly visited and exploited marine ecosystem (Miller et al. 2008).

Vessel groundings in the Florida Keys occur regularly, and each impacts the benthic environment. The significance of these groundings, and associated restoration alternatives, was detailed in the Florida chapter of the "State of the Coral Reef Ecosystems of the United States and Pacific Freely Associated States: 2005" (Andrews et al. 2005). In the Florida Keys, the number of reported vessel groundings decreased annually from 2002 to 2006 (from 721 groundings in 2002 to 301 in 2006). However, it is not possible to determine if this trend is a result of fewer boaters in the sanctuary, higher fuel costs, increased boater awareness, or a decreased willingness to call for assistance if boaters run aground. Generally, there has been no proportional shift in impact to different habitat types, with approximately 14% of groundings in coral reef habitats, an estimated 85% in seagrass and about 1% on hard bottom (Donahue et al. 2008).

7. *What are the contaminant concentrations in sanctuary habitats and how are they changing?* Contaminants of concern that are addressed in this question include pesticides, pharmaceutical products, hydrocarbons, and heavy metals. Toxins that are produced by harmful algal blooms and other water quality parameters are addressed in other sections of this document. To date, there have only been a few studies (e.g., Glynn et al. 1989, Singh et al. 2010) investigating the effects of contaminants on marine organisms in the Florida Keys; therefore, little synthesis of information is possible at this time to indicate a) the geographic extent and spatial variation in concentrations of various contaminants, b) the temporal variability of these concentrations, and c) contaminant pervasiveness and toxicity to organisms. As a result, this question is rated as "undetermined" and similarly the trend is rated as "undetermined."

Although a comprehensive report on contaminants in the sanctuary is not available, it is known or suspected that:

■ Some nearshore waters of the Florida Keys are contaminated to an unknown extent from pharmaceuticals in sewage. Potential local sources of contamination include: solid waste and sewage disposal practices, marinas and live-aboards, seepage from municipal landfills, mosquito control programs, and surface water runoff (Rumbold and Snedaker 1999).

■ The practice of soaking wooden lobster traps in used engine oil, or similar products, prior to their deployment was outlawed in 1993. At that time, approximately 670,000 traps were fished statewide, with more than 90% of traps deployed in Monroe County (FWC Fishery Statistics); a wooden trap was estimated to soak up about a quart of oil.

■ It is still common practice in the sponge fishery to use vegetable oil as a way to increase "visibility" through the surface of the water while poling for sponges (S. Donahue, FKNMS, pers. obs.).

- Of the more than 300 small-vessel groundings that occur each year in the sanctuary, a few are associated with fuel and shipboard chemical spills (e.g., lubricants, solvents, and paints). Over time, these spills dissipate or break down, but their constituent chemicals may remain in the habitat for years.

- Because of the Florida Keys' proximity to a heavily used shipping lane, potential oil and other chemical spills from container ship and transport vessels remains a threat.

8. *What are the levels of human activities that may influence habitat quality and how are they changing?*

The level of human activity impacting sanctuary habitat quality is rated as "fair/poor," because selected activities have caused or are likely to cause severe impacts, and cases to date suggest a pervasive problem. The trend is rated as "declining" because of continued impacts from a diversity of activities and increasing levels of visitation to the Keys.

The Florida Keys and its environs have a long history (>100 years) of exploitation, thus many of this historically abundant megafauna (e.g., green turtles) and habitats have already been severely altered or reduced. As a result, resource managers are conserving pieces of the former system. For example, green sea turtles once served an important role in maintaining seagrass habitat quality; however, these turtles were extensively hunted for food in the Keys before the 19th century and suffered drastic population declines (Jackson et al. 2001). Jackson et al. (2001) suggested herds of turtles cropped the turtle grass very short when grazing, which helped keep organic matter from accumulating in the sediments. This accumulation now fuels microbial populations and promotes low-oxygen conditions in the sediments beneath the plants. Manatees, which were also more abundant in the past, played a similar role in keeping the seagrasses cropped. Because people have hunted and depleted these key species to endangered status, seagrasses often become so overgrown that they shade the bottom habitat and start to decompose in place, thus making the seagrass susceptible to wasting disease (Robblee et al. 1991).

As was previously described, habitat destruction resulting from human population increases over the past century has resulted in a decline of mangroves, corals and seagrass. These losses have cascading impacts on other ecosystem services. The construction of the Overseas Highway, uncontrolled upland development (including dredge and fill operations), and shoreline hardening (via seawall construction) are further examples of human activities that have damaged habitat quality through the 1970s. Although many of these activities still occur within sanctuary boundaries, they are now highly regulated.

Despite the fact that the human population in the Keys has decreased over the short term, coastal development and land use will continue to impact habitat quality. Urban runoff from nonpoint pollution sources can diminish water quality and transport pollutants to the marine environment. Illegal discharges also have the potential to increase nutrients in surrounding waters. Illicit discharges occurring outside sanctuary boundaries (e.g., as evidenced by tar balls) can introduce toxins to the nearshore environment. Other anthropogenically driven factors such as climate change, sea level rise and ocean acidification are large-scale issues that may also affect habitat quality.

Since the 1990s, fishing pressure from the commercial sector has decreased, although recreational and commercial fishing pressure continues to affect habitat quality. For example, damage to the benthic habitat can result when mobile fishing gear, such as trawl nets or traps, are utilized. Derelict fishing gear and other marine debris can also scar or destroy benthic habitat, such as reefs or seagrasses, when entangled or dragged on the sea floor (Donohue et al. 2001, Chiappone et al. 2005). In recent surveys, marine debris in the Florida Keys including derelict fishing gear has been recorded in similar or greater amounts when compared to surveys from the past ten years (Chiappone et al. 2005, Miller et al. 2010).

Surveys of marine debris, including derelict fishing gear, entangled on the seabed in hard-bottom and coral reef habitats have been conducted intermittently by UNCW during 2000-2001, 2008, and 2010 in the Florida Keys (Chiappone et al. 2002a, 2004, 2005). Earlier (2000-2001) surveys indicated that hook-and-line gear, especially monofilament line, and remnant lobster traps, especially buoy lines, were the predominant debris items. Debris types causing the greatest degree of abrasion damage to sessile invertebrates such as sponges and corals were hook-and-line gear (68%), especially monofilament line (58%), followed by debris from lobster traps (26%), especially rope (21%). A concerted effort to document the spatial extent, amount, and impacts of marine debris in 2008 indicated derelict angling and trap gear is ubiquitous in the sanctuary, even within no-take zones. The sheer amount of debris recovered annually is testament to an increasingly visited and exploited marine ecosystem (Miller et al. 2008).

During 2008, a total of 686 pieces representing 59 different debris items or categories were recovered from 34,800 square meters (374,600 square feet) of sampled benthic habitat at 145 sites from Key Largo to Key West, with 443 kilograms (980 pounds) (wet weight) of debris removed. Of the 686 total debris items counted and retrieved, 363 (53%) items were hook-and-line gear (monofilament, wire leaders, hooks, lead sinkers, etc.), followed by 241 trap debris items (35%), and other debris (82 items, 12%). A total of 156,515 feet (477.6 meters) of angling gear was measured and retrieved from the bottom, mostly represented by monofilament line and wire leader. Over 3,000 feet (940 meters) of trap rope, either free (not attached to something), or attached to wooden slats or metal gratings, was measured and retrieved. Hook-and-line gear was the most frequent category of marine debris in terms of the number of sites and number of items encountered. Lost angling gear is ubiquitous throughout the Florida Keys, and was present at 59% of the sites sampled. Mid-channel patch reefs (1.35 ± 0.49 items per 60square meters) and high-relief spur and groove (0.66 ± 0.15) yielded the greatest angling gear densities. No-fishing zones and corresponding reference areas were roughly similar in terms of lost hook-and-line gear densities for most habitats, and in several instances, angling gear densities were greater within sanctuary no-take zones.

Lobster and crab trap debris was the second most frequent category of marine debris encountered in 2008 in terms of the number of sites present and the number of items retrieved. Trap debris consisted of rope, wooden slats, cement slabs, plastic pot openings and metal mesh trap grating, not including intact but un-buoyed traps on the seabed. The distribution of trap debris indicates that, like trap gear, it is ubiquitous throughout the Florida Keys in all of the habitats sampled (58.6% of sites). Nearshore habitats yielded greater densities than offshore habitats, and, similar to lost hook-and-line fishing debris, no-take zones and reference areas were roughly similar in terms of trap debris for several of the habitat types.

Groundings by small vessels less than 50 feet (15 meters) in length occur regularly and cause measurable impacts to habitat quality in the Florida Keys. Grounding damage from the propeller, hull, engine, or anchor usually results in significant injury to coral reefs and seagrass habitat (NOAA 2007). Although the number of reported vessel groundings has decreased annually since 2002, unreported groundings are known to occur by the damage they leave behind. Groundings often cause immediate habitat devastation with long-term impacts that require years to decades to recover (Donahue et al. 2008, Farrer 2010).

Diver impacts from recreational snorkeling or scuba diving can damage habitat in locations that receive heavy visitation. For example, inexperienced divers often damage coral as a result of excessive contact with corals due to poor buoyancy control (Talge 1989).

Lastly, the severity of the impacts from treasure salvaging (i.e., activities by those entities with legitimate admiralty judgment and rights) on sanctuary resources is somewhat unknown, but is regulated. This activity is only allowed through a Research and Recovery Permit in areas devoid of coral, hard-bottom and seagrass communities. The use of so called "mailboxes" or blowers to remove sand from a target site on the seafloor can create

three- to five-meter diameter holes; however, the depressions are likely to fill back in over time as influenced by daily current, wave action and storm events. Most legitimate treasure salvage activity is presently occurring in the Hawk Channel and Quicksands area around the Marquesas in the lower Keys, with a limited amount occurring over sandy bottoms in the upper Keys.

Habitat Status & Trends

#	Issue	Rating	Basis for Judgment	Description of Findings
5	Abundance/ Distribution	—	In general, mangrove and benthic habitats are still present and their distribution is unchanged, with the exception of the mangrove community, which is about half of what it was historically. The addition of causeways has changed the distribution of nearshore benthic habitats in their vicinity.	Selected habitat loss or alteration has taken place, precluding full development of living resource assemblages, but it is unlikely to cause substantial or persistent degradation in living resources or water quality.
6	Structure	▼	Loss of shallow (<10 meters) *Acropora* and *Montastraea* corals has dramatically changed shallow habitats; regional declines in coral cover since the 1970s have led to changes in coral-algal abundance patterns in most habitats; destruction of seagrass by propeller scarring; vessel grounding impacts on benthic environment; alteration of hard-bottom habitat by illegal casitas.	Selected habitat loss or alteration has caused or is likely to cause severe declines in some but not all living resources or water quality.
7	Contaminants	?	Few studies, but no synthesis of information.	N/A
8	Human Activities	▼	Coastal development, highway construction, vessel groundings, over-fishing, shoreline hardening, marine debris (including derelict fishing gear), treasure salvaging, increasing number of private boats, and consequences of long-term changes in land cover on nearshore habitats.	Selected activities have caused or are likely to cause severe impacts, and causes to date suggest a pervasive problem.

Status: Good Good/Fair Fair Fair/Poor Poor Undet.

Trends: Improving (▲), Not Changing (—), Declining (▼),
Undetermined Trend (?), Question not applicable (N/A)

Living Resources

The following information provides an assessment by sanctuary staff and experts in the field of the status and trends pertaining to the current state of the sanctuary's living resources:

9. *What is the status of biodiversity and how is it changing?* Selected biodiversity loss has caused or is likely to cause severe declines in some but not all ecosystem components and reduce ecosystem integrity; therefore, this question is rated as "fair/poor." Recently the relative abundance and diversity across a spectrum of species has been substantially altered by both natural and anthropogenic pressures, particularly large reef-building corals, long-spined sea urchins, and large-bodied fish. Combine the changes in abundance with low recruitment rates of those same species and the likelihood that those species will rebound in abundance is questionable. Furthermore, numerous fisheries[1] (e.g., lobster, crab, shrimp, sponges, fin-fish, aquarium trade) continue to remove individuals from the system, affecting sanctuary biodiversity and function. For these reasons, the trend is rated as "declining."

It is important to note that the "declining" trend rating could be open to interpretation because of the difficulty in applying a single trend rating that is representative of all individual trends in species abundance. For example, it is thought that species richness, as defined by the number of species found in a particular area, has changed little over the last four decades. Similarly, no species in the sanctuary are known to have become locally extinct during the same time period, although there are species which are threatened or endangered with extinction. At least three exotic species (described in Question 11) have also recently become established. Shifts in the relative abundance of multiple species, especially those at higher trophic levels, are indicators of compromised native biodiversity and stability in the system that can impact community and ecosystem structure and function. Understanding the degree of change in biodiversity that has occurred over time and how the coral reef ecosystem functioned in a "pre-exploitive" state can help managers and stakeholders identify realistic ecological and socioeconomic targets for maintaining or improving ecosystem services.

A historical perspective of sanctuary biodiversity suggests that many of the higher-trophic-level species, such as marine mammals and predatory fishes, were dramatically reduced by hunting and fishing prior to the sanctuary's designation. Current research on the historical ecology in the Florida Keys documents only one species extinction in the last 200 years —the Caribbean monk seal (*Monachus tropicalis*). Monk seals were historically ubiquitous and abundant in the Caribbean and the Florida Keys, but were hunted to extinction by the early 20th century (McClenachan and Cooper 2008). As such, the Caribbean monk seal was listed in the Endangered Species Act (1967-2008; 73 FR 63901). Other marine mammals found in the area of the sanctuary include cetaceans and manatees, although there is no historical record of those taxa being hunted or fished in significant numbers. However, fisheries for reef fishes and mollusk and crustacean invertebrates (conch, shrimp, stone crab, lobster) have existed in the Florida Keys in some cases for almost 300 years.

Numerous fish species in the sanctuary have been heavily exploited since the 18th century and have experienced population declines during the 20th century to unprecedented low population levels. Native Americans fished for reef fishes on Florida reefs long before the arrival of European settlers (Oppel and Meisel 1871). Reef fishing accelerated in the 1920s. Following growing public conflicts and sharp declines in catches, monitoring programs at the species level began in the early 1980s (Bohnsack et al. 1994a, Bohnsack and Ault 1996, Harper et al. 2000, Ault et al. 2005a). Ault et al. (1998) assessed the status of reef fish stocks and determined that 13 of 16 groupers, seven of 13 snappers, one wrasse (hogfish) and two of five grunts were overfished according to federal (NOAA Fisheries Service) standards (Figure 31). In addition, some stocks appeared to have been chronically overfished since the 1970s, with the largest,

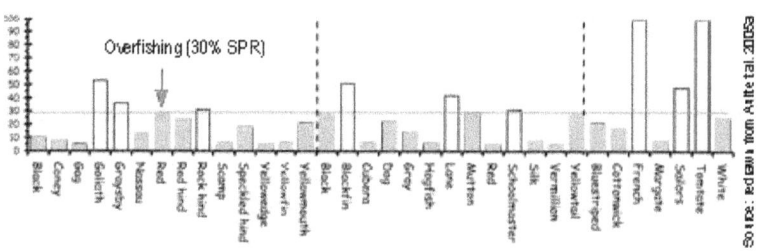

Figure 31. Spawning potential ratio (SPR) for 34 exploited species in the snapper-grouper complex from the Florida Keys from 2000-2002. Dark bars indicate overfished stocks and open bars indicate stocks that are above the 30% spawning potential ratio standard.

---

[1] Fisheries are not regulated by NOAA's Office of National Marine Sanctuaries but are regulated by FWC and NOAA Fisheries Service.

most desirable species depleted first, followed by increasingly smaller and less desirable species with time (Ault et al. 1998). The average size of adult black grouper in the upper Keys was about 40% of its 1940 value, and the spawning stock for this species was less than 5% of its historical, unfished maximum potential (Ault et al. 2001). In subsequent analyses, Ault et al. (2005a and 2005b) determined that 25 of the 34 species within the snapper-grouper complex for which sufficient data were available were experiencing overfishing. Closures of the fisheries at the state and federal levels for goliath (*Epinephelus itajara;* 1990) and Nassau (*Epinephelus striatus,* 1992) grouper remain in effect, although the goliath grouper stock continues to indicate signs of slow recovery (Porch et al. 2003, 2006) to the extent that considerable debate occurs regarding re-opening of that fishery. In its 2010 report to Congress, the NOAA Fisheries Service classified nine species that are landed in the Florida Keys as overfished (i.e., depleted below minimum standards), and 11 species as subject to overfishing (i.e., being fished at a rate that would lead to being overfished), with some overlap between the two categories (NMFS 2010) (Table 1).

The resulting reduction in numbers of large fishes and loss of spawning aggregations affects ecosystem integrity and biodiversity. Former spawning aggregation sites are not functioning the way they did historically and quantitative anecdotes from experienced fishers point towards reduced numbers of spawning aggregations and fewer, smaller individuals within those that

Table 1. Southeast regional stocks that are subject to overfishing or are overfished as defined by NOAA Fisheries Service. Although the sanctuary does not manage fisheries, it straddles both the South Atlantic and Gulf of Mexico fisheries management council jurisdictions. The below list includes species in both the South Atlantic and Gulf of Mexico fishery management council jurisdictions as of 2009. (Source: NMFS 2010)

Subject to Overfishing	Overfished
Vermilion snapper (South Atlantic only)	Red snapper
Red snapper	Snowy grouper (South Atlantic only)
Snowy grouper (South Atlantic only)	Black sea bass (South Atlantic only)
Red grouper (South Atlantic only)	Red porgy (South Atlantic only)
Black sea bass (South Atlantic only)	Pink shrimp (South Atlantic only)
Gag grouper	Red grouper (South Atlantic only)
Speckled hind (South Atlantic only)	Gag grouper (Gulf of Mexico only)
Warsaw grouper (South Atlantic only)	Gray triggerfish (Gulf of Mexico only)
Tilefish (South Atlantic only)	Greater amberjack (Gulf of Mexico only)
Greater amberjack (Gulf of Mexico only)	
Gray triggerfish (Gulf of Mexico only)	

are still present. Researchers from NOAA Fisheries Service and Florida's Fish and Wildlife Research Institute have been monitoring one recovering spawning aggregation for mutton snapper (*Lutjanus analis*) at Riley's Hump in the Tortugas Ecological Reserve (South) since 2004. According to observers in 2009, "thousands" of mutton snapper (*Lutjanus analis*) aggregated for spawning purposes at this site (Figure 32; Burton et al. 2005).

Sea turtles have been hunted for centuries throughout the Caribbean and have lost essential nesting beaches throughout their range. McClenachan et al. (2006) showed that although some nesting sea turtle populations are beginning to recover, the long-term effect of reduced numbers of sea turtles and nesting beaches will delay the recovery of the green and hawksbill species in the Caribbean basin. American crocodiles also utilize components of the sanctuary for their survival. They were listed as endangered species in 1975 due to the loss of critical habitat from coastal development, but have been gradually recovering throughout its range. The species was recently upgraded on the federal listing to "threatened" but remains on the state of Florida's endangered list.

The smalltooth sawfish once ranged from New York to Florida to the U.S. Gulf Coast. It was listed as an endangered species in 2003. Its decline was the result of habitat degradation and loss and mortality resulting from both targeted fishing and by-catch from other fisheries (Carlson et al. 2007). The smalltooth sawfish was the first cartilaginous fish to be included on the Endangered Species List. Today, the population center is located in Florida Bay and the Ten Thousand Islands area of the Everglades National Park, but individuals are occasionally encountered in the sanctuary as far west as the Marquesas.

Biodiversity change is hard to measure for seabirds in the sanctuary. In recent times, no seabird species have been lost or

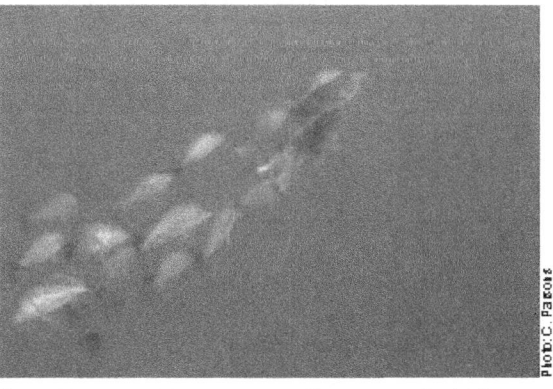

Photo: C. Parsons

Figure 32. Mutton snapper (*Lutjanus analis*) spawning inside the Tortugas Ecological Reserve (South) at Riley's Hump.

extirpated from sanctuary waters. Nesting species, roosting species, wintering species and species migrating through are still being recorded in roughly the same numbers. The sanctuary has more information for coastal species such as magnificent frigatebirds, least terns (*Sternula antillarum*), roseate terns (*Sterna dougallii*), bridled terns (*Onychoprion anaethetus*), sooty terns (*Onychoprion fuscatus*), brown noddies (*Anous stolidus*) and masked boobies (*Sula dactylatra*), but little to no information on most pelagic species (those which spend most of their life at sea and do not breed in Florida) such as shearwaters and petrels.

Invertebrate biodiversity has changed during the last century. Studies of invertebrate populations have shown that:

■ The long-spined sea urchin is considered an important herbivore on Caribbean coral reefs. Populations, especially in areas where overfishing has reduced populations of herbivorous fishes, suffered a mass mortality event in the Caribbean basin, including the Florida Keys, from 1983 to 1984 (Lessios et al. 1984, Lessios et al. 2001). This mortality event is recognized as "one of the most spatially expansive and prolonged disturbances to reef ecosystems in the region" (Carpenter 1988, Lessios 1988, 2005, Miller et al. 2008). The Florida Keys population suffered a second die-off event in 1991 (Forcucci 1994). Although long-term monitoring shows increased long-spined sea urchin occurrence and average size since 1999, there has been slow recovery of adult long-spined sea urchins in most habitats, with the exception of patch reefs (Miller et al. 2008, Chiappone et al. 2008).

■ Sponge populations in hard-bottom areas have been periodically decimated since 1844 (Donahue 2008), most recently by two *Synnechococcus* sp. cyanobacterial blooms in 1995 and 2007. The historical sponge fishery also greatly reduced the density and abundance of certain sponge species. Over the entirety of the intensive sponge fishery (ca. 1850 to 1940), it is estimated that 1.5 billion pounds of sponges were removed from the northern Caribbean (McClenachan 2008). The decline of the sponge population has impacted ecosystem services, such as water filtration and ontogenetically important shelter habitat for fishes and invertebrates.

■ Queen conch were commercially and recreationally fished until a moratorium was instituted by the state of Florida in 1985 due to concerns of overfishing. Results of a long-term monitoring program show adult queen conch density and abundance have increased at least three-fold from 1992 to 2006, but greater increases were negated due to the active

hurricane seasons of 2004 and 2005 (Hunt 1987, Glazer and Delgado 2003). The ecosystem effects of a reduced queen conch population are not definitively known. However, researchers (Stoner et al. 1995, Torres 2003) have shown that queen conch strongly affect community structure, through their roles as herbivores and detritivores, by influencing the vegetative structure that provides forage and shelter for other benthic invertebrates. The removal of such a previously abundant invertebrate may also have an impact on species (e.g., Caribbean spiny lobster, loggerhead turtles, other marine snails) that use queen conch as prey.

■ The commercial collection and sale of live reef species is a small but well-managed fishery in the Florida Keys (otherwise known as the marine aquarium or ornamental trade). State-wide landings in 2005 included 147,290 total finfish and 8,611,912 individual invertebrates (e.g., polychaete worms, tunicates, crabs, sea stars and anemones). The fishery has been regulated by the state fisheries agency (currently the FWC) since 1991. Although Florida Keys fishermen have been exemplary in initiating regulations for their fishery, and noting fluctuations in the variety of species they fish, there are currently no independent stock assessments for the species they target. Approximately 147 endorsements (permits) were issued for the live collection of ornamental vertebrates and invertebrates for sale in the aquarium industry in Monroe County in 2007.

Lastly, it should be noted that the status and changes to the biodiversity of habitat-forming organisms (e.g., coral, seagrass) were described in the "Habitat" section of this report.

10. What is the status of environmentally sustainable fishing and how is it changing? The status and trend ratings for this question are based on the available scientific knowledge from published studies, unpublished data, and expert opinion for targeted and non-targeted living resources that are directly and indirectly affected by fishing. Because this is the sanctuary's first condition report, the rating combines the historical view of the potential effects of fishing activity on biological community development, and ecosystem function and integrity, with the targeted research of species-specific fisheries over the last three to four decades. The rating reflects conditions in the sanctuary but does not serve as an assessment of the status of current fisheries management practices in the region. However, the determination of the trend rating for this question reflects recent changes in fisheries management practices that may have potential beneficial effects on living resources in the sanctuary. The response to this question is a rating of "fair/poor" because fisheries extraction has caused or is likely to cause severe declines in some but not all ecosystem components and reduce ecosystem integrity. The trend is rated as "unde-termined" because predictions are difficult to make regarding potential ecological gains resulting from newer fishing regula-tions and sanctuary zones that prohibit extraction. Benefits of recent management changes could be offset by illegal fishing practices, changing patterns and amounts of recreational fishing effort, chronic marine debris in the form of trap fishery losses and illegal casitas placement, and invasive marine species (e.g., Indo-Pacific red lionfishes *Pterois volitans* and *P. miles* and or-ange cup coral *Tubastrea coccinea*). Less than 6% of the sanc-tuary's waters are considered "no-take."

Environmentally sustainable fishing or ecologically sustain-able fishing may be defined as fishing at a level that the ecosys-tem can sustain without shifting to an alternative or undesirable state. To determine if environmental sustainable fishing is oc-curring, one has to simultaneously consider the impacts of all exploited species on an ecosystem, including its stability and resilience (Zabel et al. 2003). In addition, fishery yield and the integrity of ecosystem structure, productivity, function, and biodi-versity (including habitat and associated biological communities) must also be considered. The past decade has seen a para-digm shift in the management focus of fisheries from manag-ing individual target stocks for maximum sustainable yield to ecosystem-based fisheries management. This shift leads to a more holistic consideration of sustaining fishery yield, as well as maintenance of marine ecosystems and their function. Some fishery data were described in other questions of this document (see Questions 6 and 9 on pages 40 and 46 respectively) and that information should be considered along with the additional detail provided here. Generally, fishing can reduce ecosystem integrity in three ways: first, removing targeted species and killing non-target species (as bycatch) may result in cascading ecological effects (Frank et al. 2005). Second, because fishing is size-selective, concerns exist about ecosystem disruption by removal of ecologically important species such as top-level predators (e.g., groupers, snappers, sharks, jacks) and prey (e.g., shrimps, baitfish) of certain sizes. Third, fishing can stress all habitat types in the sanctuary in the form of physical impacts of fishing gear to the habitat and by introducing marine debris. For example, regular yet unintended trap loss in the lobster and stone crab trap fisheries results in trap ropes wrapping around coral heads and abrading or killing coral colonies. Combined, the two fisheries utilize approximately 815,000 traps per season in addition to an unknown number of recreational stone crab traps (five per person allowable with a Florida saltwater fishing license) have the same potential for habitat impact. In addition, lobster or stone crab traps can continue "fishing" even after they have been lost, which leads to continued mortality of marine or-ganisms that are too large to escape the traps after capture.[6]

For the 1996 to 2006 period, Murray (2007) summarized various measures of fishing effort for Monroe County relative to "other Florida counties" (Table 2). Over this period, all measures of fishing effort declined more rapidly in Monroe County relative to all other counties in Florida, except for stone crab permits.

Table 2. Changes in commercial fishing effort in Monroe County be-tween 1996 & 2006. (Source: in Murray 2007, data from FWC)

Effort Measure/Area	1996	2006	Change between 1996 and 2006
Saltwater Product Licenses	2,895	1,636	-43.49 %
Commercial boats	4,194	2,921	-30.35 %
Commercial Fishing Trips	67,773	35,811	-47.16 %
Stone Crab Permits	1,198	459	-61.69 %
Lobster Permits	1,270	704	-44.57 %
Lobster Fishing Trips	29,039	14,278	-50.83 %

Generally, there is a very high exploitation rate in the Keys from both recreational effort and commercial effort. Trends in reef fish landings from 1981 to 1992 were reported for the Flor-ida Keys by Bohnsack et al. (1994a). Depending on the year, recreational landings comprised between 40% and 66% of total landings. Reef fishes accounted for 58% of total fish landings, 69% of recreational landings, and 16% of commercial landings. Commercial landings were dominated by invertebrates (Carib-bean spiny lobster, shrimp, and stone crabs), which comprised 63% of total landings. But trends in recreational and commercial fishing pressure in Monroe County/Florida Keys are in decline due to a number of fishery and extra-fishery factors, including stagnant ex-vessel values (the revenue the fisherman receives for his catch) resulting from low demand, higher landside prices such as cost of living, gear, crew, etc., and less waterfront space availability (Leeworthy and Wiley 1996, Leeworthy 1996, Lee-

---

[6] Plastic traps are required to have a degradable wooden panel; thus, there is a lifespan after which traps degrade (unlike other lost gear that may ghost fish for longer periods of time).

worthy et al. 2010, Leeworthy and Morris 2010, Murray 2007, Sharp et al. 2005). Commercial fishing catch declined from 21.8 million pounds in 1995-1996 to 9.6 million pounds in 2008, a 56% decrease. Fishing trips also declined 56% over this period, from 67,422 trips in 1995-1996 to 29,681 trips in 2008. This was a greater decline than what occurred across the entire state of Florida. Florida's total catch declined about 34% during the same period, while trips declined about 47%. The decline was due in part to changes in fishery management designed to reduce overall fishing effort, as well as decreasing demand for Caribbean spiny lobsters, which is the dominant fishery in the Florida Keys. The Florida Keys historically account for 89% of commercial Caribbean spiny lobster catch. (FWRI 2010)

Ault et al. (1998) assessed the status of multiple reef fish stocks in the Florida Keys and determined that 13 of 16 groupers, seven of 13 snappers, one wrasse (hogfish) and two of five grunts were overfished, according to federal (NOAA Fisheries Service) standards (see Figure 31, page 46). They suggested that some stocks appeared to have been chronically overfished since the 1970s, and that the Florida Keys fishery exhibits classic "serial overfishing" in which the largest, most desirable species are depleted by fishing (Ault et al. 1998), followed by sequentially smaller species. Ault et al. (2001) found that the average size of adult black grouper (*Mycteroperca bonaci*) in the upper Keys was about 40% of its 1940 value, and that the spawning stock for this species is now less than 5% of its historical, unfished maximum. In subsequent analyses, Ault et al. (2005a, 2005b) determined that, of 34 species within the snapper-grouper complex for which sufficient data were available, 25 were experiencing overfishing. Another game fish that has declined in numbers is the bonefish (*Albula vulpes*), which is at approximately 5% of historic levels primarily because of habitat and food loss (Ault 2008). Although additional, long-term monitoring is necessary to adequately understand the impacts of new fishery regulations, initial research has shown that certain fish species (e.g., black and red groupers, *Epinephelus morio*, and mutton snapper) have responded positively to the combination of stronger regulations and larger ecological reserves within the sanctuary. These results will be further detailed in the "Response" section of this document.

The commercial and recreational lobster fisheries are regulated by the FWC. Due to the Spiny Lobster Trap Certificate Program (370.142)[7] the total number of commercial lobster traps allowed in the fishery has declined from about 750,000 in 1993 and 1994 to about 480,000 in 2010 (FWC Fishery Statistics). The Florida lobster trap fishery is unique in that it allows the use of sub-legal lobsters as a "live attractant." The consequences of this practice are well-documented in literature and include increased stress and mortality from confinement to traps (SEDAR 8 2005) and potential spread of a lethal lobster virus (Behringer et al. 2008). Fishery managers suspect that more protection for sub-legal-sized lobsters should improve landings in Florida's lobster fishery (Matthews 2001), and improve the fishery sustainability.

The queen conch is a large, marine gastropod that inhabits the tropical western Atlantic including the Florida Keys. It once supported significant commercial and recreational fisheries in south Florida; however, the ease of capture and the desirability of the shell and meat resulted in a severe depletion of the local population to the point that a ban was instituted in 1985 in state waters and then in 1986 in federal waters. When the ban was established, less than 6,000 adult conch remained in the Florida Keys (Glazer and Delgado 2003). Since then, ongoing surveys have shown a slow and very limited recovery with an estimated 33,500 adults in 2010 (FWC unpublished data).

In addition to the traditional "hook and line" and trap fishing pressure, biodiversity in the sanctuary is also affected by the aquarium trade. The collection and sale of living corals and hard substrate with attached organisms ("live rock") has been prohibited in state waters of Florida since 1995 and in federal waters since 1997. The state and federal government both regulate a small but viable fishery based in live rock aquaculture, where geologically unique limestone is placed on sandy, barren ocean floor areas and acts as a recruitment site for hard and soft corals and other marine invertebrates. This fishery remains commercial in nature because the mature live rock is sold in the aquarium trade.

Similar to live rock aquaculture, the collection and sale of live reef species comprises a small but well-managed fishery, most notably in the Florida Keys. This fishery has been regulated by the FWC since 1991, and there is currently a moratorium on the issuance of new marine life endorsements (permits). Approximately 80 commercial endorsements were renewed for the live collection of ornamental vertebrates and invertebrates for sale in the aquarium industry in Monroe County during each year from 2006 to 2009. Combined commercial landings in the Keys during the same time period included 291,672 total finfish and 14,584,831 individual invertebrates (e.g., polychaete worms, tu-

---

[7] The Spiny Lobster Trap Certificate Program was established in 1990 to stabilize the spiny lobster fishery by reducing the total number of traps used in the spiny lobster fishery to the lowest number in order to increase the yield per trap and maintain or increase overall catch levels, promote economic efficiency in the fishery, and conserve natural resources. This program controls the number of traps in the lobster fishery using trap certificates that are issued to individual lobster fishers by the Fish and Wildlife Conservation Commission (FWC). Fishers receive one lobster trap tag for each certificate they own.

nicates, crabs, sea stars and anemones) (source: FWC). Florida Keys commercial fishermen have initiated regulations for their fishery, recognizing fluctuations in the variety of species they fish. Concerned fishermen of the Keys continue to work with the FWC to suggest rule changes to ensure sustainability of the marine life fishery. However, there is also a recreationally allowable "catch" of marine life, and there is no way to account for the level of effort or extraction this sector represents at the current time. Lastly, but most importantly, there have been no stock assessments of any of the species collected, thus it is impossible to determine whether this fishery is environmentally sustainable over the long term.

In a recent study by Rhyne et al. (2009), the Florida Marine Life Fishery landing data from 1994 to 2007 was analyzed for all invertebrate species, and it was discovered that of the 9 million individuals collected in 2007, 6 million were grazers. The results suggest the number of grazers greatly exceeds the number of specimens collected for ornamental purposes, representing a significant categorical shift, positioning the invertebrate ornamental fishery for a collapse. More targeted research would help managers determine what effect both sectors of the marine life fishery are having on ecosystem biodiversity and integrity to help more effectively manage these resources.

Although seabirds are an integral component of the food web, more studies are needed to better assess fishing impacts on prey availability in coastal and seabird populations. Many bird species forage in or around the marine environment where they can become entangled in fishing gear, hooks and line to the extent that they are unable to feed or move about freely. Bird rescue organizations regularly treat cormorants, pelicans, herons and gulls that have become entangled or injured by fishing gear.

Shrimp are important in the diet of a wide range of species including many fish and bird species; however, they are also exploited by both recreational and commercial fisheries. Recreational "shrimping" usually occurs during the wintertime, but the effort and harvest levels associated with this sector are not known. Commercially, shrimp are harvested for both food (the pink shrimp *Farfantepenaeus duorarum*) and as bait for the recreational fisheries. For example, commercial landings of pink shrimp in the Florida Keys averaged 1,165,120 lbs in the years 2006-2010 (FWC statistics). Though landings have fluctuated over the last five years, it is generally not known how shrimp fishing impacts ecological sustainability.

11. What is the status of non-indigenous species and how is it changing? Although the threats of introduced aquatic species to habitats they colonize is often unknown beforehand, some can have serious detrimental impacts, including competition with native species for food and space, alteration of

Figure 33. The venomous lionfish, which is normally found in the Pacific and Indian Oceans, is a non-native fish that has established itself in the Atlantic.

habitat, predation on native species, and introduction of diseases to which native species have no resistance (Ruiz-Carus 2006). Non-indigenous species in the sanctuary are occurring with increasing frequency and may inhibit full community development and function and may cause measurable but not severe degradation of ecosystem integrity; therefore, this question is rated "fair" and "declining." More than 30 species of non-native marine fishes have been documented in Florida waters (Schofield et al. 2009), with more than 18 species of non-native marine fish being documented in Miami/Dade, Broward and Palm Beach counties in southeast Florida (REEF database 2006). Aquarium "dumping" has been identified as the likely source of these introductions given that most of the species are popular ornamental fish.

The sanctuary has been witness to the non-indigenous Pacific orbicular batfish (*Platax orbicularis*), which was controlled, and the Indo-Pacific red lionfishes, which are presently the only non-native marine fish species known to be established along the coast of Florida (Schofield et al. 2009) (Figure 33). Red lionfish, formerly residents of the western Pacific, Red Sea, and eastern Indian Oceans only, were first reported in the 1980s along south Florida and are now well established along the Southeast U.S. and the Caribbean (Ruiz-Carus 2006, Morris et al. 2009). Reports of lionfish in the sanctuary began in January 2009, and between January 2009 and July 2010 there were approximately 500 reported lionfish sightings in the Florida Keys (250 of those were confirmed and removed from sanctuary waters) (Morris and Whitfield 2009). Since then, sighting and removal efforts have been continuously increasing. Juvenile lionfish (approximately 30 mil-

Figure 34. The non-indigenous orange cup coral (Tubastrea coccinea) has expanded its range and can now be found in portions of the sanctuary.

Figure 35. The Red-tipped Sea Goddess (Glossodoris sedna), a nudibranch native to the tropical Pacific, is now well established in the Florida Keys.

limeters in length) were observed in spring 2010 at several locations in Florida Bay (C. McHan, FWC, pers obs. and M. Butler, Old Dominion University, pers. comm.), suggesting a pervasive invasion is occurring across all the habitats of the Florida Keys ecosystem. The increasing abundance and wider distribution of lionfish in the South Atlantic Bight, Bermuda, Florida, and the Bahamas indicates that lionfish are the first marine fish species to successfully establish a breeding population in the tropical western Atlantic.

The venomous protective spines of lionfish, combined with their feeding habits, unique reproduction and few predators, contribute to their successful invasive abilities. Lionfish are ambush predators, can threaten local ecosystems by altering the structure of native reef fish communities by out-competing native reef organisms and reducing forage fish biomass (Morris and Whitfield 2009). Impacts from lionfish could include direct competition with groupers for food and predation on reef fish and crustaceans (Ruiz-Carus 2006, Albins and Hixon 2008, Morris and Akins 2009). Also, lionfish pose a danger to divers and fishermen – stings from the venomous spines of the fish may result in pain, swelling, numbness and sometimes more severe effects including paralysis and systemic effects.

One coral species is invasive and could potentially impact ecological integrity. The range of the non-indigenous orange cup coral (*Tubastraea coccinea*) (Figure 34), has expanded since it was first observed offshore of Key Largo in 1999 and now includes the Gulf of Mexico, South Florida, and the Florida Keys, including the sanctuary (Fenner and Banks 2004, Ferry 2009, Shearer 2010). Observations in the Caribbean and the Gulf of

Mexico show that this species inhabits natural reef substrates and can cause tissue necrosis and partial mortality of native corals (Creed 2006). However, in general, orange cup coral appears primarily on artificial substrates such as submerged steel wrecks (Fenner and Banks 2004, Ferry 2009, Shearer 2010). It is suspected that these artificial structures played a major role in the spread of this species. A study by Ferry (2009) indicates that orange cup coral has not yet become established in the lower Florida Keys. However, the potential for this species to impact reef communities is high due to high proliferation rates resulting from the production of asexual larvae, the ability to out-compete native species and limit substrate available for recruitment of native species, plus the lack of a natural predator.

The Red-tipped Sea Goddess, (*Glosssodoris sedna*), a nudibranch native to the tropical Pacific (Figure 35), has become well-established in the Florida Keys (K. Nedimyer, Coral Restoration Foundation, pers. comm.). Over the last three to four years it has become seasonally abundant in a variety of habitats. Although they have become well established, it is unknown if they pose a threat to any resources in the sanctuary.

12. What is the status of key species and how is it changing? The key species or taxa in the sanctuary selected for use in this report include stony corals, seagrasses, queen conch, Caribbean spiny lobster, long-spined sea urchin, the snapper-grouper complex and sea turtles. These species are important for their ecological roles, and long-term datasets are available for assessing changes for these species. With the exception of seagrasses, historical data for each of these groups show substantial declines in abundance. Therefore, the status of key species in the sanctuary is rated as "poor" because the reduced abundance of selected keystone species has caused, or is likely to cause, severe declines in ecosystem integrity; or selected key species are at severely reduced levels and recovery is unlikely. The trend is rated as "not changing" because of the reduced abundance of a limited number of key species in each habitat type. Although there are very encouraging results of increased sizes and density of select species within certain sanctuary marine zones, forecasting how these changes will affect their long-term status is challenging.

Stony Corals

As discussed in earlier questions, long-term monitoring of nearshore coral habitats indicates a decline in both species richness and coral cover at the stations surveyed, and no significant recruitment has occurred since the monitoring program began in 1996 (Ruzicka et al. 2010). The declines in abundance of two of the principal Caribbean reef-building corals, staghorn and elkhorn coral, are often-cited as examples of the changes in western Atlantic reefs that have occurred over the past several decades (Aronson and Precht 2001, Gardner et al. 2003). The causes of these declines, which began in the late 1970s, include large-scale factors such as coral bleaching and disease, especially white-band disease, as well as smaller-scale effects resulting from storms and predation by corallivorous snails and damselfishes. Both staghorn and elkhorn corals were under consideration for addition to the U.S. Endangered Species List since the early 1990s and were formally added as threatened in 2006 based on Caribbean-wide population declines and poor recovery (Williams et al. 2008). The more recent declines of the massive star corals (*Montastraea* spp.) have also led to the overall loss of coral cover both in the Florida Keys (Ruzicka 2010) and in other parts of the Caribbean (Hughes and Tanner 2000, Edmunds and Elahi 2007). As of July 2010, the NOAA Fisheries Service was conducting a status review of 82 additional coral species for ESA consideration, seven of which occur in the Caribbean and in the sanctuary (*Agaricia lamarcki, Dendrogyra cylindrus, Dichocoenia stokesii, Montastraea annularis, Montastraea faveolata, Montastraea franksi, Mycetophyllia ferox*).

Seagrass

Long-term monitoring of seagrass has shown changes in coverage and nutrient composition at some monitoring stations. These changes are consistent with model predictions of nutrient-induced changes of these systems. Although no significant overall loss of seagrass coverage in the sanctuary has occurred since monitoring began, there have been significant changes in the composition of the seagrass species found in benthic communities (Fourqurean 2009). Furthermore, shallow seagrass beds are regularly subject to injury by vessel groundings.

Queen Conch

Although queen conch densities are relatively high within the sanctuary, the modest spatial extent of the aggregations results in low estimates of overall abundance. Queen conch populations are showing signs of gradual recovery from their low abundance estimates in the 1980s. Scientists from the Fish and Wildlife Research Institute are currently investigating the cause of chronic reproductive failure of nearshore aggregations. Although queen conch have been protected from fishing since 1985, in both federal and state of Florida waters, poaching still occurs on a regular basis (G. Delgado, FWC, pers. comm.).

Caribbean Spiny Lobster

Caribbean spiny lobster in the Florida Keys experience intense fishing pressure within Florida Keys National Marine Sanctuary, both from a heavily capitalized commercial fishery and a recreational fishery that is the most intensive such fishery on the globe (Sharp et al. 2005). In addition to the direct removal of lobsters by the fishery, each fishing sector also directly affects the survival rates of Caribbean spiny lobster before they recruit to the fishery. The commercial lobster trap fishery's practice of confining sub-legal-sized lobsters within traps to serve as attractants results in an estimated 10% mortality rate among these lobsters (SEDAR 8 2005). The recreational fishery results in the catch-and-release of a large number of lobsters below the legal size limit, causing injuries that result in increased mortality (Parsons and Eggleston 2007).

Although the no-take zones within the sanctuary were not designed as a fishery management tool, results from an FWC five-year monitoring project concluded that Sanctuary Preservation Areas (SPAs) were too small to protect Caribbean spiny lobsters from the fishery, but the larger Western Sambo Ecological Reserve (WSER) did function to some degree as a fishery reserve (Cox and Hunt 2005). There, the mean size of legal-sized lobsters and the frequency of occurrence of lobsters were significantly larger than those commonly encountered within the fished areas of the sanctuary, having increased steadily after WSER establishment. Cox and Hunt (2005) also concluded the increased frequency of encountering atypically large lobsters in the areas adjacent to the WSER (including the nearby fishery-exploited areas) suggested lobsters were likely emigrating from the WSER, thus this zone may serve to some degree to enhance fishery landings. The WSER does not encompass all of the habitats utilized by adult Caribbean spiny lobsters during their life history, and inclusion of the adjacent outlier reef would serve to protect lobsters from fishery exploitation (Cox and Hunt 2005).

Long-spined sea urchins

The long-spined sea urchin *Diadema antillarum* was considered a most important herbivore (grazer) because it helped to control the amount of algae on Western Atlantic coral reefs (Lessios et al. 2001). The demise of this once-ubiquitous echinoid is considered one of several factors responsible for the changes observed on Florida Keys reefs. Historical surveys of *D. antillarum* prior to the 1983 and 1984 Caribbean-wide mass mortality event are limited for the Florida Keys and consist of data collected at a few seagrass and fore-reef sites, mostly from Indian Key to reefs offshore of Key Largo. However, the available data indicate that densities were at least as high as four or five individuals per 10 square feet (one square meter) (Chiappone et al. 2008). The Caribbean-wide mass mortality began in the Florida Keys during the summer of 1983 and presumably led to a 90% or greater reduction in population size. From 1983 to 1990, there were no published studies of *D. antillarum* density and size structure. Surveys carried out in the early 1990s suggested that the population was recovering, with densities on shallow spur and groove reefs approaching one-tenth (i.e., 0.5-0.6 individuals per 10 square feet) of their pre-1983 level, and a size distribution dominated by larger (>2 inches, or 5 centimeters) TD) individuals (Forcucci 1994). In contrast to other wider Caribbean reef ecosystems, a second mortality event struck the Florida Keys *D. antillarum* population beginning in April 1991, with similar morbidity symptoms as the 1983 event that reduced the population to one-hundredth of its pre-1983 level (Forcucci 1994). Surveys conducted within one year of the 1991 mortality indicate that very low densities (<0.1 per 10 square feet) and small test sizes (<1 inch, or 3 centimeters) in shallow fore-reef habitats characterized the *D. antillarum* population (Forcucci 1994), a pattern that continued for the next decade (Chiappone et al. 2002 b, c).

Although monitoring conducted over the past decade has detected increases in both the density and size structure of long-spined sea urchins on patch reefs, a similar trend has not been detected on offshore reef habitats. Overall, there has been slow

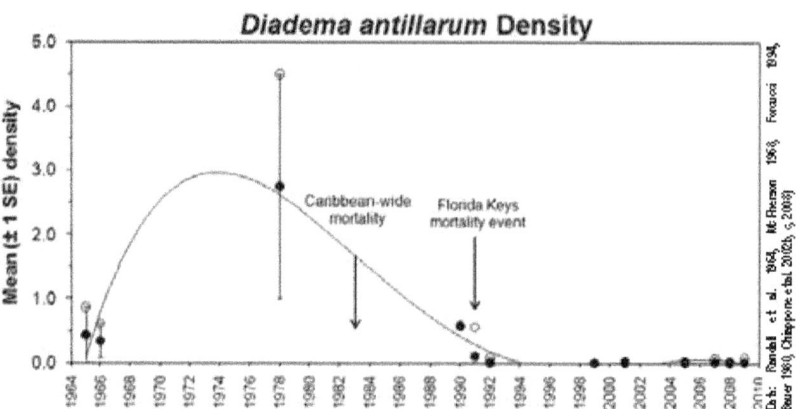

Figure 36. Temporal patterns in mean *Diadema antillarum* density on shallow spur and groove reefs in the Florida Keys.

recovery of long-spined sea urchins compared to pre die-off densities (Miller et al. 2008). Over an 11-year period (1999-2010), researchers examined densities and test sizes of *D. antillarum* and other sea urchins at more than 1,100 Florida Keys sites spanning 217 miles (350 kilometers), encompassing multiple habitat types from inshore to the deeper fore-reef slope. Surveys since 1999 indicate that current densities are still well below one individual per square meter and the maximum site-level density recorded during the 11-year period was only 0.33 individuals per 10 square feet (one square meter) (Figure 36). However, there has been a notable positive shift in their average and maximum size (Chiappone et al. 2008). Population recovery to pre-1983 levels could take decades, if not longer. Algal assemblages, in most habitats, despite reduced *D. antillarum*, are dominated by diminutive algal turfs, crustose coralline, and to a lesser extent macroalgae, suggesting that herbivorous fish grazing is critical for maintaining low algal standing crop on Florida Keys reef. Moreover, observations of newly recruited juvenile long-spined sea urchins have been largely confined to reef-rubble zones. However, because of the highly dynamic nature of the substrate resulting from wave and storm surge in this habitat, the mortality rate of these recruits is potentially substantial.

Groupers and other fishes

Previous sections of this report review the status of select species of finfish (see Questions 9 and 10). Even though sanctuary zones were not established to protect individual species, there have been encouraging observations of increased abundance and sizes of select finfish inside Tortugas Ecological Reserve (a no-take zone). Groupers in the Florida Keys have been historically exploited, and in a study by Ault et al. (1998) it was determined that 13 of 16 grouper species were overfished according to NOAA Fisheries Service standards. As of 2010, the status of grouper species has improved and according to the NOAA Fisheries Service, only three species of grouper (snowy, red, and gag) are still considered to be overfished in the same area (NOAA Fisheries Service fourth quarter 2010 "overfished map").

Specifically, the goliath grouper was targeted by commercial and recreational fishing since the late 1800s. They are extremely susceptible to exploitation due to a mixture of life history traits such as slow growth, long life, delayed sexual maturity, and the pattern of spawning aggregations. These characteristics, in association with escalating fishing pressure, led to the fishery closure in 1990 and the subsequent listing of goliath grouper as a candidate for the Species of Concern List under the U.S. Endangered Species Act. Fishery closures and designating some sanctuary zones as no-take have helped to increase the goliath grouper population as well as expand its geographic distribution. However, it is not clear as to when the population may be fully recovered, or when the fishery will be reopened if it were to be (Collins 2009, Porch et al. 2003, 2006). It is hoped that more examples of positive finfish responses to sanctuary zones continue, but the damaging ecological effects of the invasive red lionfishes could counteract management efforts.

Another study on the social structure of hogfish (e.g., harems) showed a difference between Western Sambo Ecological Reserve and the adjacent "fished" areas; spawning was only observed inside Western Sambo Ecological Reserve during a recent study (Muñoz et al. 2010).

Sea turtles

Sea turtle species frequenting the Florida Keys that are listed as endangered under the U.S. Endangered Species Act include the green, leatherback, hawksbill, and Kemp's Ridley turtles. Green sea turtles were hunted for their meat to the brink of extinction during the late 1800s and early 1900s in south Florida, and their numbers in the Florida Keys continue to remain low today. Systematic monitoring of green turtle nests on islands of the Key West National Wildlife Refuge show nearly a doubling since 1990; however, the number of nests still remains low (USFWS unpubl. data). These low population numbers affect seagrass beds, as these reptilian herbivores serve an important role in maintaining seagrass habitat quality by keeping the organic matter from accumulating in the sediments through continuous grazing. Green sea turtles are also affected by fibropapillomatosis (FP), a disease that forms large tumors on soft and hard tissues of turtles (Herbst 1994, Ene et al. 2005). In the Indian River

Lagoon, Florida Bay, and the Florida Keys, 50-70% of the green turtles are affected (Ene et al. 2005) and since the early 1980s, the percentage of green turtles stranded in Florida with FP has been increasing each year (Foley et al. 2005).

Loggerhead turtles, listed as threatened, also frequent the Florida Keys. However, an updated analysis of Florida's long-term loggerhead sea turtle nesting data reveals that loggerhead nest counts have declined 25% over the last 10 years (Witherington et al. 2009). Systematic monitoring of loggerhead turtle nests on islands of the Key West National Wildlife Refuge indicates a more than 50% decline since 1990. This marked decline in the number of breeders and nests, low productivity, a high proportion of false crawls, tidal flooding coupled with ongoing beach erosion, and sea level rise collectively threaten the future of the nesting loggerhead turtle population in the sanctuary (USFWS unpubl. data). In 2010, NOAA Fisheries Service and the U.S. Fish and Wildlife Service proposed to list nine Distinct Population Segments (DPS) of loggerhead sea turtles under the U.S. Endangered Species Act. Under this proposal, the South Atlantic Ocean DPS is being considered to go from "Threatened" status to "Endangered".

In January 2010, the Florida Keys experienced record low temperatures, causing many sea turtles to become stunned by cold-water temperatures. More than 250 cold stunned turtles were recorded in January 2010, the majority of which were green turtles, with smaller numbers of loggerheads and Kemp's Ridleys. NOAA and the FWC helped to coordinate the rescue of hundreds of sea turtles to help them recover from the cold shock. Rescued turtles from the Florida Keys were housed and rehabilitated at the Sea Turtle Hospital in Marathon. The hospital is a non-profit facility that has been in operation since 1986.

Seabirds

The populations of most of the state and federally listed seabird species seem to be stable. The least tern and roseate tern nesting populations are stable but low in numbers. The roseate tern population dropped drastically after the 2005 hurricanes but has since rebounded. This was notably due to the disappearance of Pelican Shoal in the lower Keys. That site was a coral-rubble and sand island where roseate and bridled terns were nesting and the island is now underwater. The birds have shifted to nesting on roofs of large buildings in the Keys. There are no similar ground nesting sites (islands) throughout sanctuary boundaries (R. Zambrano, FWC, pers. comm.).

Manatees

The West Indian manatee includes two distinct subspecies, the Florida manatee (*Trichechus manatus latirostris*) and the Antillean manatee (*Trichechus manatus manatus*). The Florida manatee's range is confined to the southeastern U.S., while Antillean manatees are found throughout the Caribbean. Due to a variety of human activities, like coastal development, this important herbivore has declined in numbers and their distribution is patchy throughout Florida.

A U.S. Fish and Wildlife Service survey estimated there were at least 3,800 Florida manatees in 2009. Even though this population number is low compared to historic records, the population is stable due to effective management of human-related threats (e.g., establishing watercraft speed limits to prevent propeller strikes). However, the Florida manatee population was negatively affected by the prolonged cold event in January 2010, when 244 deaths (13 of which were newborns) were recorded statewide (FWC statistics).

13. What is the condition or health of key species and how is it changing? The condition and health of key species in the sanctuary is rated as "fair/poor" because the comparatively poor condition of selected key resources makes prospects for their recovery uncertain. For example, the effect of diseases on hard and soft corals has caused substantial declines in coral cover (biomass) over the last two decades, yet there has been no significant coral recruitment recorded at any long-term monitoring station. Likewise, long-spined sea urchins have yet to recover from a 1980s Caribbean-wide disease outbreak. Generally, the health of selected key species has been compromised by factors including exposure to algal blooms (including harmful algal blooms), fishing, entanglement in active and lost fishing gear, ingestion of marine debris, and disease. Due to persistence, and accumulating effects of these problems, the trend is considered to be "declining."

Large, persistent phytoplankton blooms resulting in part from eutrophic conditions have been associated with fish kills and sponge and seagrass die-offs (Butler et al. 1995, Fourqurean and Robblee 1999, Hunt and Nuttle 2007). Cyanobacterial blooms have been especially prevalent in central Florida Bay during the past two decades and at times have been carried by the tidal currents to the ocean side of the Keys. Blooms are not necessarily triggered or sustained by a single change in nutrient load; rather, a combination of multiple biotic and abiotic factors contribute to their intensity and duration. Unfortunately, there is currently insufficient data to predict cyanobacterial bloom initiation or longevity, thus there is a need to integrate existing biological, climatological, and oceanographic research efforts so that predictive models can be further developed and refined.

A health concern for key species in the sanctuary, including ma-

rine mammals, seabirds, sea turtles and corals, is interaction with active and lost fishing gear. Results from a recent study on marine debris prevalence in the sanctuary showed "marine debris, most of which is derelict angling and trap gear, is ubiquitous in the sanctuary, even within no-take zones. The sheer amount of debris recovered is testament to an increasingly visited and exploited marine ecosystem" (Miller et al. 2008). Marine debris poses entanglement threats not only to highly migratory species (e.g., sea turtles and manatees) but also to sessile species (e.g., coral and sponges). Lost fishing gear can wrap around coral heads and cause injury, mainly from abrasion caused by wave action. Likewise, sponges can be literally cut in half by the combination of derelict gear and wave energy. In addition, ingestion of plastic marine debris is a health concern for a number of sea turtle and seabird species in the sanctuary. Although there are no quantitative studies on the frequency and severity of this occurring, it is well known that sea turtles will ingest plastic bags and balloons, mistaking the debris as prey items.

Corals throughout the Caribbean and Atlantic region have suffered from numerous diseases over the past several decades, and disease has been implicated in the demise of a number of reef-building species. Studies in the Florida Keys track disease prevalence at monitoring stations throughout the archipelago. For example, the Fish and Wildlife Research Institute's Coral Reef Evaluation and Monitoring Project has shown the prevalence of diseases to vacillate over time, and from 2002 to 2006 generally decreased at monitored stations within the sanctuary and at the Dry Tortugas. The number of stations affected with white diseases peaked to more than 80% in 2002, subsided to 35% in 2005, then increased again to 50% in 2006. The number of stations affected with "other" diseases peaked to 90% in 2001, but declined to 57% by 2006 (Ruzicka et al. 2009). A second study, which was conducted in August 2006, focused on diseases affecting two species of coral (elkhorn and staghorn coral) that had been recently listed as threatened on the U.S. Endangered Species List. One hundred and seven sites along approximately 29 miles (46 kilometers) of coastline in the upper Keys were surveyed, and no evidence of white-band or any other diseases affecting either species was observed (Miller et al. 2008). Though they are the best datasets available to resource managers, it should be noted that these types of annual surveys do not necessarily capture the real trends of disease impacts (or trends thereof) to coral populations because of the acute nature of the disease outbreaks.

Other diseases[8] impacting key species include fibropapillomatosis and PaV1. Fibropapillomatosis (FP) most commonly af-

---

[8] Researchers from the Florida State University are also tracking the prevalence of a common tumor in Grey snapper (*Lutjanus griseus*), but as of 2010 no peer reviewed information had been published.

fects juvenile green turtles in nearshore habitats. It is estimated that 50% to 70% of the green turtles in the Indian River Lagoon, Florida Bay, and the Florida Keys are affected and since the early 1980s, the percentage of green turtles stranded in Florida with FP has been increasing 1.2% each year (Ene et al. 2005, Foley et al. 2005). Another key species impacted by disease is Caribbean spiny lobster, which is susceptible to the *Panulirus argus* virus 1 (PaV1 (Behringer et al. 2006).

Studies on queen conch have shown nearshore populations are no longer reproductive. Nearshore water quality is suspected to be the cause of nearshore individuals experiencing rapid loss of gonadal tissue (Delgado et al. 2004, Spade et al. 2010).

The condition or health of seabirds is unknown, although their populations seem to be stable. However, as previously mentioned, birds are as susceptible to contaminants (e.g., oil, plastic, heavy metals), as are fish and corals. Impacts to small fish will obviously reduce food for terns and thereby reduce nesting productivity (R. Zambrano, FWC, pers. comm.).

During January and February 2010, the Florida Keys and the rest of Florida experienced severe, extended cold periods that caused drastic drops in seawater temperatures, especially in nearshore waters of Florida and Biscayne Bays. Such bouts of extreme cold are uncommon, but have occurred in the recent past (1977). The cold fronts during this time period moved in rather quickly, causing fish kills in nearshore waters and cold-water bleaching of corals that resulted in nearly 100% mortality of the colonies at the locations surveyed. Results from remote sensing data (NOAA and USF) and in-water surveys (managed by the Nature Conservancy) indicated that the coldest water was in the bays and flowed to the ocean side. Mid-channel reefs in Hawk Channel were particularly affected by cold-water stress and underwent extensive bleaching. Studies have shown that these same reefs are known to be more resilient to summertime warm-water bleaching events than many other coral communities within the sanctuary (see Response section, under climate change). Many sea turtles, manatees, and American crocodiles were also affected and suffered mortality. The long-term impacts of the loss of these animals, along with the numerous fish and coral losses, are unknown at the time of this writing and somewhat difficult to predict.

14. What are the levels of human activities that may influence living resource quality and how are they changing? Human activities affect the quality of living resources in the sanctuary directly and indirectly. Direct impacts to living resource quality include commercial and recreational fishing, vessel grounding, anchoring, propeller scarring, disposal of

marine debris, and disturbance from recreational diving, snorkeling, or boating. Indirect activities result in nonpoint source pollution and illegal discharges.

Many activities, such as those related to vessel groundings, caused or are likely to cause severe impacts to sanctuary resources, and cases to date suggest a pervasive problem. Therefore, the response to this question is rated as "fair/poor." However, the trend is rated as "not changing" because all water-based human activities, whether engaged in by residents or by visiting tourists, have been decreasing in Florida Keys National Marine Sanctuary since the 1990s (Leeworthy 1996, Leeworthy et al. 2010, Leeworthy and Morris 2010).

Despite the human population decrease and overall reduction in fishing in the Florida Keys since the 1990s, heavy recreational and commercial fishing pressure continues to suppress biodiversity, affecting the abundance and distribution of key species (see Question 12). Fishing stress can disrupt living resource quality by removing ecologically important top-level predators and, therefore, shifting reef ecosystem dynamics (Frank et al. 2005).

Fishing methods can also impact living resource quality. For example, damage to the benthos can result when traps or mobile fishing gear, such as trawls, are used. Marine debris, in the form of derelict fishing gear, can destroy benthic organisms and entangle mobile fauna, including endangered species, such as manatees and sea turtles (Donohue et al. 2001). When combined with high wave energy, lost, or, "ghost" crab and lobster traps can damage corals, and sever sponges (Chiappone et al. 2005) over a large area due to trap movement in high-wind-induced wave events (Lewis et al. 2009). In a recent report by Miller et al. (2010), a survey in the Florida Keys generally found similar or greater amounts of marine debris, especially derelict fishing gear, in no-take zones, when compared to baseline data from 2000, 2001 and 2008. Entanglement and vessel strikes also pose a threat to marine mammals (such as dolphins and manatees) and sea turtles because they often inhabit overlapping fishing areas.

In addition to fishing threats, vessel groundings occur regularly within the sanctuary, causing measurable impacts to living resources. Since 1998, almost all groundings have involved small (<50 feet, or 15 meters), privately owned vessels. Groundings often result in significant injury to corals, seagrasses, and other benthic organisms (NOAA 2007). Furthermore, vessels that try to "power off" the grounding site can cause significantly more injury.

In the Florida Keys, the number of reported vessel groundings decreased annually from 2002 to 2006 (from 721 groundings in 2002 to 301 in 2006), but it is not possible to determine if this trend is a result of fewer boaters using the resource because of higher fuel costs, increased boater awareness of the sensitivity of the environment, or a reduced willingness to call for assistance if boaters run aground. Generally, there has been no proportional shift in impact to different living resource types: approximately 14% of groundings impact coral, an estimated 85% impact seagrasses, and about 1% impact hard-bottom habitat (Donahue et al. 2008). Because corals and seagrasses grow in shallow water they are also susceptible to a variety of other direct impacts from smaller commercial and recreational vessels such as damage from the propeller, hull, engine, and anchoring. Despite the fact that the number of reported vessel groundings in the Florida Keys is decreasing, anchor damage, groundings, and propeller scarring still occur frequently and often result in immediate resource devastation with long-term impacts (Farrer 2010).

From the beginning of 1994 through 2010, the Florida Department of Environmental Protection reported approximately 2,500 incidents of spills in the Florida Keys. The annual mean number of petroleum and chemical spills was around 150 over the same period, with diesel fuel, motor oil, and gasoline representing 49% of these incidents, collectively. Spills in the sanc-

tuary can have an impact on living resource quality. Whether associated with fuel discharges from small vessel groundings, or larger oil or chemical spills resulting from offshore shipping traffic, offshore drilling operations, or land-based sources, spills have the potential to adversely impact corals, foraging birds, marine mammals, fishes, seagrasses and mangroves.

Diver impacts from recreational snorkeling or scuba diving can negatively impact corals in locations that are heavily utilized. Other ecotourism activities in the Florida Keys, such as dolphin-watching boats, can disrupt natural activities of these animals.

Even though the human population recently decreased in the Florida Keys, indirect impacts from urbanization and use of coastal areas will continue to impact living resource quality. Runoff from nonpoint sources of pollution diminishes water quality. Illegal discharges (e.g., discharging or depositing sewage into all waters) can also create excessive amounts of nutrients, stimulating the rapid growth of algae, which in turn smother and kill live coral.

Both direct and indirect impacts can adversely affect living resource quality in the Florida Keys. However, over the long term, localized direct impacts may be overwhelmed by the adverse and wide-ranging indirect effects of anthropogenically caused climate change resulting in sea level rise, abnormal air and water temperatures, and changing ocean chemistry.

Living Resources Status & Trends

#	Issue	Rating	Basis for Judgment	Description of Findings
9	Biodiversity	▼	Relative abundance across a spectrum of species has been substantially altered, with the most significant being large reef-building corals, large-bodied fish, sea turtles, and many invertebrates, including, the long-spined sea urchin. Recovery is questionable.	Selected biodiversity loss has caused or is likely to cause severe declines in some but not all ecosystem components and reduce ecosystem integrity.
10	Extracted Species	?	Historical effects of recreational and commercial fishing and collection of both targeted and non-targeted species; it is too early to determine ecosystem effects of new fishery regulations and new ecosystem approaches to fishery management.	Extraction has caused or is likely to cause severe declines in some but not all ecosystem components and reduce ecosystem integrity.
11	Non-Indigenous Species	▼	Several species are known to exist; lionfish have already invaded and will likely cause ecosystem level impacts; impacts of other non-indigenous species have not been studied.	Non-indigenous species may inhibit full community development and function, and may cause measurable but not severe degradation of ecosystem integrity.
12	Key Species	—	Reduced abundance of selected key species including corals (many species), queen conch, long-spined sea urchin, groupers and sea turtles.	The reduced abundance of selected keystone species has caused or is likely to cause severe declines in ecosystem integrity, or selected key species are at severely reduced levels, and recovery is unlikely.
13	Health of Key Species	▼	Hard coral and gorgonian diseases and bleaching frequency and severity have caused substantial declines over the last two decades; long-term changes in seagrass condition; disease in sea turtles; sponge die-offs; low reproduction in queen conch; cyanobacterial blooms; lost fishing gear and other marine debris impacts on marine life.	The comparatively poor condition of selected key resources makes prospects for recovery uncertain.
14	Human Activities	—	Despite the human population decrease and overall reduction in fishing in the Florida Keys since the 1990s, heavy recreational and commercial fishing pressure continues to suppress biodiversity. Vessel groundings occur regularly within the sanctuary. Annual mean number of reported petroleum and chemical spills were around 150 during that time period, with diesel fuel, motor oil, and gasoline representing 49% of these incidents collectively. Over the long term, localized direct impacts may be overwhelmed by the adverse and wide-ranging indirect effects of anthropogenic climate change resulting in sea level rise, abnormal air and water temperatures, and changing ocean chemistry.	Selected activities have caused or are likely to cause severe impacts, and cases to date suggest a pervasive problem.

Status: Good   Good/Fair   Fair   Fair/Poor   Poor   Undet.

Trends: Improving (▲), Not Changing (—), Declining (▼), Undetermined Trend (?), Question not applicable (N/A)

NOTE: Judging an ecosystem as having "integrity" implies the relative wholeness of ecosystem structure and function, along with the spatial and temporal variability inherent in these characteristics, as determined by the ecosystem's natural evolutionary history. Ecosystem integrity is reflected in the system's ability to produce and maintain adaptive biotic elements. Fluctuations of a system's natural characteristics, including abiotic drivers, biotic composition, complex relationships, and functional processes and redundancies are unaltered and are either likely to persist or be regained following natural disturbance.

Maritime Archaeological Resources

The following information provides an assessment by sanctuary staff and experts in the field of the status and trends pertaining to the current state of sanctuary maritime archaeological resources:

15. What is the integrity of known maritime archaeological resources and how is it changing? There is some uncertainty regarding the integrity of submerged maritime archaeological resources in the Florida Keys sanctuary. Organic, ferrous, and other manmade materials associated with maritime archaeological resources (wood, iron, copper, brass, leather, twine, and fabric) are non-renewable resources. To varying extents, they are all subject to deterioration from corrosive and chemical reactions involving seawater (e.g., salts and oxygen), movement caused by storms, and marine life impacts (e.g., sea turtles scratching or cleaning their carapaces, stone crabs eating wood). Sediment movement can also affect resources by subjecting them to shifting foundations, exposure, or abrasion. Storms such as hurricanes can also influence resource integrity by covering or uncovering resources with sediment. In addition, looters have been taking artifacts from archaeological sites in the Keys for many years. Because of these factors, the rating for this question is "fair/poor" because the diminished condition of selected archaeological resources has substantially reduced their historical, scientific or educational value and is likely to affect their eligibility for listing in the National Register of Historic Places. The trend rating is "declining" because anecdotal evidence suggests human impacts to maritime archeological resources has increased in the form of recreational and commercial fishing gear entanglement and multiple reported vessel groundings that occur on or near maritime archeological resources.

16. Do known maritime archaeological resources pose an environmental hazard and how is this threat changing? No environmentally dangerous levels of hazardous material leakages have occurred in association with any maritime archeological resources in the sanctuary; however, some maritime archeological resources have been dislodged and fragmented during storm events. These fragments and pieces have the potential to come into contact with and impact the surrounding habitat. Therefore, our rating for this question is "good/fair" because selected maritime archaeological resources may pose isolated or limited environmental threats, but substantial or persistent impacts are not expected. Furthermore, there is no evidence to suggest that the environmental threat of sanctuary maritime archeological resources is changing.

17. What are the levels of human activities that may influence maritime archaeological resource quality and how are they changing? Volunteers with Florida Keys National Marine Sanctuary Submerged Resources and

Inventory Team have documented more than 400 underwater historical sites in the sanctuary, and it is assumed there are many resources yet to be discovered and documented. More than 300 vessel groundings are reported in the sanctuary every year and some may impact maritime archaeological resources. In addition, the availability of inexpensive, off-the-shelf underwater technologies now affords the public the opportunity to locate and visit archaeological resources, thus increasing the potential for looting and other unauthorized human activities that can further affect the rate of deterioration and scientific value of maritime archaeological resources in the sanctuary. In addition, hook-and-line and commercial fishing tackle are also regularly found on submerged resources. Because reports of looting and vessel grounding cases involving potential maritime archaeological resources are increasing, the response to this question is rated "fair/poor" as these activities have caused or are likely to cause severe impacts, and cases to date suggest a pervasive problem. Although the intensity of these impacts varies year-to-year, the resulting trend suggests that conditions appear to be "declining."

Maritime Archaeological Resources Status & Trends

#	Issue	Rating	Basis for Judgment	Description of Findings
15	Integrity	▼	Resources are non-renewable and are subject to deterioration or loss resulting from looting, chemical processes, shifting sediments, marine life, fishing gear entanglement and vessel groundings (the last two are increasing in frequency).	The diminished condition of selected archaeological rezsources has substantially reduced their historical, scientific, or educational value and it likely to affect their eligibility for listing in the National Register of Historic Places.
16	Threat to Environment	—	Movement of sunken vessels during storm threatens nearby resources.	Selected maritime archaeological resources may pose isolated or limited environmental threats, but substantial or persistent impacts are not expected.
17	Human Activities	▼	Reports of looting and vessel grounding cases involving potential resources are increasing.	Selected activities have caused or are likely to cause severe impacts, and cases to date suggest a pervasive problem.

Status: Good Good/Fair Fair Fair/Poor Poor Undet.

Trends: Improving (▲), Not Changing (—), Declining (▼), Undetermined Trend (?), Question not applicable (N/A)

Response to Pressures

F lorida Keys National Marine Sanctuary uses an ecosystem approach to comprehensively address the variety of impacts, pressures, and threats to the Florida Keys marine ecosystem. It is only through this inclusive approach that the complex problems facing the sanctuary can be adequately addressed. The goal of the sanctuary is to protect the marine resources of the Florida Keys by interpreting the marine environment for the public and facilitating human uses of the sanctuary that are consistent with the primary objective of sanctuary resource protection.

The sanctuary was created and exists under federal law. It became effective in state waters with the consent of the Board of Trustees of the Internal Improvement Trust Fund of the state of Florida, which is comprised of the governor and cabinet. It is administered by NOAA and is jointly managed with the state of Florida under a co-trustee agreement, specifically through the Florida Department of Environmental Protection (FDEP). In addition, the Florida Fish and Wildlife Conservation Commission (FWC) enforces sanctuary regulations in partnership with sanctuary managers and the NOAA Office of Law Enforcement (NOAA 2007).

Regulations are an integral component of the sanctuary management process. They make up an important part of sanctuary management by regulating certain activities on a sanctuary-wide basis and others depending on how an area of the sanctuary has been categorized or zoned. Permitting, authorization, notification and review processes allow certain activities that are otherwise prohibited to take place under carefully controlled circumstances (NOAA 2007).

An enforcement presence in sanctuary waters is necessary in order to protect and conserve resources. Sanctuary law enforcement has traditionally been accomplished through a Cooperative Enforcement Agreement between NOAA and the state of Florida. Beginning in 1981, NOAA and the state entered into an agreement in which the Florida Park Service, previously responsible for managing the John Pennekamp Coral Reef State Park, continued to provide management services to NOAA, including enforcement of sanctuary regulations. The state, now in the form of the FWC, continues as the sanctuary's primary enforcement arm. A recent example of this cooperative enforcement agreement includes two of Florida's largest illegal lobster fishing cases on record that took place in 2009. In these cases, divers were caught and later convicted of taking more than 10,000 pounds of lobsters off of illegal artificial structures known as casitas in the Great White Heron National Wildlife Refuge. These two separate cases were built by NOAA Fisheries Service agents

and the U.S. Fish and Wildlife Service Office of Law Enforcement, and FWC played an important role in executing the resulting search and seizure warrants[9].

In addition to traditional law enforcement activities, the sanctuary relies heavily on "interpretive enforcement," which seeks voluntary compliance primarily through education. The goal of interpretive enforcement is to gain the greatest level of compliance through understanding and public support of sanctuary goals. Interpretive enforcement emphasizes informing the public through educational messages and literature about responsible behavior before resources can be adversely impacted. Sanctuary law enforcement officers, staff and volunteers talk directly with users and distribute brochures in the field and throughout the community. Such encounters allow officers to make direct, informative contact with visitors and local residents while conducting routine enforcement activity. Preventive enforcement is achieved by maintaining sufficient presence within the sanctuary to deter violations. Successful enforcement relies on frequent water patrols and routine vessel boardings and inspections. Water patrols ensure that sanctuary users are familiar with regulations in order to deter willful or inadvertent violations and provide quick response to violations and emergencies (NOAA 2007).

The following section describes current or proposed management responses to pressures impacting sanctuary resources.

Marine Zoning

Marine zoning[10] is being employed in the sanctuary to assist in the protection of the biological diversity of the marine environment in the Keys. Zoning is critical to achieving the sanctuary's primary goal of resource protection. Its purpose is to protect and preserve sensitive components of the ecosystem by regulating activities within the zoned areas, while facilitating activities compatible with resource protection. Zoning ensures that areas of high ecological importance will evolve in a natural state, with minimal human influence. Zoning also promotes sustainable use of the sanctuary resources, and pro-

---

[9] It is illegal to catch lobster from artificial structures in Florida waters, except from fishing gear allowed by FWC, FDEP or Army Corps on permitted artificial reefs (e.g. Duane, Eagle, Thunderbolt). Furthermore, sanctuary regulations (§922.163 (a)(3)) prohibit "...placing or abandoning any structure, material, or other matter on the seabed."

[10] Marine zone efficacy is currently being evaluated by sanctuary staff and partners. Results are expected to be released to the public in 2012.

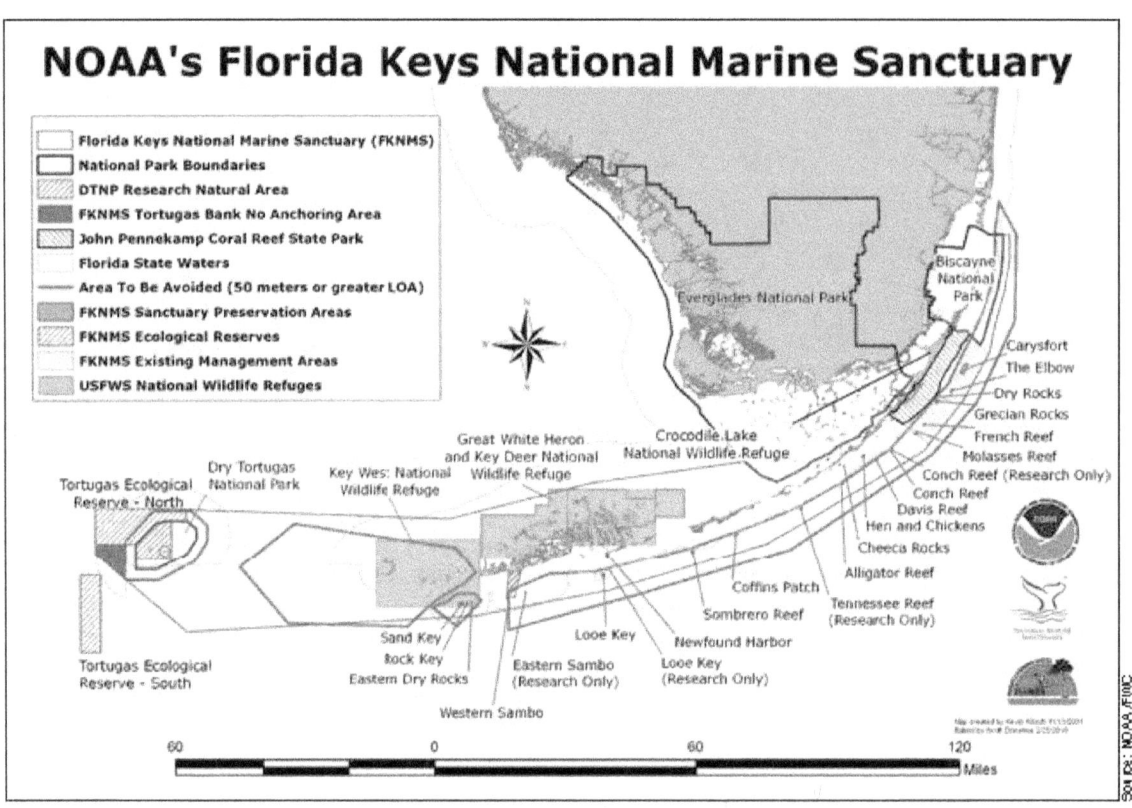

Figure 37. A map of many (not all) of the jurisdictions and zones in south Florida and the Florida Keys.

tects areas that represent diverse habitats and areas important for maintaining natural resources (e.g., fishes, invertebrates, etc.) and ecosystem functions.

In 1997, the sanctuary implemented its management plan that created special areas of varying sizes and purposes, and prohibited extractive activities within them. These areas were designated as types of marine zones in order to reduce pressures in heavily used areas, protect critical habitats and species, and reduce user conflicts. The efficacy of the marine zones is monitored sanctuary-wide under the Research and Monitoring Action Plan. The implementing regulations for this system of marine zones were instituted in the sanctuary in 1997. Three of the zone types (Sanctuary Preservation Areas, Ecological Reserves, and Special-use areas) are fully protected no-take areas, where all consumptive activities (e.g., lobstering, fishing, spearfishing, shell collecting) are prohibited. In July 2001, the 151-square-nautical-mile (518 square kilometers) Tortugas Ecological Reserve was implemented and is the largest of the sanctuary's fully protected zones. All fully protected no-take zones combine to protect 6% of sanctuary wa-

ters, and encompass 65% of the spur and groove shallow coral reef habitat (Figure 37).

The zone types within the Sanctuary include:

- **Areas to Be Avoided (ATBA)** – These areas prohibit the operation of a tank vessel or vessels greater than 50 meters in registered length, with a few exceptions (e.g., national defense, law enforcement, responses to emergencies). Some ATBA boundaries buffer those of the sanctuary (Figure 37).

- **Existing Management Areas (EMA)** – These areas were established either by NOAA or another federal agency prior to 1997 when sanctuary zoning regulations went into effect. EMAs delineate the existing jurisdictional authority of other agencies and have their own protections and restrictions above and beyond those that apply sanctuary-wide. Examples include Looe Key National Marine Sanctuary, Key Largo National Marine Sanctuary, Key West National Wildlife Refuge, and Great White Heron National Wildlife Refuge.

- **Wildlife Management Areas** – These areas minimize disturbance to especially sensitive wildlife populations and their habitats. Examples of such areas include bird nesting, resting, or feeding areas and turtle nesting beaches. Regulations governing access are designed to protect endangered or threatened species or their habitats, while providing opportunities for public use. Access restrictions can include no-access buffer zones, no-motor zones, idle speed only/no wake zones, and closed zones. There are 27 wildlife management areas, 20 of which are under the management of the U.S. Fish and Wildlife Service as units of the National Wildlife Refuge System. These areas are located within the Great White Heron, Key West, Key Deer, and Crocodile Lake National Wildlife Refuges.

- **Ecological Reserves** – These areas encompass large, contiguous and diverse habitats. They provide natural spawning, nursery, and permanent residence areas for the replenishment and genetic protection of marine life and to protect and preserve all habitats and species, particularly those not protected by fishery management regulations. Two ecological reserves protect areas that represent the full range of diversity of resources and habitats found throughout the sanctuary. These areas limit consumptive activities, while continuing to allow activities that are compatible with resource protection. This provides the opportunity for these areas to evolve in a natural state, with minimal human influence.

- **Sanctuary Preservation Areas (SPA)** – These areas protect shallow reefs along the reef tract. SPAs encompass discrete, biologically important areas that help sustain critical marine species and habitats. Regulations for this zone type are designed to limit consumptive activities and to separate users engaged in different kinds of activities. Diving, snorkeling and boating are allowed inside these zones. SPAs have mooring buoys for boaters to use in order to prevent anchor damage to corals. The actual size and location of these zones was determined by examination of user patterns, aerial photography, and ground-truthing of specific habitats. Some SPAs allow limited baitfishing by permit only.

- **Special-use Areas** – These areas are set aside for scientific research, restoration, and monitoring. They can be used for specific uses such as long-term research and monitoring and/or minimizing the adverse environmental effects of high-impact activities. Currently, there is only one type of Special-use Area being utilized in the sanctuary; there are four small Research-Only areas (totaling less than three square nautical miles) located between Key West and Key Largo.

- **Tortugas Bank "No Anchor Area"** – Vessels 50 meters in length are prohibited from anchoring on the portion of Tortugas Bank within the sanctuary west of Dry Tortugas National Park and south of Tortugas Ecological Reserve (North).

- **General-use Area** –Though not specifically identified in the sanctuary management plan, this zone includes the (remaining) areas in which general sanctuary regulations apply.

Research and Monitoring

The marine ecosystem of the Florida Keys is diverse and complex, and many of its ecological processes and their interrelationships are not well known. Although many resource impacts are obvious and severe, they are often not documented or quantified, and in addition, their causes may be unknown. As a result, the goal of the Florida Keys National Marine Sanctuary Research and Monitoring Action Plan (NOAA 2007) is to provide the knowledge necessary to make informed management decisions concerning the protection of the sanctuary's resources. Monitoring enables the establishment of baseline information on natural resources and other components of the ecosystem, and allows for the measurement of changes over time. As monitoring studies gather data, they have the potential to detect significant changes in natural resources that result from management actions or from other causes. The findings of research projects must also help managers and scientists identify cause-and-effect relationships that generate ecological patterns and trends, and stressors and other factors that threaten the health of the coral reef ecosystem.

A few examples of monitoring programs that provide sanctuary managers with basic information about the state of the Florida Keys coral reef ecosystem include:

- **Water Quality Protection Program** – since 1995, has conducted comprehensive, long-term monitoring of three ecosystem components: water quality, coral reefs and hard bottom communities, and seagrasses.

- **Ecological Research and Monitoring Program** – detects status and trends of various ecological parameters (e.g., habitats such as coral reef and hard-bottom communities, seagrasses, and mangroves; episodic events such as algal blooms and fish kills; ecosystem indicators such as sedimentation rates and turbidity) in order to discern local and system-wide effects of human and natural disturbances on natural resources and to assess the overall health of the ecosystem.

- **Marine Zone Monitoring Program** – documents the effectiveness of 24 marine zones established in 1997 and 2001, including the Tortugas Ecological Reserve, that are protected from consumptive activities ("no-take zones"). Monitoring projects document trends in ecological processes, reef fishes, Caribbean spiny lobster, queen conch, other invertebrates, and benthic community structure within fully protected marine zones and nearby reference areas.

■ **Social and Economic Monitoring** – documents the levels of use and changes in those levels of use and researches the socioeconomic impacts of management decisions on user groups, including determining the knowledge, attitudes, and perceptions of sanctuary management strategies and regulations by commercial fishermen, dive shop owners and operators, and members of local environmental groups. The 2007-2008 study on recreation and tourism in the Florida Keys/Key West extended this to all residents and visitors, however the results are not yet available.

Management Responses to Water Quality Pressures

Point and Nonpoint Sources of Pollution

The sanctuary, in partnership with the EPA and the FDEP, has implemented a Water Quality Protection Program aimed at addressing point and nonpoint sources of pollution in order to restore and maintain the chemical, physical, and biological integrity of the sanctuary. This includes restoration and maintenance of a balanced, indigenous population of corals, shellfish, fish, and wildlife, along with recreational activities in and on the water. A variety of research has been and is being conducted under the Water Quality Protection Program umbrella. Most studies have been funded by EPA, but funding has also been provided by the US Fish and Wildlife Service and FDEP.

Some of these are special studies designed to document the fate and ecological impacts of non-wastewater pollutants originating from sources such as permitted discharges, stormwater runoff, groundwater leachates, and marinas. Pollutants may include hydrocarbons, heavy metals, and pesticides (NOAA 2007). The research also includes wastewater pollutants and ecological studies, eutrophication gradient studies, comparative studies of impacted and non-impacted sites, historical studies, and use of sewage tracers (NOAA 2007).

Further efforts to address water quality issues reached a significant milestone in 1999, when the state of Florida requested a No Discharge Zone (NDZ) for city of Key West waters out to 600 feet (183 meters) from shore, prohibiting discharge of treated or untreated sewage from vessels, and the EPA concurred with this request. At the recommendation of the Water Quality Protection Program Steering Committee and the request of the Florida governor, in 2002 the EPA and the state of Florida established a NDZ for state waters within the sanctuary. The Steering Committee requested NOAA establish a similar zone for federal waters of sanctuary. As of December 2010, NOAA amended the sanctuary regulations to prohibit discharge or deposit of sewage from marine sani-

tation devices (MSDs) within the boundaries of the sanctuary and would require MSDs be secured to prevent sewage discharge or deposit.

Sanctuary educators have incorporated messages about water quality into their presentations and programs in the community and have reached out to local media to publicize this information as part of an annual water quality awareness campaign.

Lastly, Monroe County and local municipalities are undergoing extensive upgrades in wastewater infrastructure that provide advanced wastewater treatment, significantly reducing wastewater impacts and pressures in the area. As part of this upgrade, old plants are being closed down and the new plants use deep-well injection or shallow-water injection instead of nearshore outfalls. All residences and businesses in the Florida Keys will be connected to central sewer by 2015.

Swimming Advisories

The Florida Department of Health has been monitoring beach water quality in the Florida Keys since 2000, as part of the "Florida Healthy Beaches Program." This program tests on a weekly basis for the presence of fecal coliform and enterococci bacteria in beach water. High concentrations of these bacteria may indicate the presence of microorganisms that could cause disease, infections or rashes. When high levels of these bacteria are detected a "swimming advisory" is issued. The cause of each advisory is normally unknown; however, possible sources of pollution have been determined for most beaches in the state. The passage of new state legislation in the summer of 2009 requires the FDEP to investigate public wastewater treatment facilities within one mile of a beach when an advisory is issued for that beach. There are currently 17 beaches tested every week in Monroe County, five of which are within the city of Key West.

External Input

The sanctuary is partnering with the EPA and the FDEP to conduct research to understand the effects of water transported from Florida Bay on water quality in the sanctuary. Specifically, circulation studies have been conducted to estimate present-day, long-term net transport and episodic transport from Florida Bay to the sanctuary. In addition, studies have also been conducted to document any ecological impacts of Florida Bay water on sanctuary communities and potentially endangered or threatened species.

Harmful Algal Blooms

The sanctuary provides support and coordination to Mote Marine Lab's Tropical Research Center's Marine Ecosystem Event Response and Assessment (MEERA) Project. The MEERA Project is designed to provide early detection and assessment of biological events occurring in the Florida Keys and surrounding waters. The goal is to help the scientific community better understand the nature and causes of events, such as coral bleaching and disease outbreaks, fish kills, harmful algal blooms, "red tides," and other events that adversely affect marine organisms. Understanding the events will help scientists and managers determine if they are natural or linked to human activities. The project relies on observations made by people who are frequently on the water, such as charter boat captains, recreational boaters, environmental professionals, and law enforcement personnel (NOAA 2007).

Marinas and Boats

It has been documented that nutrients being introduced into nearshore waters have resulted in water quality degradation. One source of these nutrients is sewage discharge from boats and live-aboard vessels. As a result, in 2002 all state waters in the sanctuary were designated as "no-discharge" zones for sewage (treated or untreated) from all vessels. This designation was made by the EPA under the Clean Water Act. This designation requires that all boats store their sewage in a holding tank, to be pumped out at an approved facility. Mobile pump-out facilities were established to support compliance with this designation (NOAA 2007). Furthermore, NOAA initiated a rule in December 2010 that prohibits boaters from discharging or depositing sewage into both state and federal waters of the sanctuary. Pump-out locations have been identified in the *Upper Keys Boater Guide* (published by FWC and Monroe County) and a sanctuary one-page science summary that explains the new 2010 rule.

The sanctuary has also worked with the city of Key West and Reef Relief to develop and implement a "Pump It, Don't Dump It!" boater-education program.

> *In order to manage discharge into the sanctuary, a new NOAA rule, initiated in December 2010, prohibits boaters from discharging or depositing sewage into both state and federal sanctuary waters.*

Cruise Ships

Cruise ships started visiting the Port of Key West in the late 1980s and by 2008, 346 ships arrived with nearly 740,000 passengers (Leeworthy et al. 2010). At the peak, cruise ship passengers exceeded 1 million passengers, but this concerned the Key West local government. Local officials felt the city was too dependent on the cruise ship industry for their revenues, and they were concerned about the impact on the quality of life in Key West (Leeworthy et al. 2010). As a result, the Key West Port Authority has since attempted to restrict cruise ship visitation to fewer than 750,000 passengers per year.

Although large cruise vessels are the equivalent of small cities in regard to waste production, they are not subject to the strict environmental regulations and monitoring requirements imposed on

land-based facilities, such as obtaining discharge permits, meeting numerous permit conditions and monitoring discharges while at sea. Though all ocean-going carriers (cruise ships included) are subject to numerous international and federal waste disposal regulations, such as the Act to Prevent Pollution from Ships (APPS), the International Convention for the Prevention of Pollution from Ships (MARPOL) and the Marine Plastic Pollution Research and Control Act, it is a legal option for any large ship to dispose of blackwater (sewage), graywater (waste from showers, sinks, laundries and kitchens), and most other solid waste except plastics while at sea.

The Florida Keys Sanctuary Advisory Council formed a Large Vessel Working Group, which was tasked with investigating the impacts of cruise ships on sanctuary resources (NOAA 2007). The working group collaborated closely with the cruise ship industry and ultimately agreed to support the city of Key West's effort to develop fair and effective environmental practices for large ships. The working group also supported the expansion of the No Discharge Zone into all sanctuary waters for all vessels, including cruise ships.

Petroleum (hydrocarbons) or Chemical Spills

A ban on oil drilling and hard mineral mining was established when the sanctuary was created. Also, in November 2002, the United Nations International Maritime Organization approved designation of the Florida Keys as a Particularly Sensitive Sea Area (PSSA). PSSAs are areas that need special protection because of their significance for recognized ecological, socioeconomic or scientific reasons, and which may be vulnerable to damage by international maritime activities. Such designation is not accompanied by additional rules and regulations, but rather seeks to elevate public awareness of the threat of oil spills and hazardous materials to sensitive marine environments.

Despite these measures, the potential for spills still poses a signifi-

> *The Deepwater Horizon (DWH) Oil Spill in 2010 was of an unprecedented magnitude and beyond the scope and design of local ACPs. It also posed an ecological and economic threat to the Florida Keys. During the oil spill response, sanctuary staff and SCAT (Shoreline Cleanup and Assessment Technique) teams monitored shorelines for tarballs. Because the Loop Current never connected to the spill area in the Gulf of Mexico, there was no evidence that any DWH related pollution or contaminants reached the Florida Keys. However, long-term impacts to the overall area, if they occur, will remain unknown for some time.*

cant threat to sanctuary resources. Spill response is structured via the Incident Command System (ICS) for the legal protection of the trustees of the resource, as well as the "responsible party." As such, the general public is usually not directly involved in the response process, with few exceptions. Response to significant spills is led by the U.S. Coast Guard and the FDEP, with NOAA's Office of Response & Restoration and the sanctuary participating at their request to provide relevant spill trajectory information and to assess damage to marine resources. The primary guidance documentation used by all parties during a spill is the local Area Contingency Plan, which for Sector Key West (includes the Florida Keys) can be found on line at http://ocean.floridamarine.org/ACP/KWACP. This document was developed as a result of the Oil Pollution Act of 1990, has been in place since 1996, and has been regularly updated.

In an effort to streamline communications between responding and trust agencies, NOAA initiated "Safe Sanctuaries 2005" in the sanctuary, which simulated a tanker grounding within the sanctuary that injured coral habitat and historical artifacts and spilled oil that threatened other sanctuary resources. This exercise provided training in emergency response management, including sanctuaries-specific training in the use of the Sanctuaries Hazardous Incident Emergency Logistics Database System (SHIELDS) and in the Incident Command System (ICS); this hypothetical spill scenario was the most realistic at the time (i.e., one tanker spilling a known quantity of a known material). The exercise involved more than 150 people, including representatives from the U.S. Coast Guard, the U.S. Department of the Interior, the FDEP, the FWC, Monroe County, and various NOAA programs. In addition, in February 2010 staff from the sanctuary participated in the Coast Guard Sector Key West's "Combined Preparedness for Response Exercise Program Full Scale Oil Spill Drill." Sanctuary personnel provided natural resource expertise and guidance to the various response teams, helping identify and prioritize marine habitats in need of protection during the drill. In turn, exercises such as these helped the sanctuary and its agency partners during the response to the Deepwater Horizon oil spill April – July 2010. For smaller spill events and vessels, the sanctuary has often assumed a lead role in ensuring that fuel, oil, and vessel debris is removed to minimize further damage to sanctuary resources. The sanctuary has a dedicated team of biologists that handle these occurrences.

Commercial and Recreational Fishing

Florida Keys National Marine Sanctuary does not manage any aspect of commercial or recreational fisheries. Fisheries management agencies with jurisdiction in sanctuary waters are FWC, Gulf of Mexico and South Atlantic Fishery Management Councils, and NOAA Fisheries Service. Current involvement of the sanctuary in issues related to fishing is primarily through use of marine zones.

Marine fishes depend on healthy habitats to survive and reproduce. Throughout their lives, fishes use many types of habitats including seagrass, salt marsh, coral reefs, kelp forests and rocky intertidal areas, among others. Various activities on land and in the water constantly threaten to alter, damage, or destroy these habitats. NOAA's Fisheries Service, regional fishery management councils, and federal and state agencies work together to address these threats by identifying Essential Fish Habitat (EFH) and Habitat Areas of Particular Concern (HAPC) for each federally managed fish species and developing conservation measures to protect and enhance these habitats. Productive commercial and recreational fisheries are inextricably linked to healthy marine habitats; protecting these habitats will help support fishing communities now and for generations to come. Federal agencies that fund, permit, or carry out activities that may adversely affect seagrass, mangrove, coral, live/hard-bottom, or other habitats that are designated EFH or HAPC by the South Atlantic Fishery Management Council are required to consult with NOAA Fisheries Service regarding the potential impacts of their actions on these areas. Through this consultation requirement, NOAA Fisheries Service may recommend measures to avoid, minimize, mitigate or otherwise offset adverse effects on EFH. The South Atlantic Fishery Management Council has designated Florida Keys National Marine Sanctuary as HAPC for coral, coral reef and live/hard-bottom, and areas within the sanctuary as HAPC for coastal migratory pelagic species, such as mackerel and cobia.

The regional fisheries councils and state of Florida have prohibited destructive or wasteful fishing gear, established minimum size and bag limits, as well as seasonal closures, and restricted the take of some species. As mandated by the Florida Keys National Marine Sanctuary and Protection Act (public law 101-605), six types of marine zones were established throughout the sanctuary to reduce user group conflicts and protect resources. These zones were designed to reduce damage to resources and threats to environmental quality, while allowing uses that are compatible with resource protection. The zones protect habitats and species by limiting consumptive or conflicting user activities, allowing resources to evolve in a natural state, with minimal human influence. Exploited species have shown positive responses in these areas (e.g., yellowtail snapper, mutton snapper, black grouper), but monitoring and appropriate regulation must be maintained to prevent overfishing. Distribution of fishing rules and information about marine zones and their regulations is a regular component of the sanctuary's education and outreach program, especially at events and festivals and presentations in the community.

As mentioned in Question 12 in the "State of Sanctuary Resources" section of this report, the no-take zones within the sanctuary were not designed as a fishery management tool; however, at the sanctuary's urging, the FWC's Fish and Wildlife Research Institute initiated a long-term monitoring project designed to assess if and to what degree these areas served to provide protection of Caribbean spiny lobsters from fishery exploitation. The project was designed to compare the abundance and size-structure of Caribbean spiny lobster observed within the protected area with those encountered at adjacent "reference" sites that were subject to fishing pressure. The general expectation was that if these reserves provided protection from fishing, then the abundance and size-structure of the lobsters encountered within the reserves should increase relative to the adjacent reference sites. The initial five-year monitoring effort concluded that the SPAs were too small to adequately protect Caribbean spiny lobsters from the fishery, but the larger Western Sambo Ecological Reserve (WSER) did function to some degree as a fishery reserve (Cox and Hunt 2005). There, the mean size of legal-sized lobsters and the frequency of occurrence of lobsters significantly larger than those commonly encountered within the fished areas of the sanctuary increased steadily after its establishment.

Continued monitoring of lobsters within the WSER, a smaller adjacent protected area, and nearby fishery-exploited areas found these atypically large lobsters in the areas adjacent to the WSER with increased frequency, suggesting that they were likely emigrating from the WSER. Additional research using acoustic marking to examine the movement patterns of Caribbean spiny lobsters within WSER revealed that Caribbean spiny lobsters do indeed commonly move across the boundaries of the WSER. The increased abundance of these large lobsters within the exploited areas of the sanctuary suggests that the WSER may serve to some degree to enhance fishery landings. Additionally, this study also revealed that female Caribbean spiny lobsters commonly cross the boundary of the WSER to the outlier reef lying seaward of the offshore bank reef to spawn. Although these reproductive-related movement patterns occur primarily during the fishery's spawning season closure, these findings revealed that the WSER does not encompass all of the habitats utilized by adult Caribbean spiny lobsters during their life history, and inclusion of the adjacent outlier reef would serve to enhance lobsters from fishery exploitation.

Lastly, as the Federal agency responsible for ensuring the long-term sustainability of our nation's ocean resources, NOAA continually evaluates the quality of recreational fishing data collected and reported. Considering the ever more detailed uses of NOAA's data in stock assessments and fisheries management decision-making, in 2006 the National Research Council of the National Academy of Sciences recommended an overhaul of NOAA's data program in order to provide more detailed and timely information to managers, fishermen and other stakeholders. One of the NRC's recommendations was the creation of a universal "phone book" - or registry - of current saltwater anglers. This system will replace the previous method of randomly dialing coastal households, providing a far more efficient and effective way to determine the number of people fishing and the number of trips they take, or what is known as the overall fishing effort. That information is a crucial part of our ability

to estimate the health of fish stocks, and to check that protections put in place to preserve fisheries will be fair, effective, and based on sound science. Registration is also a way for NOAA and anglers to work together to help ensure the long-term future of saltwater fishing. As the first comprehensive accounting of the scope of recreational saltwater fishing in the U.S., the registry will help to more fully demonstrate anglers' economic, conservation and marine stewardship impacts. More information about the NRC's recommendations and how NOAA is working to implement them can be found at www.countmyfish.noaa.gov.

Climate Change, Bleaching Events, and Weather Disturbances

Extreme water temperature fluctuations in the sanctuary have been linked to bleaching and disease in reef corals and mass mortality of seagrass in Florida Bay. Beginning in 1989, recording thermographs have been deployed by the sanctuary in strategic areas throughout the Florida Reef Tract to monitor water temperature over the long term, and make that information available to management and research user groups. In addition to these thermographs, other state and academic researchers collect in-situ water temperature data and efforts are currently underway by the sanctuary and FWC to build a website that facilitates data sharing and collaboration.

With support from the Mote Marine Laboratory a program was created and modeled after the Great Barrier Reef Marine Park Authority's "Bleach Watch" program. The Florida Keys "Bleach Watch" Program utilizes volunteers to provide reports from the reef on the actual condition of corals throughout the bleaching season. These field observations help to monitor for signs of coral bleaching. There are two facets to the program: the Professional Program and the Community Program. The Professional Program is for divers who visit a particular reef on a regular schedule and can provide weekly monitoring of the reefs to help gauge the pre-bleaching coral composition and help determine the susceptibility of a site to bleaching. The Community Program is designed for observers who make occasional reef trips or do not frequent the same reef sites. Information gathered from both programs is compiled into a "Current Conditions Report" that provides a comprehensive overview of current conditions throughout the sanctuary (see http://isurus.mote.org/Keys/current_conditions.phtml).

As mentioned in the "Harmful Algal Blooms" section of this report, the sanctuary also provides support and coordination to Mote Marine Lab's Tropical Research Center's Marine Ecosystem Event Response and Assessment (MEERA) Project. One of the goals of the MEERA Project is to provide early detection and assessment of coral bleaching events in the sanctuary (NOAA 2007).

Sanctuary staff have also supported the Ocean Conservancy and the EPA in implementing the Reef Ecosystem Condition Monitoring Program (RECON). The RECON program trains volunteer

Figure 38. A diver performs regular maintenance on *Acropora cervicornis* fragments at a permitted coral nursery funded by the American Reinvestment and Recovery Act.

divers to collect information about the reef environment, the health of stony corals, the presence of key reef organisms and obvious human-induced impacts. The goals of RECON are to broaden the scope of available information about bottom-dwelling organisms on coral reefs, to alert local researchers and managers of changing reef conditions such as coral bleaching and nuisance algal blooms, and to increase public understanding of these threats to coral reef ecosystems (NOAA 2007).

The sanctuary is also a partner in the Florida Reef Resilience Program (FRRP). This program is managed by The Nature Conservancy, with support from the state of Florida, NOAA and the Great Barrier Reef Marine Park Authority. A parallel program is in progress at Australia's Great Barrier Reef, and the two programs are designed to complement one another and to inform coral-reef conservation around the globe. Specific to the field component of FRRP, sanctuary staff participate in the disturbance response monitoring efforts, which rapidly assess coral condition and health along the Florida Reef Tract during peak annual water temperatures, as well as after disturbances like the cold-water event of January 2010 (see Question 13).

Diseases of Marine Organisms

The Florida Keys sanctuary has been collaborating with partners to better understand and document diseases plaguing the ecosystem. For example, a collaboration between EPA, NOAA, and Mote Marine Lab began epizootiological assessments of coral disease along the Florida Reef Tract in 1998. This research is ongoing, and aims to assess the prevalence of coral diseases as a function of time, the location within the Florida Reef Tract, and the reef type. Nine disease conditions described in the literature, two additional syndromes and "other disease" affecting scleractinian coral species and sea fans, are used in these assessments. Santavy et al. (2005) describes the epizootiological trends of coral disease from the first four years of this project, and a more comprehensive analysis of similar trends from 2005 to 2009 are in preparation.

In 2009, NOAA awarded The Nature Conservancy and its partners $3.3 million to support threatened coral recovery and restoration in Florida (including the Keys) and the U.S. Virgin Islands. The goal of this project is to recover one acre of coral reefs in each of eight distinct areas of the Caribbean by growing *Acropora* coral in seafloor nurseries and transplanting them to depleted reef sites (Figure 38).

This project will provide significant and tangible ecological impacts through an increase in local biodiversity, as well as enhanced ecosystem services for various user groups, including recreational divers and snorkelers, commercial dive tour operators, commercial fishers and recreational anglers. This funding is a direct result of the American Recovery and Reinvestment Act of 2009.

In response to the large die-off of long-spined sea urchins in the 1980s, husbandry techniques are currently being refined to produce laboratory-reared individuals to increase sea urchins densities throughout the Florida Keys. Experimental manipulations are also being conducted to compare the behavior of these individuals to wild *D. antillarum*. The goal of this work is to produce large numbers of ecologically competent hatchery-reared *D. antillarum* that can be released into the wild as part of a comprehensive reef restoration effort. This is a collaborative effort with Mote Marine Laboratory, and the FWC's Fish and Wildlife Research Institute.

Vessel Use

In 1990, as part of the sanctuary management plan, several areas were declared off-limits to tankers and other vessels over 164 feet (50 meters) in length. The Areas to Be Avoided (ATBAs) were developed in response to the region's many historical groundings, and large vessels have been discouraged from operating in those located along the Florida Reef Tract. Four ATBAs account for 1,561 square nautical miles (5,354 square kilometers) of waters within and adjacent to the sanctuary. In addition, sanctuary staff use a database to assess trends in vessel groundings, identify "hot spots" where education and outreach activities can be enhanced, and determine what solutions, such as waterway marking, may be appropriate. The sanctuary is authorized to assess civil penalties and recover the cost of response, assessment, and restoration from the responsible parties. The sanctuary has Damage Assessment, Restoration and Resource Protection (DARRP) teams in the upper Keys and the lower Keys. In conjunction with sanctuary education and outreach staff, managers, and law enforcement personnel, DARRP staff develop grounding prevention measures, minimize impacts, assess impacts, repair injuries where possible, and support the associated legal processes. DARRP team members also conduct seagrass restoration using techniques developed by NOAA's National Centers for Coastal Ocean Science.

Since 1981, mooring buoys have been installed and maintained throughout the sanctuary with the intent to reduce vessel damage to sensitive marine habitats, specifically coral reef formations and seagrass beds, and to submerged archeological resources. There are currently nearly 500 mooring buoys within the boundaries of the sanctuary. While mooring buoys are excellent management tools, other management programs must accompany a mooring buoy program, including education, outreach, research and monitoring. The Mooring Buoy Action Plan, part of the 2007 Florida Keys National Marine Sanctuary Management Plan (NOAA 2007), establishes a methodology for identifying areas appropriate for mooring buoys and managing boating activities near coral reefs so that detrimental impacts are minimized. By allowing or directing access at selected locations, a Mooring Buoy Program can limit resource use conflicts and damage to the resources. In addition, sanctuary staff travels worldwide, assisting groups with mooring buoy installations that protect natural resources from anchor damage.

The state of Florida and the sanctuary have also been educating boaters to limit risks and improve navigation in coral reef areas. Large vessel avoidance and Racon beacons in lighthouses have resulted in declines in large vessel groundings. State and sanctuary officials have improved their response to grounding events and improved their restoration methods of damaged sites, thereby reducing the extent of damage. Reef restoration is a fertile field of study necessary to determine effective and efficient ways to restore degraded coral reef ecosystems.

Sanctuary education and outreach efforts include resource and safety education for boaters in sanctuary waters. Education is accomplished through information booths at outdoor events and festivals; presentations given to boating, fishing and community clubs and organizations; distribution of boater education materials to businesses in the Keys; and many other programs. FWC provides some of the boater education materials that are distributed. Media outreach on vessel injury prevention and shallow-water boating techniques is accomplished through the Seagrass Outreach Partnership. The partnership is an interagency group that began in the Keys under sanctuary education and outreach leadership, but now has partners statewide. The sanctuary implemented a grant through the Coastal Zone Management Program that identified sensitive areas in need of additional marking by spar buoys to prevent vessel injuries and installed the needed spar buoys in conjunction with Monroe County.

Coastal Development

Hydrology

Today, the South Florida Water Management District is responsible for operating and maintaining the Project to continue to provide for urban and agricultural development in coordination with flood and water supply protection (NOAA 1996). To address the priorities of returning more natural water flows to the Everglades and restoring the varied habitats from Kissimmee Chain of Lakes through the Florida Keys, Congress established the South Florida Ecosystem Restoration Task Force in 1996. Task force members include federal, state, local and tribal representatives who coordinate numerous restoration initiatives. At the forefront of these undertakings is the Comprehensive Everglades Restoration Plan, a hydrologic plan that hopes to reverse the unintended consequences resulting from the original flood control project of the U.S. Army Corps of Engineers. Restoration projects, guided by task force strategic planning and success criteria, include land acquisition, invasive species management, water storage, and stormwater treatment, among others. Restoration projects are expected to take 40 to 50 years to accomplish. Sanctuary staff regularly participate in task force-related committees and actively track the progress of water management and restoration projects designed to restore freshwater flows to two important estuaries adjacent to sanctuary waters: Florida Bay and Biscayne Bay.

Nearshore Construction and Dredging

The U.S. Army Corps of Engineers, FDEP, South Florida Water Management District (SFWMD) and NOAA Fisheries Service serve lead roles in reviewing projects for nearshore construction that trigger federal and state dredge and fill regulations, including the Clean Water Act (33 U.S.C. §1344), Rivers and Harbors Act (33 U.S.C. §403), and Section 373 and Section 403 Florida Statutes of the Magnuson-Stevens Fishery Conservation and Management Act (16 U.S.C. §1801 et seq.). Waters of Monroe County have also been designated as Outstanding Florida Waters (62-302.700 Florida Administrative Code), which provides additional protections to water quality. Furthermore, the majority of dredge and fill projects associated with coastal residential and commercial development are regulated under Florida Statutes Chapter 37, while dredging and construction related to deep-water ports is also addressed in Chapters 161 and 403 FS. Construction projects that are not exempted by the sanctuary regulations (those not listed at 15 CFR 922.163(a)(3)(i) – (v)) or that trigger other sanctuary prohibitions are reviewed by the sanctuary. Conditions requiring avoidance of certain species during construction (e.g., stony corals), modification of project design to reduce impacts, or removal of sensitive organisms from the site may be included in any given permit or authorization that the sanctuary issues for a project. To the extent possible, DEP, SFWMD, NOAA Fisheries Service, U.S. Army Corps of Engineers, and sanctuary staff work collaboratively to comprehensively review projects and provide consistent determinations. NOAA also participates in the Naval Air Station Key West Partnering Team, an interagency group formed in 2004 to review large-scale projects, including continued maintenance of water depths in Key West Harbor, which support Navy and Homeland Security operations.

The sanctuary Coral Rescue and Nursery Program was developed in 2003 in response to repairs by the U.S. Navy at Key West Truman Harbor Mole Pier, which threatened thousands of stony corals growing on the wharf. Sanctuary staff have developed protocols for coral risk assessment, rescue and transplantation when corals are found growing on government or private structures that are slated for repair. Preferentially, corals removed from construction sites are transplanted back to the area once activities are complete, or are moved to a nearby location to preserve functional resource value. In instances where on-site relocation is not a viable option, corals are placed in the sanctuary coral nursery at the Dr. Nancy Foster Florida Keys Environmental Complex in Key West or at an offshore nursery managed by Mote Marine Laboratory. Corals receive routine husbandry until such time that they can be used for beneficial projects, including educational display and exhibition, basic and applied research, and restoration of damaged areas. Use of rescued corals for research purposes reduces the pressure on natural habitats, providing scientists with an alternate and viable source of samples. Rescued corals are also used in management-directed research that will help protect coral reefs in the future.

Beach Nourishment

Similar to other nearshore construction projects, beach nourishment or restoration in the Florida Keys is regulated by U.S. Army Corps of Engineers and Florida DEP Bureau of Beaches and Coastal Systems (BBCS). BBCS has developed strict metrics for sediment grain composition, turbidity allowances, toe of fill effects, and time of year restrictions for these projects. These metrics are outlined in Chapter 161 of Florida Statutes, which addresses beach nourishment and protection structures. Through their permit process, the Army Corps is required to consult with the U.S. Fish and Wildlife Service and NOAA Fisheries Service and consider impacts of proposed beach nourishment on species and habitats managed by those agencies, including sea turtles, manatees and essential fish habitat.

Non-Indigenous Species

Eradication of introduced species is difficult and often impossible, and management practices focus largely on prevention of introductions. However, in one successful example of eradicating an invasive exotic finfish, four Pacific orbicular batfish were captured at Molasses Reef and given to the New England and Florida Aquariums for display.

In June 2008, representatives from approximately 30 state, federal and non-profit institutions met during a workshop to develop an early detection and rapid response (ED/RR) program for non-native marine fish introductions in south Florida. This program identified ED/RR processes from sighting to removal. Since then, staff from NOAA's Office of National Marine Sanctuaries and NOAA's National Centers for Coastal Ocean Science (NCCOS) have been partnering with the U.S. Geological Survey (USGS), Reef Environmental Education Foundation (REEF), and Mote Marine Lab to test and further refine ED/RR protocols for South Florida (Morris and Whitfield 2009). As part of this endeavor, Florida Keys sanctuary staff recently collaborated with REEF and NCCOS to develop an action plan for the control and management of lionfish within sanctuary waters. This plan outlines a detection, control and management strategy for lionfish that will control the densities and impacts of invasive lionfish in the sanctuary (Morris and Whitfield 2009). Between January 2009 and July 2010, there were more than 500 reported sightings and 250 confirmed removals.

As part of the effort to increase detection, reporting and response, REEF has worked with the sanctuary to conduct public workshops and training sessions for on--water professionals. The sanctuary has issued permits to these professionals to remove lionfish in Sanctuary Preservation Areas (no-take zones). Additional workshops continue to train and engage local communities in collecting and handling techniques in efforts to effect successful removals. In addition to tracking done by USGS, sightings of non-native marine fishes are also being tracked through the REEF Volunteer Fish Survey Project in partnership with federal and state agencies in the hope of preventing additional successful invasions in Florida's marine waters.

To help prevent the establishment of new non-native fishes in Florida's marine waters, NOAA's NCCOS, the USGS and REEF recently published the "Field Guide to Nonindigenous Marine Fishes of Florida" as part of their efforts to detect and remove non-native marine fishes as soon as they are discovered. The guide provides descriptions and illustrations of non-native marine fish species that have been seen along Florida's coasts, and includes maps of the sightings. It is hoped that divers, fishermen, and others will use the guide to report non-native species immediately in order to help prevent their rapid establishment (Schofield et al. 2009).

Wildlife Disturbance

Until recently, the combination of the sanctuary's marine zones (see Figure 37 on page 62) and its general regulations were the primary tools used to minimize wildlife disturbance. In an effort to augment these regulatory tools, two education and outreach programs were developed and implemented specifically to promote responsible visitor usage of sanctuary resources: the Dolphin SMART and the Blue Star programs.

A special area of the sanctuary is home to a resident group of bottlenose dolphins (*Tursiops truncatus*). It is also where many businesses conduct dolphin tours in a small geographic area. This may cause unnecessary stress to the local dolphin population by disrupting their natural behaviors. Therefore, conservation agencies including NOAA's Office of National Marine Sanctuaries and NOAA Fisheries Service, the Dolphin Ecology Project, and the Whale and Dolphin Conservation Society, as well as local businesses and members of the public, teamed up in 2007 to launch the Dolphin SMART program — a unique, multifaceted program encouraging responsible viewing of wild dolphins and recognizing businesses that partici-

pated. Program participation is intended for commercial businesses conducting wild dolphin tours, or any commercial vessel that may opportunistically view wild dolphins. Dolphin SMART offers participation incentives for businesses that follow the program criteria and educate their customers about the importance of minimizing wild dolphin harassment. It also includes an important research component that provides insight about the daily lives of the local, wild dolphin populations. The acronym "SMART" in Dolphin SMART is a reminder of the basic principles of dolphin watching: Stay at least 150 feet (45 meters) from dolphins; Move away slowly if the dolphins seem disturbed; Always put your vessel engine in neutral when dolphins are near; Refrain from feeding, touching or swimming with wild dolphins; and Teach others to be Dolphin SMART. The program has recognized five operators in the Keys, as well as operators in other areas in southwest Florida and Alabama. A list of Dolphin SMART operators also is available online at http://sanctuaries.noaa.gov/dolphinsmart/welcome.html.

The Blue Star Program, launched in 2009, was established by the sanctuary to reduce the impact of divers and snorkelers on the local coral reef ecosystem. Blue Star is a voluntary education and recognition program for commercial dive and snorkel operators who are committed to coral reef conservation and education. By forming a partnership with commercial operators to educate their customers about the fragile nature of the coral reef ecosystem, the purpose and goals of the sanctuary, and diving and snorkeling etiquette individuals can use to make a difference. Specific goals of the program include:

- Reduce the amount of damage to coral reefs caused by divers and snorkelers by emphasizing proper etiquette and empowering individual divers with the right information.

- Increase knowledge among divers, snorkelers, and charter boat owners and staff about the purpose, goals and objectives of Florida Keys National Marine Sanctuary and engage them as partners in coral reef conservation.
- Educate the public about the importance of responsible diving and snorkeling in the coral reef ecosystem.

In 2010, British researcher Emma Camp conducted a study analyzing diver interactions with coral reefs, documenting how divers either purposely or incidentally come into contact with coral. Touching coral has been shown to have a cumulative damaging effect on coral polyps. Camp observed more than 80 divers diving with four different dive shops. One of the conclusions of her study indicates that increased conservation education, such as that offered by the Blue Star program, can significantly reduce these diver touches and incidental interactions with the coral reef (Camp 2011).

Artificial Reefs

NOAA supports a precautionary approach when considering the deployment of artificial reefs, and will continue to emphasize the protection, restoration, and enhancement of natural habitats, as opposed to constructing artificial habitats, as a general matter of policy consistent with the Coral Reef Conservation Act, Magnuson-Stevens Fishery Conservation and Management Act, and the National Marine Sanctuaries Act when reviewing related permit applications. The sanctuary recognizes that additional research is needed to better understand both the socioeconomic and coral reef ecosystem impacts of artificial reefs.

In 2006 research was done by NOAA to investigate the hypothesis that the introduction of the USS *Spiegel Grove* as an artificial reef off Key Largo would alter use patterns on the surrounding natural reefs. The results showed a 13% reduction in diver use on the surrounding natural reefs, a 160.5% increase in artificial reef use, and a net increase in total artificial and natural reef use of 9% (Leeworthy et al. 2006). This represents a positive increase in total business, while reducing pressure on the natural reefs. Concurrently, REEF implemented a five-year monitoring plan to document fish species, sighting frequency and estimated abundance over time at the *Spiegel Grove* site and at seven nearby natural and artificial reef sites. The primary goal of the monitoring was to document fish recruitment to the artificial reef, detect changes over time in the assemblage and compare patterns of select species between sites. Though the final report does not compare the change in abundance of all species surveyed between natural habitat and artificial structures over time, it does document that the *Spiegel Grove* had a slightly lower species richness than six of the other seven study sites by the end of the five-year project, which could be related to the impact of Hurricane Dennis in 2005. Similar research is underway by NOAA and REEF for the USS *Vandenberg*, which was sunk off Key West in 2009.

The revised sanctuary management plan also outlines a strategy related to researching the impacts of artificial reefs. In this strategy, there are three activities that must be carried out by the artificial reef permit holders with oversight from sanctuary staff. The first activity will guide the assessment of effects of artificial reefs on fish and invertebrate abundance and community composition and on other sanctuary resources. Further, the longevity of artificial reefs composed of different materials will be evaluated, and appropriate artificial reef locations will be determined, based in part on these findings. The second activity complements the first; information on habitat modifications caused by artificial reefs is a necessary element of evaluating consistency of artificial reefs with sanctuary goals and objectives. Soft sediments may be altered during installation of artificial reefs, and water flows around these structures are likely to continue to modify soft sediments and their associated communities. Nearby hard-bottom habitats may also experience modifications as a result of altered flows and other factors associated with artificial reefs, thus these factors need to be adequately studied. The third activity will assess and develop regulations for artificial reef construction and evaluate habitat suitability for artificial reef placement.

Marine Debris

Since 1994, the sanctuary has helped to organize the Adopt-a-Reef Program, an annual volunteer reef cleanup effort. The program targets recreational divers and provides data placards for recording debris collected at designated locations, usually popular dive sites, coordinated through local dive shops. The types of data collected include date and location of the cleanup, diver name, bottom time, number of trash bags filled, a rank-order of the five most important debris items, and an estimated weight of debris collected. From 1994 to 2000, 866 divers collected 16,535 pounds (7,500 kilograms) of debris, with hook-and-line gear, aluminum cans, plastic, cardboard, wood, and rope from lobster pots constituting the most common items. The materials removed from the sanctuary are prevented from causing further impact to sanctuary resources and the data collected regarding the type and distribution of debris are being used by sanctuary staff for other marine debris response activities.

Shoreline and water cleanups are a regular part of the sanctuary's education and outreach Team OCEAN program. Significant amounts of marine debris have been retrieved from sanctuary waters over the years by volunteers and student groups using kayaks to collect debris from shallow waters and larger, recreational vessels to transport it back to shore. Since the sanctuary began tracking the amount removed from this effort (2007), more than 30,000 pounds (13,608 kilograms) of marine debris have been hauled to a land-based solid waste facility. Lost fishing gear, polypropylene rope, Styrofoam buoys, plastic traps, and plastic trap throats constitute the majority of the debris collected by sanctuary staff and volunteers.

The sanctuary has also worked with Monroe County and FWC to identify derelict vessels for removal, and has administered funds for this purpose.

During the 2005 hurricane season, the Florida Keys were subjected to several major storms that mobilized and damaged commercial lobster and stone crab traps, making it practically impossible for fishermen to locate and retrieve their fishing gear. Florida state regulations (Chapter 68B-55 FAC), which normally prohibits removal of commercial traps by anyone other than their owner or law enforcement officers, threatened to hinder removal efforts. Ultimately, the state of Florida partnered with Monroe County to recover more than 45,000 traps from Monroe County waters, at a cost of more than $1.8 million. Marine debris removal also occurs on a smaller

Team OCEAN is an on-the-water education and information program aimed at protecting the natural marine resources of the Florida Keys, while enriching the experiences of visitors to Florida Keys National Marine Sanctuary. It involves the stationing of trained volunteer teams at heavily visited reef sites throughout the Keys during peak recreational boating seasons to serve as educators and inform other boaters about the unique nature of the coral reef habitat, share their knowledge of the best approach to certain areas, demonstrate the use of a mooring buoy, and distribute safety information.

scale, as community coastal cleanup events are regularly organized throughout the year. These non-sanctuary-sponsored events help eliminate trap-related debris that has washed onto mangrove islands and beaches.

Summer 2009 also marked the end of a three-year debris removal project in which remote sensing was used to locate illegal lobster-attracting structures, called "casitas." The NOAA Fisheries Service Restoration Center, with support from the NOAA Marine Debris Program, the sanctuary and other state and federal agencies, oversaw the identification and removal from sanctuary waters of 89 tons of casita material placed illegally.

Lastly, marine debris removal efforts have been directed as part of compensatory restoration in vessel grounding settlements.

Military Use

Military activities that were specifically identified in the Environmental Impact Statement (EIS) and management plan for the sanctuary are exempt from sanctuary regulations. For new activities, or activities that were not identified in the EIS and management plan, the military is required to consult with the sanctuary (as directed by Section 304(d) of the NMSA) to ensure that the proposed activities are carried out in a manner that minimizes impacts to sanctuary resources.

The most significant military activity occurring in the sanctuary since its designation has been ongoing maintenance of the Key West harbor by the U.S. Navy. In 2003, the sanctuary consulted with the U.S. Army Corps of Engineers, EPA and Florida DEP when the Navy proposed maintenance dredging in the Key West harbor, shipping channel and turning basins. The removal of approximately 1 million cubic yards of sediment was permitted by the Army Corps in July 2003 to restore the charted depth and facilitate safe transit of deeper-draft Navy vessels through the area, and has been success-

ful in reducing sediment plumes created by the propellers of these and other larger vessels such as cruise ships. Sanctuary conditions requiring avoidance of known coral areas, and dredge effect monitoring, among others, were incorporated into the Army Corps permit to protect resources. Additional dredging was conducted by the Navy in 2007 to address sedimentation that occurred as a result of the hurricane seasons of 2004 and 2005. The Naval Air Station Key West Natural Resources and Environmental Compliance Partnering Team, an interagency group that includes the sanctuary, was formed in 2004 by the Navy to review large-scale projects, including continued maintenance of the Key West harbor.

The U.S. Coast Guard Sectors Key West and Miami coordinate with the sanctuary on multiple initiatives and provide significant protection to the marine environment of the Florida Keys. Coast Guard maintained navigation aids, including warning markers, delineate popular reef sites, many of which are protected by the sanctuary as Sanctuary Preservation Areas, Ecological Reserves, and Special Use Areas. The Coast Guard works with the sanctuary and other federal, state and local jurisdictions to develop interagency response plans to oil spills or other environmental threats, which includes participation in the National Preparedness for Response Exercise Program (NPREP). This program was developed to establish a workable exercise schedule meeting the requirements of the Oil Pollution Act of 1990 and the Clean Water Act. The NPREP sets forth exercise requirements ranging from small internal or external notification exercises to full-scale, area-wide exercises involving personnel and equipment from federal, state, and local government and industry. The Coast Guard also consults the sanctuary for geographic information system (GIS) support during actual pollution response activities, migrant interdiction operations, and to assist with the development of map products for inclusion in Area Contingency Plans or other response planning documents. More recently, Coast Guard personnel led the Unified Command for intergovernmental response to the Deepwater Horizon MC252 oil spill. The Coast Guard also coordinates closely with the sanctuary through their marine event permitting program, ensuring that authorized events (such as boat races, regattas, fireworks displays and other public and private activities) comply with the sanctuary regulations and include conditions for resource protection.

Management Responses to Pressures Impacting Maritime Archaeological Resources

Proactive management of submerged archaeological resources in sanctuary waters occurs through a Programmatic Agreement involving the sanctuary, the state of Florida, and the Advisory Council on Historic Preservation. This partnership is responsible for managing cultural resources in the sanctuary consistent with the Federal Archaeology Program, the Abandoned Shipwreck Act of 1987 and the National Historic Preservation Act. Maritime heritage resources in the sanctuary encompass a broad historical range. Because of the Keys' strategic location on early European shipping routes, the area's shipwrecks reflect the history of the entire period of discovery and colonization. Currently, 14 shipwrecks within the sanctuary are listed on the National Register of Historic Places. This richness of historical resources brings a corresponding responsibility to protect and preserve resources of national and international interest. Long-term protection requires a precautionary approach to historical resource management, particularly when information or artifacts may be destroyed or lost through direct or indirect activities. Accordingly, the resources are managed for public benefit and enjoyment, while the historical and cultural heritage is preserved for the future. As with all sanctuary resources, submerged archaeological resources are managed to facilitate multiple uses that are compatible with resource protection. (NOAA 2007)

It is an integral part of the sanctuary mission to protect and preserve maritime heritage resources for the public trust while still allowing for the private salvage of publicly owned historical resources. This is accomplished through a rigorous permit system which adheres to the Federal Archaeology Program guidelines. The three-tiered permit system allows for the private sector and institutions such as universities to survey, inventory, research, and recover maritime heritage resources in the sanctuary. The three types of permits available are the Survey and Inventory Permit, the Research and Recovery Permit, and the Deaccession/Transfer Permit. Proper standards of conservation, cataloguing, display, curation and publication must be assured before permitting disturbance of any maritime heritage resources. Such projects are expensive and labor-intensive, sometimes requiring specialists in the fields of archaeology, conservation, museum work, historic shipwreck research, and recovery. Sanctuary staff continues to explore public and private partnerships for management and consider private-sector implementation, when appropriate. A comprehensive GIS database is used to track and monitor permits as well as other maritime heritage resources.

Commercial salvage in the sanctuary can be allowed by permit for abandoned shipwrecks in federal waters. For wrecks in state waters, the state of Florida must be consulted due to their jurisdiction over abandoned shipwrecks through the Abandoned Shipwreck Act. There will be no commercial salvage of maritime archaeological resources of high historical significance, however commercial salvage for objects of low-to-moderate historical significance in areas relatively devoid of significant natural resources can be permitted. The recording and reporting of recovery operations, as well as the curation of representative samples of artifacts, must be consistent with the Programmatic Agreement for Maritime Archaeological Resources Management, as well as the Federal Archaeological Program or equivalent standards. The federal program was developed by the National Park Service by Presidential Order, and includes a collection of historical and archaeological resource-protection laws to which federal managers are required to adhere. The National Historic Preservation Act (NHPA) requires federal agencies to develop programs to inventory and evaluate historic resources. NHPA Section 106 requires review of each recovery permit by the State Historic Preservation Office and the Advisory Council on Historic Preservation. Permits within the scope of, and which adhere to all provisions of, the Programmatic Agreement need not go through an additional NHPA 106 review process. The Abandoned Shipwreck Act requires that state's management practices protect shipwrecks, natural resources and habitat areas, and guarantee recreational access to shipwreck sites. Sanctuary management also preserves selected shipwrecks in the sanctuary for research and recreation whereas some artifacts are recovered and preserved in museums with public access (NOAA 2007).

The sanctuary also has an extensive education and volunteer program in maritime heritage resources. Volunteers on the Submerged Resources Inventory Team have documented more than 400 underwater historical sites in the sanctuary. The three-volume inventory entitled "Underwater Resources of the Florida Keys National Marine Sanctuary" is available in public libraries throughout the Florida Keys. The education team has also developed a historic Shipwreck Trail which highlights nine historic vessels that sank in sanctuary waters and represents three broad periods of Florida Keys maritime history: European Colonial, American, and Modern. Brochures and underwater site guides for each vessel have been distributed to area dive operators and are also available in two sanctuary offices. The sites on the trail are marked with spar buoys and offer mooring buoys to eliminate damages from anchoring. The sanctuary also manages 189 Collection-type Heritage Assets, and by way of a Curatorial Services Agreement, more than 100 of these artifacts are on loan to various organizations including the Mel Fisher Maritime Heritage Society and Historical Museum in Key West, the Florida Keys Land and Sea Trust/Crane Point Museum and Nature Center in Marathon, and the Key Largo Chamber of Commerce. Of the remaining artifacts, some can be viewed on display in the Florida Keys National Marine Sanctuary Upper Region Office.

Concluding Remarks

This is the first attempt to comprehensively describe the status, pressures and trends of resources in the sanctuary. At its core, this document is an executive-level summary of research that describes the status and condition of sanctuary resources and should be used in conjunction with the more detailed summaries of the individual monitoring and research programs (e.g., zone monitoring program, water quality protection program, etc.). Additionally, this report helps identify strengths in current monitoring efforts, as well as causal factors that may require monitoring and potential remediation in the years to come. The data discussed will enable resource managers and stakeholders not only to acknowledge prior changes in resource status, but will provide guidance for future management challenges. For example, this report supports the need for additional management actions that address the degraded conditions of some key habitats and living resources in the sanctuary.

In this era of significant decline of coral reefs throughout the world, resilience is the key to survival of this critical ecosystem. It has been estimated that coral cover on reefs in the Caribbean has declined by an average of 80% in the last three decades (Gardner et al. 2003). It is generally agreed that these declines are not due to a single cause, but have resulted from multiple stressors acting together to alter ecosystem conditions and resulting in widespread deterioration. In turn, resource "managers may be able to increase the resilience of the system to climate change...by reducing impacts of local- and regional-scale stressors, such as fishing, input of nutrients, sedimentation and pollutants, and degraded water quality" (Keller et al. 2009). Many areas within the sanctuary, especially patch reefs and the deeper, fore-reef environment, continue to exhibit relatively high cover (>25%) by reef-building corals, and this may provide important insight in understanding resilience and other factors that sustain coral reef vitality. Therefore, it is more important than ever to protect remaining healthy reefs from impacts that can be addressed through management actions, both for their own sake and in order to help us promote the recovery of other coral reefs.

Because of the recreational and commercial importance of the marine resources of the Florida Keys, protecting these sanctuary resources is valuable not only for the environment but also for the economy. The special marine resources of the region, which led to the area's designation as a national marine sanctuary, contribute to the high quality of life for residents and visitors. Without these unique marine resources, the quality of both life and the economy of the Keys would decline.

Acknowledgements

The staff of Florida Keys National Marine Sanctuary would like to acknowledge the assistance and efforts of subject area experts who, by participating in meetings in March 2008, provided responses to questions that guided the drafting of the "State of Sanctuary Resources" section of this report: Alejandro Acosta (FWC), Lad Akins (REEF), Jerald Ault (UM-RSMAS), Erich Bartels (MML), James Bohnsack (NOAA Fisheries Service), Joseph Boyer (FIU), Joseph Cavanaugh (REEF), Leda Cunningham (REEF), Bob Glazer (FWC), John Hunt (FWC), G. Todd Kellison (NOAA Fisheries Service), Tom Matthews (FWC), Margaret Miller (NOAA Fisheries Service), Steven Miller (UNCW), and Cory Walter (MML). The authors would also like to recognize the extensive contributions of Mark Chiappone (UNCW) to this document.

The report benefited significantly from the following individuals who either provided a preliminary review of the report or contributed comments, content, images and data: Lad Akins (REEF), Jerry Ault (RSMAS), Carrie Backlund (Naval Air Station, Key West), Edward Barham (Naval Air Station, Key West), Rick Beaver (FWC), Cathy Becky (USGS Sirenia Project), Donald Behringer (UFL), Heather Blough (NOAA NMFS), Geoffrey Bock (Dept. of Primary Industries & Fisheries), Jim Bohnsack (NOAA NMFS), Theo Brainerd (NOAA NMFS), Mark Chiappone (UNCW), Gabriel Delgado (FWC), Michael Feeley (FWC), Roland Ferry (Wetlands, Coastal and Oceans Branch, EPA, Region 4), Megan Forbes (NOAA Marine Debris Program), Karen Fox (Clancy Environmental Consultants, Inc., a Tetra Tech Company), Todd Hitchins (NOAA), John Hunt (FWC), Bill Kiene (ONMS Southeast Region), William Kruczynski (Special Studies, EPA, Region 4), Gang Liu (NOAA Coral Reef Watch Program), Jerry Lorenz (Audubon Society), Margaret Miller (NMFS), Anne Morkill (FWS), Ken Nedimyer (Coral Restoration Foundation), David Polk (Florida Department of Health), Rob Ruzicka (FWC), Joe Schittone (formerly of ONMS), David A. Score (NOAA Corps), William Sharp (FWC), Tonya Shearer (Georgia Institute of Technology), Manoj Shivlani (RSMAS), and Ricardo Zambrano (FWC). Current and former staff of Florida Keys National Marine Sanctuary also provided preliminary reviews of the report or contributed comments, content, images and data: Brenda Altmeier, Jeff Anderson, Michael Buchman, Karrie Carnes, Joanne Delaney, Nancy Diersing, Kent Edwards, Alicia Farrer, Lilli Ferguson, William Goodwin, John Halas, Todd Hitchins, J. Harold Hudson, Robert Keeley, Lauri MacLaughlin, Sean Morton, William Precht, Benjamin Sniffen, Steve Werndli, and Fiona Wilmot.

Finally, our sincere thanks are extended to the peer reviewers of this document: John F. Bruno, Ph.D. (Associate Professor, University of North Carolina at Chapel Hill), Richard E. Dodge, Ph.D. (Dean, Nova Southeastern University Oceanographic Center), Paul Sammarco, Ph.D. (Professor, Louisiana Universities Marine Consortium), and Rob van Woesik, Ph.D. (Professor, Florida Institute of Technology).

Cited Resources

Abbott, G.M., J.H. Landsberg, A.R. Reich, K.A. Steidinger, S. Ketchen, C. Blackmore. 2009a. Resource guide for public health response to harmful algal blooms in Florida. Fish and Wildlife Research Institute Technical Report TR-14. viii + 132 p.

Abbott, J.P., L.J. Flewelling, J.H. Landsberg. 2009b. Saxitoxin monitoring in three species of Florida puffer fish. Harmful Algae 8:343-348.

Acosta, A., C. Bartels, J. Colvocoresses, M.F.D. Greenwood. 2007. Fish assemblages in seagrass habitats of the Florida Keys, Florida: spatial and temporal characteristics. Bull Mar Sci 81(1):1-19.

Adams, C. 1992. Economic activities associated with the commercial fishing industry in Monroe County, Florida. Staff Paper SP92-27, Food and Resource Economics Department, Institute of Food and Agricultural Sciences, University of Florida, Gainesville, FL.

Albins, M. and M. Hixon. 2008. Invasive Indo-Pacific lionfish *Pterois volitans* reduce recruitment of Atlantic coral-reef fishes. Marine Ecology Progress Series 367:233-238.

Andrews, K., L. Nall, C. Jeffrey, S. Pittman (eds). 2005. The state of coral reef ecosystems of Florida. pp. 150 – 200. *In* J. Waddell (ed.). The State of Coral Reef Ecosystems of the United States and Pacific Freely Associated States: 2005. NOAA Technical Memorandum NOS NC-COS 11. NOAA/NCCOS Center for Coastal Monitoring and Assessments Biogeography Team. Silver Spring, MD. 522pp.

Antonius, A. 1973. New observations on coral destruction in reefs. Abstract. Tenth meeting of the association of island marine laboratories of the Caribbean, University of Puerto Rico, Mayaguez, PR. pp. 3.

Antonius, A. 1981 [1982]. The "band" diseases in coral reefs. pp. 7-14. *In* E.D. Gomez, C.E. Birkeland, R.W. Buddemeier, R.E. Johannes, J.A. Marsh, Jr. and R.T. Tsuda (eds.) Proceedings of the 4th International Coral Reef Symposium Vol. 2. Marine Science Center, University of the Philippines, Manila, Philippines.

Aronson, R.B. and W.F. Precht. 2001. White-band disease and the changing face of Caribbean coral reefs. Hydrobiologia 460:25–38.

Ault, J.S., J.A. Bohnsack, G. Meester. 1998. A retrospective (1979-1995) multispecies assessment of coral reef fish stocks in the Florida Keys. Fish. Bull. 96(3):395-414.

Ault, J.S., S.G. Smith, G.A. Meester, J. Luo, J.A. Bohnsack. 2001. Site characterization for Biscayne National Park: assessment of fisheries resources and habitats. NOAA Technical Memorandum NMFS SEFSC 468. Miami, FL. 185pp.

Ault, J.S., S.G. Smith, J.A. Bohnsack. 2005a. Evaluation of average length as an indicator of exploitation status for the Florida coral-reef fish community. ICES J. Mar. Sci. 62:417-423.

Ault, J.S., J.A. Bohnsack, S.G. Smith, J. Luo. 2005b. Towards sustainable multispecies fisheries in the Florida, USA, coral reef ecosystem. Bull. Mar. Sci. 76(2):595-622. Electronic document available from: http://femar.rsmas.miami.edu/Publications/BMS_76%282%29_2005_Ault%20et%20al.pdf

Ault, J.S. (ed.). 2008. Biology and management of the world tarpon and bonefish fisheries . Taylor & Francis Group, CRC Series in Marine Science, Volume 9. Boca Raton, Florida . ISBN 084932792X. 441pp.

Baird, A.H. and P.A. Marshall. 2000. Mass bleaching of corals on the Great Barrier Reef: differential susceptibilities among taxa. Coral Reefs 19:155-163.

Bauer, J.C. 1980. Observations on geographical variations in population density of the echinoid *Diadema antillarum* within the western north Atlantic. Bull Mar Sci 30:509-515.

Behringer, D.C., M.J. Butler, J.D. Shields. 2006. Avoidance of disease by social lobsters. Nature 441(421).

Behringer, D.C., M.J. Butler, J.D. Shields. 2008. Ecological and physiological effects of PaV1 infection on the Caribbean spiny lobster (*Panulirus argus* Latreille). Journal of Experimental Marine Biology and Ecology 359:26-33.

Bohnsack, J.A. and D.L. Sutherland. 1985. Artificial reef research: a review with recommendations for future priorities. Bulletin of Marine Science 37(1):11-39.

Bohnsack, J.A., D.E. Harper, D.B. McClellan. 1994a. Fisheries trends from Monroe County Florida. Bulletin of Marine Science 54:982–1018.

Bohnsack, J.A., D.E. Harper, D.B. McClellan, M. Hulsbeck. 1994b. Effects of reef size on colonization and assemblage structure of fishes at artificial reefs off southeastern Florida, U.S.A. Bulletin of Marine Science 55(2-3): 796-823.

Bohnsack, J.A. and J.S. Ault. 1996. Management strategies to conserve marine biodiversity. Oceanography 9(1):73-82. Electronic document available from: http://femar.rsmas.miami.edu/Publications/Oceanography9(1)_1996_Bohnsack.pdf

Boyer, J.N. and H.O. Briceño. 2009. 2009 Annual report of the water quality monitoring project for the Florida Keys National Marine Sanctuary. Southeast Environmental Research Center Technical Report T-497. Florida International University. Miami, FL. 91pp. Electronic document available from: http://serc.fiu.edu/wqmnetwork/Report%20Archive/2009FKNMS.pdf

Brooks, G.R. and C.W. Holmes. 1990. Modern configuration of the southwest Florida carbonate slope: development by shelf margin progradation. Marine Geology 94(4)301-315.

Bruckner, A.W. 2000. Black-band disease (BBD) of scleractinian corals: occurrence, impacts, and mitigation. University of Puerto Rico, Mayaguez. PhD Dissert. 286pp.

Burns, C.D. 1981. A report on the 1980 fish kill along the Florida reef track. pp 36-41. *In:* D.K. Atwood. (ed.) Unusual mass fish mortalities in the Caribbean and. Gulf of Mexico. Atlantic Oceanographic and Meteorological Laboratories, Miami, Florida.

Burton, M.L., K.J. Brennan, R.C. Muñoz, R.O. Parker, Jr. 2005. Preliminary evidence of increased spawning of mutton snapper (Lutjanus analis) at Riley's Hump two years after the establishment of the Tortugas South Ecological Reserve. Fish. Bull. 103(2):404-410.

Butler, M.J., J.H. Hunt, W.F. Herrnkind, M.J. Childress, R. Bertelsen, W.C. Sharp, T.R. Matthews, J.M. Field, H.G. Marshall. 1995. Cascading disturbances in Florida Bay, USA: cyanobacteria blooms, sponge mortality, and implications for juvenile spiny lobsters *Panulirus argus* Mar. Ecol. Prog. Ser. 129:119-125.

Butler, M.J., D.C. Behringer, J.D. Shields. 2008. Transmission of *Panulirus argus* virus 1 (PaV1) and its effect on the survival of juvenile Caribbean spiny lobster. Diseases of Aquatic Organisms 79:173-182.

Bythell, J.C., E.H. Gladfelter, M. Bythell. 1993. Chronic and catastrophic natural mortality of three common Caribbean reef corals. Coral Reefs 12: 143–152.

Camp, E. 2011. A study of factors affecting the interactions divers make with coral reefs: a case study of diving in Key Largo. MSc. dissertation, Sheffield Hallam University.

Carlson J.K., J. Osborne, T.W. Schmidt. 2007. Monitoring the recovery of smalltooth sawfish, *Pristis pectinata*, using standardized relative indices of abundance. Biol. Conserv. 136:195-202.

Carpenter, R.C. 1988. Mass mortality of a Caribbean sea urchin: Immediate effects on community metabolism and other herbivores. Proc Natl Acad Sci USA 85:511-515.

Carr, R.S. 1991. Prehistoric settlement of the Florida Keys. pp. 54-96 *In:* J. Gato and D. Gallagher (eds.). The Monroe County Environmental Story. Monroe County environmental Education Task Force, Big Pine Key, Florida.

Causey, B.D. 2001. Lessons learned from the intensification of coral bleaching from 1980-2000 in the Florida Keys, USA. *In:* R.V. Salm and S.L. Coles (eds). Coral Bleaching and Marine Protected Areas. Proceedings of the Workshop on Mitigating Coral Bleaching Impact Through MPA Design, Bishop Museum, Honolulu, Hawaii, 29-31 May 2001. Asia Pacific Coastal Marine Program Report # 0102, The Nature Conservancy, Honolulu, Hawaii, U.S.A.

Causey, B.D. 2008. Coral reefs of the U.S. Caribbean; the history of massive coral bleaching and other perturbations in the Florida Keys. *In*. C. Wilkinson and D. Souter (eds.). Status of Caribbean coral reefs after bleaching and hurricanes in 2005. Global Coral Reef Monitoring Network and Reef and Rainforest Research Centre, Townsville, Queensland, Australia. 152pp.

CEMR (Center for Economic and Management Research).1995. Economic impact of commercial fisheries in the Florida Keys: case study-Florida Keys National Marine Sanctuary draft management plan. Tampa, FL: published for the Monroe County Commercial Fishermen.

Chesher, R.H. 1974. Canal survey: Florida Keys. Marine Research Foundation, Key West, Florida. 73pp.

Chiappone, M., A. White, D.W. Swanson, S.L. Miller. 2002a. Occurrence and biological impacts of fishing gear and other marine debris in the Florida Keys. Marine Pollution Bulletin 44(7):597-604.

Chiappone, M., D.W. Swanson, S.L. Miller. 2002b. Density, spatial distribution and size structure of sea urchins in coral reef and hard bottom habitats of the Florida Keys. Marine Ecology Progress Series 235:117-126.

Chiappone, M., D.W. Swanson, S.L. Miller, S.G. Smith. 2002c. Large-scale surveys on the Florida Reef Tract indicate poor recovery of the long-spined sea urchin *Diadema antillarum*. Coral Reefs 21:155-159.

Chiappone, M., H. Dienes, D.W. Swanson, S.L. Miller. 2004. Spatial distribution of lost fishing gear on fished and protected reefs in the Florida Keys National Marine Sanctuary. Caribbean Journal of Science 40(3) 312-326.

Chiappone, M., H. Dienes, D.W. Swanson, S.L. Miller. 2005. Impacts of lost fishing gear on coral reef sessile invertebrates in the Florida Keys National Marine Sanctuary. Biological Conservation 121(2):221-230.

Chiappone, M., L.M. Rutten, S.L. Miller, D.W. Swanson. 2007. Large-scale distributional patterns of the encrusting and excavating sponge *Cliona delitrix* pang on Florida Keys coral substrates. *In*: Porifera Research - Biodiversity, Innovation, Sustainability. M.R. Custodio, G. Lobo-Hajdu, E. Hajdu, G. Muricy (eds), Museu Nacional, Rio de Janeiro, pp 255-263

Chiappone, M., L.M. Rutten, D.W. Swanson, S.L. Miller. 2008. Population status of the urchin *Diadema antillarum* in the Florida Keys 25 years after the Caribbean mass mortality. Proceedings of the 11th International Coral Reef Symposium, Ft. Lauderdale, pp 706-710

City of Key West, Finance Department. 2005. The Impact of the Cruise Ship Industry on the Quality of Life in Key West. RFQ No: 04-001 City of Key West Naval Properties Local Redevelopment Authority.

Clark, C. 2006. Lobster fishermen stake it all on 2006 season. Miami Herald. Miami, FL.

Clavero, M. and E. García-Berthou. 2005. Invasive species are a leading cause of animal extinctions. Trends in Ecology and Evolution 20:110.

Cochard R., S.L. Ranamukhaarachchi, G.P. Shivakoti, O.V. Shipin, P.J. Edwards, K.T. Seeland. 2008. The 2004 tsunami in Aceh and Southern Thailand: A review on coastal ecosystems, wave hazards and vulnerability. Perspectives in Plant Ecology Evolution and Systematics 10:3-40.

Collins, A.B. 2009. A preliminary assessment of the abundance and size distribution of goliath grouper Epinephelus itajara within a defined region of the central eastern Gulf of Mexico. 6st Gulf and Caribbean Fisheries Institute Proceedings: 184-190.

Corbett, D.R., K. Dillon, W. Burnett, J. Chanton. 2000. Estimating the groundwater contribution into Florida Bay via natural tracers, 222Rn and CH4. Limnol. Oceanogr. 45(7):1546–1557.

Cowen, R. K., C. B. Paris, A. Srinivasan. 2006. Scaling of connectivity in marine populations. Science. 311(5760):522-527

Cox, C. and J.H. Hunt. 2005. Change in size and abundance of Caribbean spiny lobsters *Panulirus argus* in a marine reserve in the Florida Keys National Marine Sanctuary, USA. Mar Ecol-Prog Ser 294:227-239.

Creed, J.C. 2006. Two invasive alien azooxanthellate corals, *Tubastraea coccinea* and *Tubastraea tagusensis*, dominate the native zooxan-thellate *Mussismilia hispida* in Brazil. Coral Reefs 25: 350.

Cross, J.A. 1980. Residents' concerns about hurricane hazard within the Lower Florida Keys. National Conference on Hurricanes and Coastal Storms Proceedings. pp. 156-161.

Davis, G.E. 1977. Anchor damage to a coral reef on the coast of Florida. Biol. Conserv. 11(1)29-34.

Davis, G.E. 1982. A century of natural change in coral distribution at the Dry Tortugas: a comparison of reef maps from 1881 and 1976. Bulletin of Marine Science 32(2)608-623.

De'Ath, G., J.M. Lough, K.E. Sabricius. 2009. Declining coral calcification on the Great Barrier Reef. Science 323:116-119. doi:10.1126/science.1165283

Delgado, G. A., C. T. Bartels, R. A. Glazer, N. J. Brown-Peterson, K. J. McCarthy. 2004. Translocation as a strategy to rehabilitate the queen conch (*Strombus gigas*) population in the Florida Keys. Fish. Bull. 102: 278-288.

Denner, E.B.M., G.W. Smith, H. Busse, P. Schumann, T. Narzt, S.W. Polson, W. Lubitz, L.L. Richardson. 2003. Aurantimonas coralicida gen. nov., sp. nov., the causative agent of white plague type II on Caribbean scleractinian corals. International Journal of Systematic and Evolutionary Microbiology 53:1115–1122.

Derraik, J.G. 2002. The pollution of the marine environment by plastic debris: a review. Marine Pollution Bulletin 44(9):842-852.

de Sylva, D. P. 1994. Distribution and ecology of ciguatera fish poisoning in Florida, with emphasis on the Florida Keys. Bull. Mar. Sci. 54(3): 944—954.

DiDomenico, G., 2001. Storm Trap Debris Generated From Lost and Abandoned Lobster and Stone Crab Traps in Monroe County. Environmental Problem Solving Group, Florida Department of Environmental Protection, Florida.

Donahue, S. 2008. Influences of the Loggerhead sponge (*Spheciospongia vesparium*) and the Vase sponge (*Ircinia campana*) on nearshore hard bottom community development in the Florida Keys. MS Thesis, Old Donimion University. Norfolk, VA.

Donohue, M., R. Boland, C. Sramek, G. Antonelis. 2001. Derelict fishing gear in the northwestern Hawaiian Islands: diving surveys and debris removal in 1999 confirm threat to coral reef ecosystems. Marine Pollution Bulletin 42:1301–1312.

Donahue, S., A. Acosta, L. Akins, J. Ault, J. Bohnsack, J. Boyer, M. Callahan, B. D. Causey, C. Cox, J. Delaney, G. Delgado, K. Edwards, G. Garrett, B. D. Keller, G. T. Kellison, V. R. Leeworthy, L. MacLaughlin, L. McClenachan, M. W. Miller, S. L. Miller, K. Ritchie, S. Rohmann, D. Santavy, C. Pattengill-Semmens, B. Sniffen, S. Werndli, and D. E. Williams. 2008. The state of coral reef ecosystem of the Florida Keys. pp. 161-187. *In:* J.E. Waddell and A.M. Clarke (eds.), The State of Coral Reef Ecosystems of the United States and Pacific Freely Associated States: 2008. NOAA Technical Memorandum NOS NCCOS 73. NOAA/NCCOS Center for Coastal Monitoring and Assessment's Biogeography Team. Silver Spring, MD. 569 pp.

Drew, C.A. and D.B. Eggleston. 2008. Juvenile fish densities in Florida Keys mangroves correlate with landscape characteristics. Mar Ecol-Prog Ser 362:233-243.

Dunlap, M. and J.R. Pawlik. 1998. Spongivory by parrotfishes in Florida mangrove and reef habitats. Mar. Ecol. PSZNI 19:325-337.

Dustan, P. 1977. Vitality of reef coral populations off Key Largo, Florida: recruitment and mortality. Environ Geol 2:51-58.

Dustan, P. and J.C. Halas. 1987. Changes in the reef-coral community of Carysfort Reef, Key Largo, Florida: 1974 to 1982. Coral Reefs 6:91-106.

Edmunds, P.J. and R. Elahi. 2007. The demographics of a 15-year decline in cover of the Caribbean reef coral *Montastraea annularus*. Ecological Monographs 77(1):3–18.

Ene, A., M. Su, S. Lemaire, C. Rose, S. Schaff, R. Moretti, J. Lenz, L.H. Herbst. 2005. Distribution of chelonid fibropapillomatosis-associated herpesvirus variants in Florida: molecular genetic evidence for infection of turtles following recruitment to neritic developmental habitats. Journal of Wildlife Diseases 41(3):489-497. Electronic document available from: http://www.jwildlifedis.org/cgi/content/abstract/41/3/489

Enos, P. 1977. Holocene sediment accumulations of the South Florida shelf margin. *In:* P. Enos and R.D. Perkins (eds.). Quaternary Sedimentation in South Florida; Geological Society of America Memoir 147. Boulder, CO, p. 1-130.

Farrer, A.A. 2010. *N-Control* seagrass restoration monitoring report, monitoring events 2003-2008. Florida Keys National Marine Sanctuary, Monroe County, Florida. Marine Sanctuaries Conservation Series ONMS-10-06. U.S. Department of Commerce, National Oceanic and Atmospheric Administration, Office of National Marine Sanctuaries, Silver Spring, MD. 32pp.

FDER (Florida Department of Environmental Regulation). 1987. Florida Keys Monitoring Study: Water quality assessment of five selected pollutant sources in Marathon, Florida. FDER, Marathon Office, 187 pp.

Fenner, D. and K. Banks. 2004. Orange cup coral *Tubastraea coccinea* invades Florida and the Flower Garden Banks, Northwestern Gulf of Mexico. Coral Reefs 23:505-507.

Ferry, R. 2009. Range expansion of an invasive coral species into South Florida and the Florida Keys National Marine Sanctuary: investigating the ecological impact and source of the invasion. Wetlands, Coastal and Oceans Branch, EPA, Region 4. 6pp.

FFWC (Florida Fish and Wildlife Conservation Commission), Florida Marine Research Institute and National Oceanic and Atmospheric Administration. 1998. Benthic Habitats of the Florida Keys. FMRI Technical Report No. TR-4. 52 pp.

Foley, A.M., B.A. Schroeder, A.E. Redlow, K.J. Fick-Child, W.G. Teas. 2005. Fibropapillomatosis in stranded green turtle (*Chelonia mydas*) from the eastern United States (1980-98): Trends and associations with environmental factors. Journal of Wildlife Disease 41:29-41.

Fong, P. and D. Lirman. 1994. Damage and recovery on a coral reef following hurricane Andrew. Research & Exploration 10(2):246-248.

Fong, P. and D. Lirman. 1995. Hurricanes cause population expansion of the branching coral *Acropora palmata* (Scleractinia): Wound healing and growth patterns of asexual recruits. Marine Ecology 16(4):317-335.

Forcucci, D.1994. Population density, recruitment and 1991 mortality event of *Diadema antillarum* in the Florida Keys. Bull Mar Sci 54:917-928.

Fourqurean, J.W. 2009. FY2008 Annual report of seagrass monitoring in the Florida Keys National Marine Sanctuary. Contracts: NOAA - NA04NOS4780024, NA06NOS54780105; EPA X97468102-7.

Fourqurean, J.W. and M.B. Robblee. 1999. Florida Bay: a history of recent ecological changes. Estuaries 22(2B):345-357.

Fourqurean, J.W., M.J. Durako, L.X. Hefty. 2002. Seagrass distribution in south Florida: a multi-agency coordinated monitoring program. *In:* J.W. Porter and K.G. Porter (eds.), Linkages between ecosystems in the south Florida hydroscape: the river of grass continues. CRC Publ., Boca Raton, FL, pp. 489-514.

Fourqurean, J.W., J.N. Boyer, M.J. Durako, L.N. Hefty, B.J. Peterson. 2003. Forecasting Response of Seagrass Distributions to Changing Water Quality Using Monitoring Data. Ecological Applications 13(2)474-489.

Frank, K.T., B. Petrie, J.S. Choi, W.C. Leggett. 2005. Trophic cascades in a formerly cod-dominated ecosystem. Science 308:1621–1623.

Furman, B.T. and K.L. Heck. 2008. Effects of nutrient enrichment and grazers on coral reefs: an experimental assessment. Mar Ecol Prog Ser 363:89-101.

FWRI (Florida Fish and Wildlife Research Institute). 2010. Commercial fishing fish ticket information system. Florida Fish and Wildlife Conservation Commission, Fish and Wildlife Research Institute, St. Petersburg, Florida.

Gardner, T. A., I. M. Côté, J. A. Gill, A. Grant, A. R. Watkinson. 2003. Long-term region-wide declines in Caribbean corals. Science 301(5635):958-960.

Gardner, T.A., I.M. Côté, J.A. Gill, A. Grant, A.R. Watkinson. 2005. Hurricanes and Caribbean coral reefs: Impacts, recovery patterns, and role in long-term decline. Ecology 86:174-184.

Geiser, D.M., J.W. Taylor, K.B. Ritchie, G.W. Smith. 1998. Cause of sea fan death in the West Indies. Nature 394:137–138.

Gerard, S. 1992. Caribbean treasure hunt. Sea Frontiers. pp. 49-62.

Ginsburg, R.N. and E.A. Shinn. 1964. Distribution of the reef building community in Florida and the Bahamas [abs]: American Association of Petroleum Geologists 48:527.

Gladfelter, W.B., 1991. Population structure of *Acropora palmata* on the windward forereef, Buck Island National Monument: Seasonal and catastrophic changes 1988-1989. Chapter 5. *In:* Ecological Studies of Buck Island Reef National Monument, St. Croix, US. Virgin Islands. U.S. Department of the Interior, National Park Service, U.S. Virgin Islands.

Glazer, R.A. and G.A. Delgado. 2003. Towards a holistic strategy to managing Florida's queen conch (*Strombus gigas*) population. pp. 73-80. *In:* D. Aldana Aranda (ed.). El Caracol *Strombus gigas:* Conocimiento Integral para su Manejo Sustentable en el Caribe. CYTED, Programa Iberoamericano de Ciencia y Technología para el Desarrollo. Yucatán, México. 165 pp.

Glazer, R., N. Denslow., N. Brown-Peterson, P. McClellan-Green, D. Barber, N. Szabo, G. Delgado, K. Kroll, I. Knoebl, D. Spade. 2008. Anthropogenic effects on queen conch reproductive development in South Florida, a final report. Florida Fish and Wildlife Conservation Commission, Fish and Wildlife Research Institute. 73pp. Electronic document available from: http://ocean.floridamarine.org/the sanctuary_wqpp/products/special_projects/2009/glazer_denslow.pdf

Glynn, P., A.M. Szmant, E.F. Corcoran, S.V. Cofer-Shabica. 1989. Condition of coral reef cnidarians from the northern Florida reef tract: Pesticides, heavy metals, and histopathological examination. Marine Pollution Bulletin 20(11):568-576.

Gómez, R., D. Erpenbeck, T. Van Dijk, E. Richelle-Maurer, C. Devijver, J.C. Braekman, C. Woldringh, R.W.M. Van Soest. 2004. Identity of cyanobacterial symbionts of *Xestospongia muta*. Boll. Mus. Ist. Biol. Univ. Genova 66-67:82-83.

Goreau, T.J., J. Cervino, M. Goreau, R. Hayes, M. Hayes, L. Richardson. G. Smith, K. DeMeyer. I. Nagelkerken. J. Garzón-Ferreira, D. Gil. G. Garrison, E. H. Williams, L. Bunkley-Williams. C. Quirolo, K. Patterson, J. Porter, K. Porter. 1998. Rapid spread of Caribbean coral reef diseases. Rev. Biol. Trop. 46:157-171. Electronic document available from: http://www.globalcoral.org/Rapid%20Spread%20of%20Diseases%20in%20Caribbean%20Coral%20Reefs.pdf

Halas, J.F. 1988. An inventory of shipwrecks, grounding, and cultural marine resources within the Key Largo National Marine Sanctuary Region: Preliminary Report. NOAA Technical Memorandum NOA MEMD # NA87AA-H-CZ007, Key Largo National Marine Sanctuary.

Hammerstrom, K.K., J.W. Kenworthy, P.E. Whitfield, M.F. Merello. 2007. Response and recovery dynamics of seagrasses *Thalassia testudinum* and *Syringodium filiforme* and macroalgae in experimental motor vessel disturbances. MEPS 45:83-92.

Harmelin-Vivien, M.L. 1994. The effects of storms and cyclones on coral reefs: a review. Journal of Coastal Research Special Issue 12:211-231.

Harper, D.E., J.A. Bohnsack, B. Lockwood. 2000. Recreational fisheries in Biscayne National Park, Florida, 1976-1991. Mar. Fish. Rev. 62:8-26.

Harvell, C.D., K. Kim, J.M. Burkholder, R.R. Colwell, P.R. Epstein, D.J. Grimes, E.E. Hofmann, E.K. Lipp, A.D.M.E. Osterhaus, R.M. Overstreet, J.W. Porter, G.W. Smith, G.R. Vasta. 1999. Emerging Marine Diseases - Climate Links and Anthropogenic Factors.Marine Ecology 285:1505-1510. Electronic document available from: http://chge.med.harvard.edu/publications/journals/documents/harvell.pdf

Herbst, L.H. 1994. Fibropapillomatosis of marine turtles. Annual Review of Fish Diseases 4:389-425.

Hoegh-Guldberg, O. 1999. Coral bleaching, Climate change and the future of the world's coral reefs. Review, Marine and Freshwater Research 50:839-866.

Hoegh-Guldberg, O., P.J. Mumby, A.J. Hooten, R.S. Steneck, P. Greenfield, E. Gomez, C.D. Harvell, P.F. Sale, A.J. Edwards, K. Caldeira, N. Knowlton, C.M. Eakin, R. Iglesias-Prieto, N. Muthiga, R.H. Bradbury, A. Dubi M.E. Hatziolos 2007. Coral reefs under rapid climate change and ocean acidification. Science 318(5857):1737-1742. doi:10.1126/science.1152509

Hoffmeister, J.E. and H.G. Multer. 1968. Geology and Origin of the Florida Keys. GSA Bulletin 79(11):1487-1502.

Hu, C., K.E. Hackett, M.K. Callahan, S. Andrefouet, J.L. Wheaton, J.W. Porter, F.E. Muller-Karger. 2003. The 2002 ocean color anomaly in the Florida Bight: A cause of local coral reef decline? Geophys. Res. Lett. 30(3):1151.

Hughes, T.P. 1994. Catastrophes, phase shifts, and large-scale degradation of a Caribbean coral reef. Science 265:1547-1551.

Hughes, T.P. and J.E. Tanner. 2000. Recruitment failure, life histories, and long-term decline of Caribbean corals. Ecology 81(8):2250–2263.

Hunt, J.H. 1987. Status of queen conch (*Strombus gigas*) management in the Florida Keys, U.S.A. Proceedings of the Gulf and Caribbean Fisheries Institute 38: 376

Hunt, J. and W. Nuttle. 2007. Florida Bay Science Program: a synthesis of research on Florida Bay. Fish and Wildlife Research Institute Technical Report TR-11. 148pp. Electronic document available from: http://research.myfwc.com/publications/publication_info.asp?id=52697

ICES (International Council for the Exploration of the Sea). 2003. Report of the working group on pathology and diseases of marine organisms. Aberdeen, UK. 95pp. Electronic document available from: http://www.ices.dk/products/CMdocs/2003/F/F0303.PDF

IPCC (Intergovernmental Panel on Climate Change). 2001. Climate Change 2001: Synthesis Report. A Contribution of Working Groups I, II, and III to the Third Assessment Report of the Intergovernmental Panel on Climate Change [Watson, R.T. and the Core Writing Team (eds.)]. Cambridge University Press, Cambridge, United Kingdom, and New York, NY, USA, 398pp.

Jaap, W.C., 1979. Observation on zooxanthellae expulsion at Middle Sambo Reef, Florida Keys, Bull Mar. Sci. 29:414-422.

Jaap, W.C. 1984. The ecology of the South Florida coral reefs: A community profile. U.S. Department of the Interior, U.S. Fish and Wildlife Service and Minerals Management Service Publication FWS/OBS 82/08 and MMS 84-0038. 138pp.

Jaap, W.C. 1988. The 1987 zooxanthellae expulsion event at Florida reef. *In:* J.C. Ogden and R.I. Wicklund (eds.) Mass bleaching of coral reefs in the Caribbean. Report of a workshop, 9-10 December 1987, St. Croix, USVI, NURP/NOAA.

Jaap, W.C., Lyons, W.G., Dustan, P., Halas, J.C. 1989. Stony coral (Scleractinia and Milleporina) community structure at Bird Key Reef, Ft. Jefferson National Monument, Dry Tortugas, Florida. Fla. Mar. Res. Publ. No. 46. 31pp.

Jackson, J.B.C. 1992. Pleistocene Perspectives on Coral Reef Community Structure. Amer. Zool. 32(6): 719-731.

Jackson, J.B.C., M.X. Kirby, W.H. Berger, K.A. Bjorndal, L.W. Botsford, B.J. Bourque, R.H. Bradbury, R. Cooke, J. Erlandson, J.A. Estes, T.P. Hughes, S, Kidwell, C.B. Lange, H.S. Lenihan, J.M. Pandofi, C.H. Peterson,

R.S. Steneck, M.J. Tegner, R.R. Warner. 2001. Historical overfishing and the recent collapse of coastal ecosystems. Science 293:629-638.

Johns, G.M., V.R. Leeworthy, F.W. Bell, M.A. Bonn. 2003. Socioeconomic study of reefs in Southeast Florida. Hazen and Sawyer in association with Florida State University and the National Oceanic and Atmospheric Administration. 349pp. Electronic document available from: http://sanctuaries.noaa.gov/science/socioeconomic/floridakeys/pdfs/sereef2000.pdf

Jordan, L.K.B., K.W. Banks, L.E. Fisher, B.K. Walker, and D.S. Gilliam. 2010. Elevated sedimentation on coral reefs adjacent to a beach nourishment project. Marine Pollution Bulletin 60:261-271.

Keller, B.D. and B.D. Causey. 2005. Linkages between the Florida Keys National Marine Sanctuary and the South Florida Ecosystem Restoration Initiative. Ocean & Coastal Management 48: 69–900.

Keller, B.D. and S. Donahue (eds). 2006. 2002–03 sanctuary science report: an ecosystem report card after five years of marine zoning. US Department of Commerce, National Oceanic and Atmospheric Administration, National Ocean Service, Office of National Marine Sanctuaries, Florida Keys National Marine Sanctuary, Marathon.

Keller, B.D., D.F. Gleason, E. McLeod, C.M. Woodley, S. Airame, B.D. Causey, A.M. Friedlander, R. Grober-Dunsmore, J.E. Johnson, S.L. Miller, R.S. Steneck. 2009. Climate change, coral reef ecosystems, and management options for marine protected areas. Environmental Management 44:1069–1088.

Kenworthy W.J., M.S. Fonsec, P.E. Whitfield, K.K. Hammerstrom. 2002. Analysis of seagrass recovery in experimental excavations and propeller-scar disturbances in the Florida Keys National Marine Sanctuary. J Coast Res 37:75-85.

Klein III, C.J. and S.P. Orlando, Jr. 1994. A spatial framework for water-quality management in the Florida Keys National Marine Sanctuary. Bull Mar Sci 54:1036-1044.

Kruczynski, W.L. and F. McManus. 2002. Water quality concerns in the Florida Keys: sources, effects, and solutions. *In*: Porter JW, Porter KG (eds.) The Everglades, Florida Bay, and coral reefs of the Florida Keys: an ecosystem sourcebook. CRC Press, Boca Raton, pp 827–881.

Kruer, K. R. and L. G. Causey. 1992. The use of large artificial reefs to enhance fish populations at different depths in the Florida Keys. NOAA Technical Memorandum NOS NCCOS 16. NOAA/NCCOS Coastal and Estuarine Data Archaeology and Rescue Program. Silver Spring, MD. 208pp.

Landsberg, J. 1995. Tropical reef-fish disease outbreaks and mass mortalities in Florida, USA: what is the role of dietary biological toxins? Diseases of Aquatic Organisms 22:83-100.

Lapointe, B.E. and M.W. Clark. 1990. Final Report: Spatial and Temporal Variability in Trophic State of Surface Waters in Monroe County During 1989 1990. Florida Keys Land and Sea Trust, Marine Conservation Program, Marathon, Florida. 81 pp.

Lapointe, B.E. and M.W. Clark. 1992. Nutrient inputs from the watershed and coastal eutrophication in the Florida Keys. Estuaries 15(4):465-476.

Lee, T.N., C. Rooth, E. Williams, M. McGowan, A. Szmant, M. E. Clarke. 1992. Influence of Florida Current, gyres and wind driven circulation on transport of larvae and recruitment in the Florida Keys coral reefs. Cont. Shelf Res. 12:971-1002.

Lee, T.N., M.E. Clarke, E. Williams, A.F. Szmant, T. Berger. 1994. Evolution of the Tortugas gyre and its influence on recruitment in the Florida Keys. Bull. Mar. Sci. 54(3)21-646.

Lee, T.N. and E. Williams. 1999. Mean Distribution and Seasonal Variability of Coastal Currents and Temperature in the Florida Keys with Implications for Larval Recruitment. Bull. of Mar. Science 64(1)35-56.

Lee, T.N. and N. Smith. 2002. Volume transport variability through the Florida Keys tidal channels. Continental Shelf Research 22:1361–1377.

Leeworthy, V.R. 1995. Review of the economic impact of commercial fisheries in the Florida Keys: case study-Florida Keys National Marine Sanctuary draft management plan. Silver Spring, MD: National Oceanic and Atmospheric Administration.

Leeworthy, V.R. 1996. Technical appendix: sampling methodologies and estimation methods applied to the Florida Keys/Key West Visitor Surveys. Silver Spring, MD: National Oceanic and Atmospheric Administration. 170 pp. Electronic document available from: http://sanctuaries.noaa.gov/science/socioeconomic/floridakeys/pdfs/vistechappen9596.pdf

Leeworthy, V.R. 2010. Visitor Study: Selected Comparisons 1995-96 and 2007-08. Silver Spring: Office of National Marine Sanctuaries, National Ocean Service, National Oceanic and Atmospheric Administration, July 2010, 17pp. Electronic document available from: http://sanctuaries.noaa.gov/science/socioeconomic/floridakeys/pdfs/comparisons_9596_0708.pdf

Leeworthy, V.R. and P.C. Wiley. 1996. Visitor profiles: Florida Keys/Key West." Silver Spring, MD: National Oceanic and Atmospheric Administration. 159pp. Electronic document available from: http://sanctuaries.noaa.gov/science/socioeconomic/floridakeys/pdfs/visprof9596.pdf

Leeworthy, V.R. and P.C. Wiley. 1997. A socioeconomic analysis of the recreation activities of Monroe County residents in the Florida Keys/Key West. Silver Spring, Maryland: National Oceanic and Atmospheric Administration. Electronic document available from: http://sanctuaries.noaa.gov/science/socioeconomic/floridakeys/pdfs/resident9596.pdf

Leeworthy, V.R., T. Maher, E.A. Stone. 2006. Can artificial reefs alter user pressure on adjacent natural reefs. Bulletin of Marine Science, 78 (1):29-37. Electronic document available from: http://sanctuaries.noaa.gov/science/socioeconomic/floridakeys/pdfs/bms.pdf

Leeworthy, V.R. and F.C. Morris. 2010. A socioeconomic analysis of the recreation activities of Monroe County residents in the Florida Keys/Key West 2008. Silver Spring: Office of National Marine Sanctuaries, National Ocean Service, National Oceanic and Atmospheric Administration, September 2010, 61pp. Electronic document available from: http://sanctuaries.noaa.gov/science/socioeconomic/floridakeys/pdfs/floridakeysres_report.pdf

Leeworthy, V.R., D.K. Loomis, S.K. Paterson. 2010. Visitor profiles: Florida Keys/Key West 2007-08. Silver Spring: Office of National Marine Sanctuaries, National Ocean Service, National Oceanic and Atmospheric Administration and Amherst, MA: Human Dimensions of Marine and Coastal Ecosystems Program, University of Massachusetts Amherst, May 2010, 196pp. Electronic document available from:

http://sanctuaries.noaa.gov/science/socioeconomic/floridakeys/pdfs/full_visitor_08.pdf

Leichter, J. J., G. Shellenbarger, S. Jenovese, S. R. Wing. 1998 Breaking internal waves on a Florida (USA) coral reef: a plankton pump at work? Mar Ecol Prog Ser 166:83–97.

Leichter, J.L., H.L. Stewart, S.L. Miller. 2003. Episodic nutrient transport to Florida coral reefs. Limnology and Oceanography 48(4):1394-1407.

Lesser, M.P. and S. Lewis. 1996 Action spectrum for the effects of UV radiation on photosynthesis in the hermatypic coral Pocillopora damicornis. Mar Ecol Prog Ser 134:171-177.

Lessios, H.A. 1988. Mass mortality of *Diadema antillarum* in the Caribbean: What have we learned? Annu Rev Ecol Syst 19:371-393.

Lessios, H.A. 2005 *Diadema antillarum* populations in Panama twenty years following mass mortality. Coral Reefs 24:125-127.

Lessios, H.A., D.R. Robertson, J.D. Cubit. 1984. Spread of *Diadema* mass mortality through the Caribbean. Science 226(4672):335-337.

Lessios, H.A., M.J. Garrido, B.D. Kessing. 2001. Demographic history of *Diadema antillarum*, a keystone herbivore on Caribbean coral reefs. Proc R. Soc. Lond. 268:2347-2353.

Levitan, D. R. 1988. Algal-urching biomass responses following mass mortality of Diadema antillarum Phillipi at St. Johns, U.S. Virgin Islands. J. Exp. Mar. Bio Eco. 119:167-178.

Levy, J.M., M. Chiappone, K.M. Sullivan. 1996. Invertebrate infauna and epifauna of the Florida Keys and Florida Bay. Volume 5: Site characterization for the Florida Keys National Marine Sanctuary. The Preserver, Zenda, 166 p.

Lewis, C.F., S.L. Slade, K.E. Maxwell, T.R. Matthews. 2009. Lobster trap impact on coral reefs: effects of wind-driven trap movement. New Zealand Journal of Marine and Freshwater Research 43:271–282.

Lidz, B.H. and E.A. Shinn. 1991. Paleoshorelines, reefs, and a rising sea: south Florida, U.S.A. Journal of Coastal Research 7(1):203-339.

Lindeman, K. C. and D. B. Snyder. 1999. Nearshore hardbottom fishes of southeast Florida and effects of habitat burial caused by dredging Fish. Bull. 97:508-525.

Lirman, D. 2000. Fragmentation in the branching coral *Acropora palmata* (Lamarck): growth, survivorship, and reproduction of colonies and fragments. Journal of Experimental Marine Biology and Ecology 251:41-57.

Lirman, D. and P. Fong. 1997a. Susceptibility of coral communities to storm intensity, duration and frequency. Proceedings 8th International Coral Reef Symposium 1:561–566.

Lirman, D. and P. Fong. 1997b. Patterns of damage to the branching coral Acropora palmata following Hurricane Andrew: Damage and survivorship of hurricane-generated asexual recruits. Journal of Coastal Research 13(1): 67-72.

Lirman, D. and P. Fong. 2007. Is proximity to land-based sources of coral stressors an appropriate measure of risk to coral reefs? An example from the Florida Reef Tract. Marine Pollution Bulletin 54:779-791.

Longley, W.H. and S.F. Hildebrand. 1941. Systematic catalogue of the fishes of Tortugas, Florida. Carneg. Inst. Wash. Publ. 535(34)1-331.

Mace, P.M. 1997. Developing and sustaining world fisheries resources: the state of the science and management. pp 98-102. *In:* D.A. Hancock, D.C. Smith, A. Grant, J.P. Beumer (eds.). Second World Fisheries Congress. CSIRO Publishing, Collingwood, Australia, pp. 98–102.

MACTEC Engineering and Consulting, Inc. 2003. Monroe County Residential Canal Inventory and Assessment. Final Report. Volumes 1 and 2.

Maliao, R.J., R.G. Turingan, J. Lin. 2008 Phase-shift in coral reef communities in the Florida Keys National Marine Sanctuary (FKNMS), USA. Marine Biology 154:841-853.

Marszalek, D., G. Babashoff, Jr., M. R. Noel, D. R. Worley. 1977. Reef distribution in south Florida. Proceedings of the Third International Coral Reef Symposium 2:223-229

Marzyck, M. 1991. The overseas highways. *In:* J. Gato D. Galleger (eds.). The Monroe County environmental story. Big Pine Key, FL: Monroe County Environmental Education Task Force, 1991.

Matthews, T.R. 2001. Trap-induced mortality of the spiny lobster, *Panulirus argus*, in Florida, USA. Mar. Freshwater Res 52:1509–1516.

Matthews, T.R., S. Slade, J. Moore. 2004. Evaluating Trap Impacts on Essential Fish Habitat in the Florida Keys. Poster aPresentation. 57th annual Gulf and Caribbean Fisheries Institutes conference. St. Petersburg, FL.

McClenachan L, J.B.C. Jackson, M.J.H. Newman. 2006. Conservation implications of historic sea turtle nesting beach loss. Front Ecol Environ 4:290–296.

McClenachan, L. and A. Cooper. 2008. Extinction rate, historical population structure and ecological role of the Caribbean monk seal. Proceedings of the Royal Society B. 275(1641):1351-1358.

McClenachan, L. 2008. Social conflict, over-fishing and disease in the Florida sponge fishery, 1849 – 1939. *In:* D.J. Starkey, P. Holm, M. Barnard (eds). Oceans past: management insights from the history of marine animal populations. Earthscan research editions. 223pp.

McDaniel, C.J., L.B. Crowder, J.A. Piddy. 2000. Spatial dynamics of sea turtle abundance and shrimping intensity in the US Gulf of Mexico. Conservation Ecology 4, 15.

McIntyre, M., R.A. Glazer, G.A. Delgado. 2006. The effects of the pesticides Biomist 30/30 and Dibrom on queen conch (*Strombus gigas*) embryos and larvae: a pilot study. Proc. Gulf Caribb. Fish. Inst. 57:731 742.

McMurray, S.E., J.E. Blum, J.R. Pawlik. 2008. Redwood of the reef: growth and age of the giant barrel sponge Xestospongia muta in the Florida Keys. Marine Biology 155:159-171.

McPherson B. F. 1968. Contributions to the biology of the sea urchin Eucidaris tribuloides (Lamarck). Bull Mar Sci 18: 400–443

Miller S.L., D.W. Swanson, M. Chiappone. 2002. Multiple spatial scale assessment of coral reef and hard-bottom community structure in the Florida Keys National Marine Sanctuary. Proceedings of the Ninth International Coral Reef Symposium. Volume 1:69-74.

Miller S.L., M. Chiappone, L.M. Rutten. 2008. Large-scale assessment of marine debris and benthic coral reef organisms in the Florida Keys National Marine Sanctuary – 2008 Quick look report and data summary. Center for Marine Science, Univ. North Carolina-Wilmington, Key Largo, FL. 271pp.

Miller, M.W., K.L. Kramer, S.M. William, L. Johnston, A.M. Szmant. 2009. Assessment of current rates of *Diadema antillarum* larval settlement. Coral Reefs 28:511-515.

Miller, S.L., M. Chiappone, L.M. Rutten. 2010. Abundance, distribution, and condition of benthic coral reef organisms in the upper Florida Keys National Marine Sanctuary – 2010 Quick look report and data summary. Center for Marine Science, Univ. North Carolina-Wilmington, Key Largo, FL. 242pp.

Morris, J.A., Jr. and J.L. Akins. 2009. Feeding ecology of invasive lionfish (*Pterois volitans*) in the Bahamian archipelago. Environmental Biology of Fishes, DOI 10.1007/s10641-009-9538-8.

Morris, J.A., Jr., and P.E. Whitfield. 2009. Biology, ecology, control and management of the invasive Indo-Pacific lionfish: an updated integrated assessment. NOAA Technical Memorandum NOS NCCOS 99. 57pp. Electronic document available from: http://coastalscience.noaa.gov/documents/lionfish_%20ia2009.pdf

Morris, J.A., Jr., J.L. Akins, A. Barse, D. Cerino, D.W. Freshwater, S.J. Green, R.C. Munoz, C. Paris, P.E. Whitfield. 2009. Biology and ecology of the invasive lionfishes, *Pterois miles* and *Pterois volitans.* Proceedings of the 61st Gulf and Caribbean Fisheries Institute November 10 - 14, 2008 Gosier, Goudeloupe, French West Indies.

Muñoz , R.C., M.L. Burton, K.J. Brennan R.O. Parker, Jr. 2010. Reproduction, habitat utilization, and movements of Hogfish (*Lachnolaimus maximus*) in the Florida Keys U.S.A.: Comparisons from fished versus unfished habitats. Bul. Mar. Sci. 86(1):93-116.

Murray, T.J. and Associates, Inc. 2007. Socio-economic baseline development Florida Keys National Marine Sanctuary". Under contract to Socioeconomic Research and Monitoring Program for the Florida Keys National Marine Sanctuary, Commercial Fishing Panels. Silver Spring, MD: National Oceanic and Atmospheric Administration. Electronic document available from:

http://sanctuaries.noaa.gov/science/socioeconomic/floridakeys/pdfs/commfishpan7and8.pdf

Nagelkerken, I., K. Buchan, G. W. Smith, K. Bonair, P. Bush, J. Garzón-Ferreira, L. Botero, P. Gayle, C. D. Harvell, C. Heberer, K. Kim, C. Petrovic, L. Pors and P. Yoshioka. 1997. Widespread disease in Caribbean sea fans: II. Patterns of infection and tissue loss. Mar. Ecol. Prog. Ser. 160: 255–263.

Nagelkerken, I., L. Aerts., L. Pors. 2000. Barrel sponge bows out. Reef Encounter 28:14-15.

NMFS (National Marine Fisheries Service). 2010. 2010 Status of U.S. Fisheries. U.S. Department of Commerce, National Oceanic and Atmospheric Administration, NOAA Fisheries Service. 28pp. Electronic document available from: http://www.nmfs.noaa.gov/sfa/statusoffisheries/SOSmain.htm

NMSP (National Marine Sanctuary Program). 2004. A monitoring framework for the National Marine Sanctuary System. U.S. Dept. of Commerce, National Oceanic and Atmospheric Administration, National Ocean Service. Silver Spring, MD. 22 pp. Electronic document available from: http://sanctuaries.noaa.gov/library/national/swim04.pdf

NOAA (National Oceanic and Atmospheric Administration). 1996. Florida Keys National Marine Sanctuary management plan/environmental impact statement, vol II. U.S. Dept. of Commerce, National Oceanic and Atmospheric Administration, National Ocean Service. Silver Spring, MD. 251pp. Electronic document available from: http://floridakeys.noaa.gov/management/welcome.html

NOAA (National Oceanic and Atmospheric Administration). 2007. Florida Keys National Marine Sanctuary revised management plan. U.S. Dept. of Commerce, National Oceanic and Atmospheric Administration, National Ocean Service. Silver Spring, MD. 382 pp. Electronic document available from: http://floridakeys.noaa.gov/management/welcome.html

NOAA (National Oceanic and Atmospheric Administration). 2008. Marine Debris Emergency Response Planning in the North-Central Gulf of Mexico Interim Draft Report. 44pp.

Nobles, R.E., P. Brown, J. Rose, E. Lipp. 2000. The investigation and analysis of swimming-associated illness using the fecal indicator Enterococcus in Southern Florida's marine water. Fla. J. Environ. Health 169:13-19.

Ocean Acidification Reference User Group. 2009. Ocean Acidification: The Facts. A special introductory guide for policy advisers and decision makers. D. d'A. Laffoley, and J.M. Baxter (eds). European Project on Ocean Acidification (EPOCA). 12pp.

Olden, J.D., N.L. Poff, M.R. Douglas, M.E. Douglas, K.D. Fausch. 2004. Ecological and evolutionary consequences of biotic homogenization. Trends in Ecology and Evolution 19:18–24.

Ogden, J.C., J.W. Porter, N.P. Smith, A.M. Szmant, W.C. Jaap, and D. Forcucci. 1994. A long-term interdisciplinary study of the Florida Keys seascape. Bull. Mar. Sci. 54:1059–1071.

Oppel, F. and T. Meisel. 1871. Along the Florida Reef. pp. 265-309. In: Tales of Old Florida. Castle Press. Seacaucus, NJ. 480pp.

Osenberg, C. W., C. M. St. Mary, J. A. Wilson, and W. J. Lindberg. 2002. A quantitative framework to elevate the attraction-production controversy. ICES Journal of Marine Science. 59:S214 – S22.

Parks, P. 1968. The railroad that died at sea. Langley Press Inc., Key West, Florida. 44pp.

Parsons, D.M. and D.B. Eggleston. 2007. Potential population and economic consequences of sublethal injuries in the spiny lobster fishery of the Florida Keys. CISRO Marine and Freshwater Research 58:166-177

Patterson K.L., J.W. Porter, K.B. Ritchie, S.W. Polson, E. Mueller, E.C. Peters, D.L. Santavy, G.W. Smith. 2002. The etiology of white pox, a lethal disease of the Caribbean coral, Acropora palmata, Proc. Natl. Acad. Sci. 99 pp. 8725–8730.

Peters, E.C. 1997. Diseases of coral-reef organisms. In: C. Birkeland (ed.), Life and Death of Coral Reefs. Chapman and Hall, New York: 114-139.

Pomerance, R., J.K. Reaser, P.O. Thomas. 1999. Coral bleaching, coral mortality, and global climate change. Report. U.S. State Department, Coral Reef Task Force, Washington, D.C.

Porch, C.E., A.M. Eklund, G.P. Scott. 2003. An assessment of rebuilding times for goliath grouper. SEDAR6-RW-3. Sustainable Fisheries Division, NMFS Southeast Fisheries Science Center. Miami, FL. 25pp.

Porch, C.E., A.M. Eklund, G.P. Scott. 2006. A catch-free stock assessment model with application to goliath grouper (Epinephelus itajara) off southern Florida. Fish. Bull. 104:89-106.

Porter, J.W. and O.W. Meier. 1992. Quantification of loss and change in Floridian reef coral

populations. American Zoologist 32:625-640.

Powers, S. P., J.H. Grabowski, C. H. Peterson, W.J. Lindberg. 2003. Estimating enhancement of fish production by offshore artificial reefs: uncertainty exhibited by divergent scenarios. Mar Ecol Prog Ser 264: 265–277.

Randall J. E., R. E. Schroeder, W. A. Starck. 1964. Notes on the biology of the echinoid Diadema antillarum. Caribb J Sci 4(2-3):421–433.

Rhyne A, Rotjan R, Bruckner A, Tlusty M. 2009. Crawling to collapse: ecologically unsound ornamental invertebrate fsheries. PLoS ONE 4(12):e8413.

Ritchie, K.B. and G.W. Smith. 1998. Type II White-Band Disease. Revista de Biologia Tropical 46(Suppl. 5):199-203.

Robblee, M. B., T. R. Barber, P. R. Carlson, M. J. Durako, J. W. Fourqurean, L. K. Muehlstein, D. Porter, L. A. Yarbro, R. T. Zieman, J. C. Zieman. 1991. Mass mortality of the tropical seagrass Thalassia Testudinum in Florida Bay (USA). Marine Ecology-Progress Series 71(3)297-99.

Roberts, H.H., L.J. Rouse, N.D. Walker, J.H. Hudson. 1982. Cold-water stress in Florida Bay and northern Bahamas; a product of winter cold-air outbreaks. Journal of Sedimentary Research 52(1)145-155.

Rudnick, D.T., P.B. Ortner, J.A. Browder, S.M. Davis. 2005. A conceptual ecological model of Florida Bay. Wetlands 25(4):870-883.

Ruiz-Carus, R., R.E. Matheson, D.E. Roberts, P.E. Whitfield. 2006. The western Pacific red lionfish, Pterois volitans (Scorpaenidae). In: Florida: Evidence for reproduction and parasitism in the first exotic marine fish established in state waters. Biol. Conserv. 128(March):384-390.

Rumbold, D. and S.C. Snedaker. 1999. Sea-surface microlayer toxicity off the Florida Keys. Mar. Environ. Res.,47:457-472.

Rutten, L.M., M. Chiappone, D.W. Swanson, S.L. Miller. 2009. Stony coral species diversity and cover in the Florida Keys using design-based sampling. Proceedings of the 11th International Coral Reef Symposium, Ft. Lauderdale: 800-804.

Ruzicka, R., K. Semon, M. Colella, V. Brinkhuis, J. Kidney, J. Morrison, K. Macaulay, J.W. Porter, M. Meyers, M. Christman, J. Colee. 2009. Coral Reef Evaluation and Monitoring Project Annual Report. NOAA/NOS MOA-2001-683 (Amendment No. 004)/7477. 111pp.

Ruzicka, R., K. Semon, J. Kidney, M. Colella, J. Morrison, V. Brinkhuis, J. Porter, M. Meyers, M. Christman, J. Colee. 2010. Oral presentaion. Report to Florida Keys National Marine Sanctuary Water Quality Protection Program Steering Committee. July 7, 2010.

Sale, P.F. 2006. Coral Reef Fishes: Dynamics and Diversity in a Complex System. Academic Press. Burlington, MA. 149-170pp.

Santavy, D.L., E. Mueller, E.C. Peters, L. MacLaughlin, J.W. Porter, K.L. Patterson, J. Campbell. 2001. Quantitative assessment of coral diseases in the Florida Keys: strategy and methodology. Hydrobiologia 460:39-52.

Santavy, D.L., J. Campbell, R.L. Quarles, J.M. Patrick, L.M. Harwell, M. Parsons, L. MacLaughlin, J. Halas, E. Mueller, E C. Peters, and J. Hawkridge. 2005. The epizootiology of coral diseases in South Florida. EPA/600/R-05/146. U.S. Environmental Protection Agency, Gulf Ecology Division, Gulf Breeze, Florida.

Schofield, P.J., J.A. Morris, Jr., L. Akins. 2009. Field Guide to Nonindigenous Marine Fishes of Florida. NOAA Technical Memorandum NOS NCCOS 92. Electronic document available from: http://fl.biology.usgs.gov/Marine_Fish_ID/index.html

Schomer, N.S. and R.D. Drew. 1982. An ecological characterization of the Lower Everglades, Florida Bay, and the Florida Keys. Washington, DC: U.S. Fish and Wildlife Service, Office of Biological Services. 246pp.

SEDAR 8. 2005. Southeastern US spiny lobster stock assessment report.

Sharp, W.C., R.D. Bertelsen, V.R. Leeworthy. 2005. Long-term trends in recreational lobster fishery of Florida, United States: landings, effort and implications for management". New Zealand Journal of Marine and Freshwater Research, 2005, Vol. 39: 733-747. Electronic document available from: http://sanctuaries.noaa.gov/science/socioeconomic/floridakeys/pdfs/sharpleeworthy.pdf

Shearer, T. 2010. Distribution of *Tubastraea coccinea* in Florida and Flower Garden Banks: Progress Report. Georgia Institute of Technology. 14pp.

Sheridan, P., R. Hill, G. Matthews, R. Appeldoorn, B. Kojis, T. Matthews. 2005. Does trap fishing impact coral reef ecosystems? An update. pp. 511-519. *In:* Proceedings of the 56th Gulf and Caribbean Fisheries Institute. Tortola, British Virgin Islands. 851pp.

Shinn, E.A., J.H. Hudson, R.B. Halley, B. Lidz. 1977. Topographic control and accumulation rate of some Holocene coral reefs, South Florida and Dry Tortugas. Proceedings, Third International Coral Reef Symposium (Miami), 2:1-7.

Shinn, E.A. 1988. The geology of the Florida Keys. Oceanus 31:46-53.

Shinn, E.A.,B.H. Lidz, J.L. Kindinger, J.H. Hudson, R.B. Halley. 1989. A Field Guide: Reefs of Florida and the Dry Tortugas, A Field Trip to the Modern Carbonate Environments of the Florida Keys and the Dry Tortugas. International Geological Congress. IGC Field Trip T1 76. American Geophysical Union, Washington, D.C., 54pp.

Shinn, E.A., B.H. Lidz, M.W. Harris. 1994. Factors controlling distribution of Florida Keys reefs. Bull. Mar. Sci. 54:1084 (abstr.).

Shubow, D. 1969. Sponge fishing on Florida's east coast. Tequesta 1(29)3-15. Electronic document available from: http://digitalcollections.fiu.edu/tequesta/files/1969/69_1_01.pdf

Singh, S.P., A. Azua, A. Chaudhary, S. Khan, K. Willett, P. Gardinali. 2010. Occurrence and distribution of steroids, hormones, and selected pharmaceuticals in south Florida coastal environments. Ecotoxicology 19:338-350.

Smith, N.P. 1994. Long-term Gulf-to-Atlantic transport through tidal channels in the Florida Keys. Bull Mar Sci. 54(3):620-609.

Smith, N.P. and T.R. Lee. 2003. Volume transport through tidal channels in the middle Florida Keys. Journal of Coastal Research 19(2)254-260.

Spade D.J., R.J. Griffitt., L. Liu, N.J. Brown-Peterson, K.J. Kroll. 2010. Queen Conch (*Strombus gigas*) testis regresses during the reproductive season at nearshore sites in the Florida Keys. PLoS ONE 5(9): e12737. doi:10.1371/journal.pone.0012737.

Starck, W.A. 1968. A list of fishes of alligator reef, Florida with comments on the nature of the Florida reef fish fauna. Undersea Biology 1:4-40.

Steindler, L., D. Hucheon, A. Avni, M. Ilan. 2005. 16S rRNA phylogeny of sponge associated cyanobacteria. App. Environ. Microbiol. 71:4127-4131.

Stoner, A.W., M. Ray, J.M. Waite. 1995. Effects of a large herbivorous gastropod on macrofauna communities in tropical seagrass meadows. Marine Ecology Progress Series 121:125-137.

Strong, A.M. and G.T. Bancroft. 1994. Patterns of deforestation and fragmentation of mangrove and deciduous seasonal forests in the upper Florida Keys. Bulletin of Marine Science 54(3):795 804.

Szmant, A.M. and A. Forrester, A. 1996. Water column and sediment nitrogen and phosphorus distribution patterns in the Florida Keys, USA. Coral Reefs 15:21–41.

Talge, H. 1989. Observations of recreational divers on coral reefs in the Florida Keys. Final report to the Florida Keys Office of The Nature Conservancy by the University of South Florida, St. Petersburg, FL. 11pp.

Thanner, S.E., T.L. McIntosh, S.M. Blair. 2006. Development of benthic and fish assemblages on artificial reef materials compared to adjacent natural reef assemblages in Maimi-Dade county, Florida. Bull. Mar. Sci. 78(1):57-70.

Tilmant, J.T. 1989. A history and an overview of recent trends in fishes of Florida Bay. Bull Mar Sci. 44(1):3-33.

Torres, R.E. 2003. Ecological consequences and population changes from intensive fishing of a shallow-water mollusk, *Strombus gigas*: A site study of Parque Nacional del Este, Domincan Republic. University of Miami, Ph.D. dissertation. 150pp.

USACE (United States Army Corps of Engineers). 1999. C&SF Restudy final integrated feasibility report and programmatic environmental impact statement (PEIS). Jacksonville, FL: USACE.

U.S. Bureau of Economic Analysis. 2010. Regional economic accounts data: state and local area personal income and employment. U.S. Department of Commerce, Bureau of Economic Analysis, On-line Database: http://www.bea.gov/newsreleases/regional/comp/comp_news-release.htm

U.S. Census Bureau. 2010. Annual population estimates for counties. U.S. Department of

Commerce, Bureau of the Census, On-line Database: http://www.census.gov/popest/counties/counties.html

U.S. Department of the Navy. 1990. Environmental assessment of underwater explosion testing near Key West. Florida, and Amendment 1, short-term limited testing at areas D and H. Prepared for the Department of the Navy, Southern Division Naval Facilities Engineering command. Contract no. N62467-88-D-0628. 212pp + appendicies.

Valentine, J.F, K.L. Heck Jr., D. Blackmon, M.E. Goecker, J. Christian, R.M. Kroutil, B.J. Peterson, M.A. Vanderklift, K.D. Kirsh, M. Beck. 2008. Exploited species impacts on trophic linkages along reef-seagrass interfaces in the Florida Keys. Ecological Applications, 18(6):1501-1515.

Vaughn, T.W. 1918. The temperature of the Florida coral reef tract. Papers from the Tortugas

Laboratory of the Carnegie Institute of Washington 9:319-339.

Vincente, V.P. 1990. Response of sponges with autotrophic endosymbionts during the coral-bleaching episode in Puerto Rico (West Indies). Coral Reefs 8:199-202.

Voss, J.D. 2006. Coral disease dynamics and environmental drives in the northern Florida Keys and Lee Stocking Island, Bahamas. ETD Collection for Florida International University. Paper AAI3235620. Electronic document available from: http://digitalcommons.fiu.edu/dissertations/AAI3235620

Waddell, J.E. and A.M. Clarke (eds.). 2008. The State of Coral Reef Ecosystems of the United States and Pacific Freely Associated States: 2008. NOAA Technical Memorandum NOS NCCOS 73. NOAA/NCCOS Center for Coastal Monitoring and Assessment's Biogeography

Team. Silver Spring, MD. 569pp.

Wagner, D., E. Mielbrecht, R. van Woesik. 2008. Application of landscape ecology to spatio-temporal variance of water-quality parameters along the Florida Keys reef tract. Bull Marine Science 83(3):553-569.

Wagner, D., E.P. Kramer, R. van Woesik. 2010. Species composition, habitat, and water quality influence coral bleaching in south-eastern Florida. Marine Ecology Progress Series 408:65-78.

Wanless, H. R. and K. L. Maier. 2007. An evaluation of beach renourishment sands adjacent to reefal settings, Southeast Florida. Southeastern Geology 45:25-42.

Weil, E. 2004. Coral reef diseases in the wider Caribbean. *In*: E. Rosenberg and Y. Loya (Eds.). Coral health and disease. Springer: 35-68.

Wells, S.L. 1991. Notes on the history of Key West. Pgs. 80-83 *In*: The Monroe County Environmental Story. J. Gato and D. Gallagher (eds.), Monroe County Environmental Education Task Force, Big Pine Key, Florida.

Wilkinson, C., O. Lindén, H. Cesar, G. Hodgson, J. Rubens, A.E. Strong. 1999. Ecological and socioeconomic impacts of 1998 coral mortality in the Indian Ocean: an ENSO impact and a warning of future change? Ambio 28: 188-196.

Williams, D.E., M.W. Miller, K.L. Kramer. 2008. Recruitment failure in Florida Keys *Acropora palmata*, a threatened Caribbean coral. Coral Reefs 27:697-705.

Witherington, B., B. Kubilis, B. Brost, B. A. Meylan. 2009. Decreasing annual nest counts in a globally important loggerhead sea turtle population. Ecological Applications 19(1)30-54.

Witman, J.D. 1992. Physical disturbance and community structure of exposed and protected reefs: a case study. American Zoologist 32:641–654.

Witzell, W.N. 1998. The origin of the Florida sponge fishery. Marine Fisheries Review 60(1)27 – 32. Electronic document available from: http://spo.nmfs.noaa.gov/mfr601/mfr6012search.pdf

Zabel, R.W., C.J. Harvey, S.L. Katz, T.P. Good, P.S. Levin. 2003. Ecologically sustainable yield. American Scientist 9:150-157.

Zieman, J.C., J.W. Fourqurean, T.A. Frankovich. 1999. Seagrass die-off in Florida Bay: long-term trends in abundance and growth of turtle grass, *Thalassia testudinum*. Estuaries 22(2):460-470.

Additional Online Resources

Biscayne National Park: http://www.nps.gov/BISC

Coral Restoration Foundation: http://www.coralrestoration.org

Dry Tortugas National Park: http://www.nps.gov/drto

Encyclopedia of the Florida Keys: http://www8.nos.noaa.gov/onms/park/Parks/?pID=8

Everglades National Park: http://www.nps.gov/EVER

Florida Department of Environmental Protection: http://www.dep.state.fl.us/coastal/sites/keys

Florida Fish and Wildlife Conservation Commission: http://www.myfwc.com

Florida Keys Commercial Fishermen's Association: http://fkcfa.org/default.aspx

Florida Keys National Marine Sanctuary: http://floridakeys.noaa.gov

Florida Keys National Marine Sanctuary Shipwreck Trail: http://floridakeys.noaa.gov/shipwrecktrail/welcome.html

Florida Keys Online Guide: http://www.florida-keys.fl.us/history.htm

Florida Keys Sanctuary Science Summaries: http://floridakeys.noaa.gov/scisummaries/welcome.html

John Pennekamp Coral Reef State Park: http://www.pennekamppark.com

Marine Ecosystem Event Response and Assessment (MEERA) http://isurus.mote.org/Keys/meera.phtml

National Key Deer Refuge: http://www.fws.gov/nationalkeydeer

Naval Air Station (NAS) on Boca Chica: http://www.globalsecurity.org/military/facility/key_west.htm

Naval Air Station Key West: http://www.navy.mil/local/naskw

NOAA Coral Reef Watch: http://coralreefwatch.noaa.gov

NOAA Marine Debris Program: http://marinedebris.noaa.gov

NOAA National Marine Fisheries Service: http://www.nmfs.noaa.gov

NOAA National Ocean Service: http://oceanservice.noaa.gov

NOAA Office of National Marine Sanctuaries: http://sanctuaries.noaa.gov

Reef Environmental Education Foundation: http://www.reef.org

Reef Relief: http://reefrelief.org

Sanctuary Friends Foundation of the Florida Keys: http://www.sanctuaryfriends.org

State of Florida: http://www.myflorida.com

U.S. Coast Guard: http://www.uscg.mil

U.S. Fish and Wildlife Service: http://www.fws.gov

University of Miami Rosenstiel School of Marine and Atmospheric Science: http://www.rsmas.miami.edu

Appendix A:
Rating Scheme for System-Wide Monitoring Questions

The purpose of this appendix is to clarify the 17 questions and possible responses used to report the condition of sanctuary resources in "Condition Reports" for all national marine sanctuaries. Individual staff and partners utilized this guidance, as well as their own informed and detailed understanding of the site to make judgments about the status and trends of sanctuary resources.

The questions derive from the National Marine Sanctuary System's mission, and a system-wide monitoring framework (NMSP 2004) developed to ensure the timely flow of data and information to those responsible for managing and protecting resources in the ocean and coastal zone, and to those that use, depend on and study the ecosystems encompassed by the sanctuaries. They are being used to guide staff and partners at each of the 14 sites in the sanctuary system in the development of this first periodic sanctuary condition report. Evaluations of status and trends may be based on interpretation of quantitative and, when necessary, non-quantitative assessments and observations of scientists, managers and users.

Judging an ecosystem as having "integrity" implies the relative wholeness of ecosystem structure and function, along with the spatial and temporal variability inherent in these characteristics, as determined by the ecosystem's natural evolutionary history. Ecosystem integrity is reflected in the system's ability to produce and maintain adaptive biotic elements. Fluctuations of a system's natural characteristics, including abiotic drivers, biotic composition, complex relationships, and functional processes and redundancies are unaltered and are either likely to persist or be regained following natural disturbance.

Following a brief discussion about each question, statements are presented that were used to judge the status and assign a corresponding color code. These statements are customized for each question. In addition, the following options are available for all questions: "N/A" - the question does not apply; and "Undet." - resource status is undetermined.

Symbols used to indicate trends are the same for all questions: "▲" - conditions appear to be improving; "—" - conditions do not appear to be changing; "▼" - conditions appear to be declining; and "?" – trend is undetermined.

Water Stressors

1. **Are specific or multiple stressors, including changing oceanographic and atmospheric conditions, affecting water quality and how are they changing?**

This is meant to capture shifts in condition arising from certain changing physical processes and anthropogenic inputs. Factors resulting in regionally accelerated rates of change in water temperature, salinity, dissolved oxygen, or water clarity, could all be judged to reduce water quality. Localized changes in circulation or sedimentation resulting, for example, from coastal construction or dredge spoil disposal, can affect light penetration, salinity regimes, oxygen levels, productivity, waste transport, and other factors that influence habitat and living resource quality. Human inputs, generally in the form of contaminants from point or non-point sources, including fertilizers, pesticides, hydrocarbons, heavy metals, and sewage, are common causes of environmental degradation, often in combination rather than alone. Certain biotoxins, such as domoic acid, may be of particular interest to specific sanctuaries. When present in the water column, any of these contaminants can affect marine life by direct contact or ingestion, or through bioaccumulation via the food chain.

[Note: Over time, accumulation in sediments can sequester and concentrate contaminants. Their effects may manifest only when the sediments are resuspended during storm or other energetic events. In such cases, reports of status should be made under Question 7 – Habitat contaminants.]

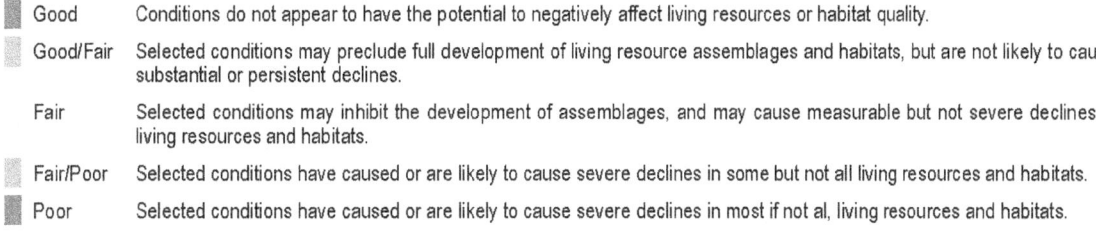

Good	Conditions do not appear to have the potential to negatively affect living resources or habitat quality.	
Good/Fair	Selected conditions may preclude full development of living resource assemblages and habitats, but are not likely to cause substantial or persistent declines.	
Fair	Selected conditions may inhibit the development of assemblages, and may cause measurable but not severe declines in living resources and habitats.	
Fair/Poor	Selected conditions have caused or are likely to cause severe declines in some but not all living resources and habitats.	
Poor	Selected conditions have caused or are likely to cause severe declines in most if not al, living resources and habitats.	

Water Eutrophic Condition

2. | **What is the eutrophic condition of sanctuary waters and how is it changing?**

Nutrient enrichment often leads to planktonic and/or benthic algae blooms. Some affect benthic communities directly through space competition. Overgrowth and other competitive interactions (e.g., accumulation of algal-sediment mats) often lead to shifts in dominance in the benthic assemblage. Disease incidence and frequency can also be affected by algae competition and the resulting chemistry along competitive boundaries. Blooms can also affect water column conditions, including light penetration and plankton availability, which can alter pelagic food webs. Harmful algal blooms often affect resources, as biotoxins are released into the water and air, and oxygen can be depleted.

	Good	Conditions do not appear to have the potential to negatively affect living resources or habitat quality.
	Good/Fair	Selected conditions may preclude full development of living resource assemblages and habitats, but are not likely to cause substantial or persistent declines.
	Fair	Selected conditions may inhibit the development of assemblages, and may cause measurable but not severe declines in living resources and habitats.
	Fair/Poor	Selected conditions have caused or are likely to cause severe declines in some but not all living resources and habitats.
	Poor	Selected conditions have caused or are likely to cause severe declines in most if not all living resources and habitats.

Water Human Health

3. | **Do sanctuary waters pose risks to human health and how are they changing?**

Human health concerns are generally aroused by evidence of contamination (usually bacterial or chemical) in bathing waters or fish intended for consumption. They also emerge when harmful algal blooms are reported or when cases of respiratory distress or other disorders attributable to harmful algal blooms increase dramatically. Any of these conditions should be considered in the course of judging the risk to humans posed by waters in a marine sanctuary.

Some sites may have access to specific information on beach and shellfish conditions. In particular, beaches may be closed when criteria for safe water body contact are exceeded, or shellfish harvesting may be prohibited when contaminant loads or infection rates exceed certain levels. These conditions can be evaluated in the context of the descriptions below.

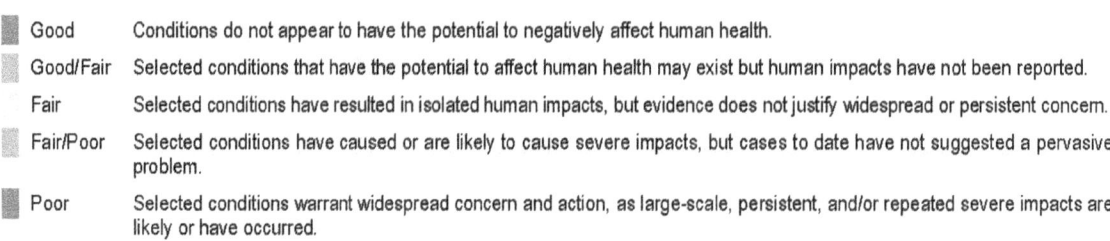

	Good	Conditions do not appear to have the potential to negatively affect human health.
	Good/Fair	Selected conditions that have the potential to affect human health may exist but human impacts have not been reported.
	Fair	Selected conditions have resulted in isolated human impacts, but evidence does not justify widespread or persistent concern.
	Fair/Poor	Selected conditions have caused or are likely to cause severe impacts, but cases to date have not suggested a pervasive problem.
	Poor	Selected conditions warrant widespread concern and action, as large-scale, persistent, and/or repeated severe impacts are likely or have occurred.

Water
Human Activities

4. What are the levels of human activities that may influence water quality and how are they changing?

Among the human activities in or near sanctuaries that affect water quality are those involving direct discharges (transiting vessels, visiting vessels, onshore and offshore industrial facilities, public wastewater facilities), those that contribute contaminants to stream, river, and water control discharges (agriculture, runoff from impermeable surfaces through storm drains, conversion of land use), and those releasing airborne chemicals that subsequently deposit via particulates at sea (vessels, land-based traffic, power plants, manufacturing facilities, refineries). In addition, dredging and trawling can cause resuspension of contaminants in sediments.

Good	Few or no activities occur that are likely to negatively affect water quality.
Good/Fair	Some potentially harmful activities exist, but they do not appear to have had a negative effect on water quality.
Fair	Selected activities have resulted in measurable resource impacts, but evidence suggests effects are localized, not widespread.
Fair/Poor	Selected activities have caused or are likely to cause severe impacts, and cases to date suggest a pervasive problem.
Poor	Selected activities warrant widespread concern and action, as large-scale, persistent, and/or repeated severe impacts have occurred or are likely to occur.

Habitat
Abundance & Distribution

5. What are the abundance and distribution of major habitat types and how are they changing?

Habitat loss is of paramount concern when it comes to protecting marine and terrestrial ecosystems. Of greatest concern to sanctuaries are changes caused, either directly or indirectly, by human activities. The loss of shoreline is recognized as a problem indirectly caused by human activities. Habitats with submerged aquatic vegetation are often altered by changes in water conditions in estuaries, bays, and nearshore waters. Intertidal zones can be affected for long periods by spills or by chronic pollutant exposure. Beaches and haul-out areas can be littered with dangerous marine debris, as can the water column or benthic habitats. Sandy subtidal areas and hardbottoms are frequently disturbed or destroyed by trawling. Even rocky areas several hundred meters deep are increasingly affected by certain types of trawls, bottom longlines, and fish traps. Groundings, anchors, and divers damage submerged reefs. Cables and pipelines disturb corridors across numerous habitat types and can be destructive if they become mobile. Shellfish dredging removes, alters, and fragments habitats.

The result of these activities is the gradual reduction of the extent and quality of marine habitats. Losses can often be quantified through visual surveys and to some extent using high-resolution mapping. This question asks about the quality of habitats compared to those that would be expected without human impacts. The status depends on comparison to a baseline that existed in the past - one toward which restoration efforts might aim.

Good	Habitats are in pristine or near-pristine condition and are unlikely to preclude full community development.
Good/Fair	Selected habitat loss or alteration has taken place, precluding full development of living resource assemblages, but it is unlikely to cause substantial or persistent degradation in living resources or water quality.
Fair	Selected habitat loss or alteration may inhibit the development of assemblages, and may cause measurable but not severe declines in living resources or water quality.
Fair/Poor	Selected habitat loss or alteration has caused or is likely to cause severe declines in some but not all living resources or water quality.
Poor	Selected habitat loss or alteration has caused or is likely to cause severe declines in most if not all living resources or water quality.

Habitat Structure

6. | **What is the condition of biologically structured habitats and how is it changing?**

Many organisms depend on the integrity of their habitats and that integrity is largely determined by the condition of particular living organisms. Coral reefs may be the best known examples of such biologically-structured habitats. Not only is the substrate itself biogenic, but the diverse assemblages residing within and on the reefs depend on and interact with each other in tightly linked food webs. They also depend on each other for the recycling of wastes, hygiene, and the maintenance of water quality, among other requirements.

Kelp beds may not be biogenic habitats to the extent of coral reefs, but kelp provides essential habitat for assemblages that would not reside or function together without it. There are other communities of organisms that are also similarly co-dependent, such as hard-bottom communities, which may be structured by bivalves, octocorals, coralline algae, or other groups that generate essential habitat for other species. Intertidal assemblages structured by mussels, barnacles, and algae are another example, seagrass beds another. This question is intended to address these types of places, where organisms form structures (habitats) on which other organisms depend.

Good	Habitats are in pristine or near-pristine condition and are unlikely to preclude full community development.
Good/Fair	Selected habitat loss or alteration has taken place, precluding full development of living resources, but it is unlikely to cause substantial or persistent degradation in living resources or water quality.
Fair	Selected habitat loss or alteration may inhibit the development of living resources, and may cause measurable but not severe declines in living resources or water quality.
Fair/Poor	Selected habitat loss or alteration has caused or is likely to cause severe declines in some but not all living resources or water quality.
Poor	Selected habitat loss or alteration has caused or is likely to cause severe declines in most if not all living resources or water quality.

Habitat Contaminants

7. | **What are the contaminant concentrations in sanctuary habitats and how are they changing?**

This question addresses the need to understand the risk posed by contaminants within benthic formations, such as soft sediments, hard bottoms, or biogenic organisms. In the first two cases, the contaminants can become available when released via disturbance. They can also pass upwards through the food chain after being ingested by bottom dwelling prey species. The contaminants of concern generally include pesticides, hydrocarbons, and heavy metals, but the specific concerns of individual sanctuaries may differ substantially.

Good	Contaminants do not appear to have the potential to negatively affect living resources or water quality.
Good/Fair	Selected contaminants may preclude full development of living resource assemblages, but are not likely to cause substantial or persistent degradation.
Fair	Selected contaminants may inhibit the development of assemblages, and may cause measurable but not severe declines in living resources or water quality.
Fair/Poor	Selected contaminants have caused or are likely to cause severe declines in some but not all living resources or water quality.
Poor	Selected contaminants have caused or are likely to cause severe declines in most if not all living resources or water quality.

Human Activities
Habitat

8. | **What are the levels of human activities that may influence habitat quality and how are they changing?**

Human activities that degrade habitat quality do so by affecting structural (geological), biological, oceanographic, acoustic, or chemical characteristics. Structural impacts include removal or mechanical alteration, including various fishing techniques (trawls, traps, dredges, longlines, and even hook-and-line in some habitats), dredging channels and harbors and dumping spoil, vessel groundings, anchoring, laying pipelines and cables, installing offshore structures, discharging drill cuttings, dragging tow cables, and placing artificial reefs. Removal or alteration of critical biological components of habitats can occur along with several of the above activities, most notably trawling, groundings, and cable drags. Marine debris, particularly in large quantities (e.g., lost gillnets and other types of fishing gear), can affect both biological and structural habitat components. Changes in water circulation often occur when channels are dredged, fill is added, coastal areas are reinforced, or other construction takes place. These activities affect habitat by changing food delivery, waste removal, water quality (e.g., salinity, clarity and sedimentation), recruitment patterns, and a host of other factors. Acoustic impacts can occur to water column habitats and organisms from acute and chronic sources of anthropogenic noise (e.g., shipping, boating, construction). Chemical alterations most commonly occur following spills and can have both acute and chronic impacts.

Good	Few or no activities occur that are likely to negatively affect habitat quality.
Good/Fair	Some potentially harmful activities exist, but they do not appear to have had a negative effect on habitat quality.
Fair	Selected activities have resulted in measurable habitat impacts, but evidence suggests effects are localized, not widespread.
Fair/Poor	Selected activities have caused or are likely to cause severe impacts, and cases to date suggest a pervasive problem.
Poor	Selected activities warrant widespread concern and action, as large-scale, persistent, and/or repeated severe impacts have occurred or are likely to occur.

Biodiversity
Living Resources

9. | **What is the status of biodiversity and how is it changing?**

This is intended to elicit thought and assessment of the condition of living resources based on expected biodiversity levels and the interactions between species. Intact ecosystems require that all parts not only exist, but that they function together, resulting in natural symbioses, competition, and predator-prey relationships. Community integrity, resistance and resilience all depend on these relationships. Abundance, relative abundance, trophic structure, richness, H' diversity, evenness, and other measures are often used to assess these attributes.

Good	Biodiversity appears to reflect pristine or near-pristine conditions and promotes ecosystem integrity (full community development and function).
Good/Fair	Selected biodiversity loss has taken place, precluding full community development and function, but it is unlikely to cause substantial or persistent degradation of ecosystem integrity.
Fair	Selected biodiversity loss may inhibit full community development and function, and may cause measurable but not severe degradation of ecosystem integrity.
Fair/Poor	Selected biodiversity loss has caused or is likely to cause severe declines in some but not all ecosystem components and reduce ecosystem integrity.
Poor	Selected biodiversity loss has caused or is likely to cause severe declines in ecosystem integrity.

Living Resources
Extracted Species

10. | **What is the status of environmentally sustainable fishing and how is it changing?**

Commercial and recreational harvesting are highly selective activities, for which fishers and collectors target a limited number of species, and often remove high proportions of populations. In addition to removing significant amounts of biomass from the ecosystem, reducing its availability to other consumers, these activities tend to disrupt specific and often critical food web links. When too much extraction occurs (i.e. ecologically unsustainable harvesting), trophic cascades ensue, resulting in changes in the abundance of non-targeted species as well. It also reduces the ability of the targeted species to replenish populations at a rate that supports continued ecosystem integrity.

It is essential to understand whether removals are occurring at ecologically sustainable levels. Knowing extraction levels and determining the impacts of removal are both ways that help gain this understanding. Measures for target species of abundance, catch amounts or rates (e.g., catch per unit effort), trophic structure, and changes in non-target species abundance are all generally used to assess these conditions.

Other issues related to this question include whether fishers are using gear that is compatible with the habitats being fished and whether that gear minimizes by-catch and incidental take of marine mammals. For example, bottom-tending gear often destroys or alters both benthic structure and non-targeted animal and plant communities. "Ghost fishing" occurs when lost traps continue to capture organisms. Lost or active nets, as well as lines used to mark and tend traps and other fishing gear, can entangle marine mammals. Any of these could be considered indications of environmentally unsustainable fishing techniques.

▦	Good	Extraction does not appear to affect ecosystem integrity (full community development and function).
▦	Good/Fair	Extraction takes place, precluding full community development and function, but it is unlikely to cause substantial or persistent degradation of ecosystem integrity.
	Fair	Extraction may inhibit full community development and function, and may cause measurable but not severe degradation of ecosystem integrity.
▦	Fair/Poor	Extraction has caused or is likely to cause severe declines in some but not all ecosystem components and reduce ecosystem integrity.
▦	Poor	Extraction has caused or is likely to cause severe declines in ecosystem integrity.

Living Resources
Non-Indigenous Species

11. | **What is the status of non-indigenous species and how is it changing?**

Non-indigenous species are generally considered problematic, and candidates for rapid response, if found, soon after invasion. For those that become established, their impacts can sometimes be assessed by quantifying changes in the affected native species. This question allows sanctuaries to report on the threat posed by non-indigenous species. In some cases, the presence of a species alone constitutes a significant threat (certain invasive algae). In other cases, impacts have been measured, and may or may not significantly affect ecosystem integrity.

▦	Good	Non-indigenous species are not suspected or do not appear to affect ecosystem integrity (full community development and function).
▦	Good/Fair	Non-indigenous species exist, precluding full community development and function, but are unlikely to cause substantial or persistent degradation of ecosystem integrity.
	Fair	Non-indigenous species may inhibit full community development and function, and may cause measurable but not severe degradation of ecosystem integrity.
▦	Fair/Poor	Non-indigenous species have caused or are likely to cause severe declines in some but not all ecosystem components and reduce ecosystem integrity.
▦	Poor	Non-indigenous species have caused or are likely to cause severe declines in ecosystem integrity.

Living Resources
Key Species

12. | **What is the status of key species and how is it changing?**

Certain species can be defined as "key" within a marine sanctuary. Some might be keystone species, that is, species on which the persistence of a large number of other species in the ecosystem depends - the pillar of community stability. Their functional contribution to ecosystem function is disproportionate to their numerical abundance or biomass and their impact is therefore important at the community or ecosystem level. Their removal initiates changes in ecosystem structure and sometimes the disappearance of or dramatic increase in the abundance of dependent species. Keystone species may include certain habitat modifiers, predators, herbivores, and those involved in critical symbiotic relationships (e.g. cleaning or co-habitating species).

Other key species may include those that are indicators of ecosystem condition or change (e.g., particularly sensitive species), those targeted for special protection efforts, or charismatic species that are identified with certain areas or ecosystems. These may or may not meet the definition of keystone, but do require assessments of status and trends.

Good	Key and keystone species appear to reflect pristine or near-pristine conditions and may promote ecosystem integrity (full community development and function).
Good/Fair	Selected key or keystone species are at reduced levels, perhaps precluding full community development and function, but substantial or persistent declines are not expected.
Fair	The reduced abundance of selected keystone species may inhibit full community development and function, and may cause measurable but not severe degradation of ecosystem integrity; or selected key species are at reduced levels, but recovery is possible.
Fair/Poor	The reduced abundance of selected keystone species has caused or is likely to cause severe declines in some but not all ecosystem components, and reduce ecosystem integrity; or selected key species are at substantially reduced levels, and prospects for recovery are uncertain.
Poor	The reduced abundance of selected keystone species has caused or is likely to cause severe declines in ecosystem integrity; or selected key species are a severely reduced levels, and recovery is unlikely.

Living Resources
Health of Key
Species

13. | **What is the condition or health of key species and how is it changing?**

For those species considered essential to ecosystem integrity, measures of their condition can be important to determining the likelihood that they will persist and continue to provide vital ecosystem functions. Measures of condition may include growth rates, fecundity, recruitment, age-specific survival, tissue contaminant levels, pathologies (disease incidence tumors, deformities), the presence and abundance of critical symbionts, or parasite loads. Similar measures of condition may also be appropriate for other key species (indicator, protected, or charismatic species). In contrast to the question about keystone species (#12 above), the impact of changes in the abundance or condition of key species is more likely to be observed at the population or individual level, and less likely to result in ecosystem or community effects.

Good	The condition of key resources appears to reflect pristine or near-pristine conditions.
Good/Fair	The condition of selected key resources is not optimal, perhaps precluding full ecological function, but substantial or persistent declines are not expected.
Fair	The diminished condition of selected key resources may cause a measurable but not severe reduction in ecological function, but recovery is possible.
Fair/Poor	The comparatively poor condition of selected key resources makes prospects for recovery uncertain.
Poor	The poor condition of selected key resources makes recovery unlikely.

Living Resources
Human Activities

14. | **What are the levels of human activities that may influence living resource quality and how are they changing?**

Human activities that degrade living resource quality do so by causing a loss or reduction of one or more species, by disrupting critical life stages, by impairing various physiological processes, or by promoting the introduction of non-indigenous species or pathogens. (Note: Activities that impact habitat and water quality may also affect living resources. These activities are dealt with in Questions 4 and 8, and many are repeated here as they also have direct effect on living resources).

Fishing and collecting are the primary means of removing resources. Bottom trawling, seine-fishing, and the collection of ornamental species for the aquarium trade are all common examples, some being more selective than others. Chronic mortality can be caused by marine debris derived from commercial or recreational vessel traffic, lost fishing gear, and excess visitation, resulting in the gradual loss of some species.

Critical life stages can be affected in various ways. Mortality to adult stages is often caused by trawling and other fishing techniques, cable drags, dumping spoil or drill cuttings, vessel groundings, or persistent anchoring. Contamination of areas by acute or chronic spills, discharges by vessels, or municipal and industrial facilities can make them unsuitable for recruitment; the same activities can make nursery habitats unsuitable. Although coastal armoring and construction can increase the availability of surfaces suitable for the recruitment and growth of hard bottom species, the activity may disrupt recruitment patterns for other species (e.g., intertidal soft bottom animals) and habitat may be lost.

Spills, discharges, and contaminants released from sediments (e.g., by dredging and dumping) can all cause physiological impairment and tissue contamination. Such activities can affect all life stages by reducing fecundity, increasing larval, juvenile, and adult mortality, reducing disease resistance, and increasing susceptibility to predation. Bioaccumulation allows some contaminants to move upward through the food chain, disproportionately affecting certain species.

Activities that promote introductions include bilge discharges and ballast water exchange, commercial shipping and vessel transportation. Releases of aquarium fish can also lead to species introductions.

	Good	Few or no activities occur that are likely to negatively affect living resource quality.
	Good/Fair	Some potentially harmful activities exist, but they do not appear to have had a negative effect on living resource quality.
	Fair	Selected activities have resulted in measurable living resource impacts, but evidence suggests effects are localized, not widespread.
	Fair/Poor	Selected activities have caused or are likely to cause severe impacts, and cases to date suggest a pervasive problem.
	Poor	Selected activities warrant widespread concern and action, as large-scale, persistent, and/or repeated severe impacts have occurred or are likely to occur.

Maritime Archaeological Resources Integrity

15. | **What is the integrity of known maritime archaeological resources and how is it changing?**

The condition of archaeological resources in a marine sanctuary significantly affects their value for science and education, as well as the resource's eligibility for listing in the National Register of Historic Places. Assessments of archaeological sites include evaluation of the apparent levels of site integrity, which are based on levels of previous human disturbance and the level of natural deterioration. The historical, scientific and educational values of sites are also evaluated, and are substantially determined and affected by site condition.

Good	Known archaeological resources appear to reflect little or no unexpected disturbance.
Good/Fair	Selected archaeological resources exhibit indications of disturbance, but there appears to have been little or no reduction in historical, scientific, or educational value.
Fair	The diminished condition of selected archaeological resources has reduced, to some extent, their historical, scientific, or educational value, and may affect the eligibility of some sites for listing in the National Register of Historic Places.
Fair/Poor	The diminished condition of selected archaeological resources has substantially reduced their historical, scientific, or educational value, and is likely to affect their eligibility for listing in the National Register of Historic Places.
Poor	The degraded condition of known archaeological resources in general makes them ineffective in terms of historical, scientific, or educational value, and precludes their listing in the National Register of Historic Places.

Maritime Archaeological Resources Threat to Environment

16. | **Do known maritime archaeological resources pose an environmental hazard and how is this threat changing?**

The sinking of a ship potentially introduces hazardous materials into the marine environment. This danger is true for historic shipwrecks as well. The issue is complicated by the fact that shipwrecks older than 50 years may be considered historical resources and must, by federal mandate, be protected. Many historic shipwrecks, particularly early to mid-20th century, still have the potential to retain oil and fuel in tanks and bunkers. As shipwrecks age and deteriorate, the potential for release of these materials into the environment increases.

Good	Known maritime archaeological resources pose few or no environmental threats.
Good/Fair	Selected maritime archaeological resources may pose isolated or limited environmental threats, but substantial or persistent impacts are not expected.
Fair	Selected maritime archaeological resources may cause measurable, but not severe, impacts to certain sanctuary resources or areas, but recovery is possible.
Fair/Poor	Selected maritime archaeological resources pose substantial threats to certain sanctuary resources or areas, and prospects for recovery are uncertain.
Poor	Selected maritime archaeological resources pose serious threats to sanctuary resources, and recovery is unlikely.

Maritime Archaeological Resources
Human Activities

17. **What are the levels of human activities that may influence maritime archaeological resource quality and how are they changing?**

Some human maritime activities threaten the physical integrity of submerged archaeological resources. Archaeological site integrity is compromised when elements are moved, removed, or otherwise damaged. Threats come from looting by divers, inadvertent damage by scuba diving visitors, improperly conducted archaeology that does not fully document site disturbance, anchoring, groundings, and commercial and recreational fishing activities, among others.

	Good	Few or no activities occur that are likely to negatively affect maritime archaeological resource integrity.
	Good/Fair	Some potentially relevant activities exist, but they do not appear to have had a negative effect on maritime archaeological resource integrity.
	Fair	Selected activities have resulted in measurable impacts to maritime archaeological resources, but evidence suggests effects are localized, not widespread.
	Fair/Poor	Selected activities have caused or are likely to cause severe impacts, and cases to date suggest a pervasive problem.
	Poor	Selected activities warrant widespread concern and action, as large-scale, persistent, and/or repeated severe impacts have occurred or are likely to occur.

Appendix B:
Consultation with Experts and Document Review

The process for preparing condition reports involves a combination of accepted techniques for collecting and interpreting information gathered from subject matter experts. The approach varies somewhat from sanctuary to sanctuary in order to accommodate differing styles for working with partners. The Florida Keys National Marine Sanctuary approach was closely related to the Delphi Method, a technique designed to organize group communication among a panel of geographically dispersed experts by using questionnaires, ultimately facilitating the formation of a group judgment. This method can be applied when it is necessary for decision-makers to combine the testimony of a group of experts, whether in the form of facts or informed opinion, or both, into a single useful statement.

The Delphi Method relies on repeated interactions with experts who respond to questions with a limited number of choices to arrive at the best supported answers. Feedback to the experts allows them to refine their views, gradually moving the group toward the most agreeable judgment. For condition reports, the Office of National Marine Sanctuaries uses 17 questions related to the status and trends of sanctuary resources, with accompanying descriptions and five possible choices that describe resource conditions.

In order to address the 17 questions, sanctuary staff selected and consulted outside experts familiar with water quality, living resources, habitat, and maritime archaeological resources. Phone calls and one-on-one meetings were convened where experts participated in discussions with sanctuary staff about each of the 17 questions. Experts represented various affiliations including Florida Fish and Wildlife Conservation Commission, Florida International University, Florida Keys National Marine Sanctuary, Mote Marine Laboratory, NOAA National Marine Fisheries Service, Reef Environment Education Foundation, University of Miami Rosenstiel School of Marine and Atmospheric Science, and the University of North Carolina Wilmington. During each consultation, experts were introduced to the questions and asked to provide recommendations and supporting arguments for their suggested rating. The ratings and text found in the report are intended to summarize the opinions and uncertainty expressed by the experts, who based their input on knowledge and perceptions of local conditions. Comments and citations received from the experts were included, as appropriate, in text supporting the ratings.

The first draft of the document was sent to various subject matter experts and important partners in research and resource management for what was called an Invited Review. Individuals included representatives from Audubon Society, Coral Restoration Foundation, Department of Primary Industries and Fisheries, Environmental Protection Agency (Wetlands, Coastal and Oceans Branch and Special Studies), Florida Department of Health, Florida Fish and Wildlife Conservation Commission, Florida Keys National Marine Sanctuary, Georgia Institute of Technology, Naval Air Station Key West, NOAA Corps, NOAA National Marine Fisheries Service, Reef Environmental Education Foundation, University of Miami Rosenstiel School of

Marine and Atmospheric Science, and the University of North Carolina Wilmington. Individuals were asked to review the technical merits of resource ratings and accompanying text, as well as to point out any omissions or factual errors. The comments and recommendations of invited reviewers were received, considered by sanctuary staff, and incorporated, as appropriate, into a final draft document.

A draft final report was then sent to John F. Bruno, Ph.D. (Associate Professor, The University of North Carolina at Chapel Hill), Richard E. Dodge, Ph.D. (Dean, Nova Southeastern University Oceanographic Center), Paul Sammarco, Ph.D. (Professor, Louisiana Universities Marine Consortium), and Rob van Woesik, Ph.D. (Professor, Florida Institute of Technology) who served as external peer reviewers. This External Peer Review is a requirement that started in December 2004, when the White House Office of Management and Budget (OMB) issued a Final Information Quality Bulletin for Peer Review (OMB Bulletin), establishing peer-review standards that would enhance the quality and credibility of the federal government's scientific information. Along with other information, these standards apply to Influential Scientific Information, which is information that can reasonably be determined to have a "clear and substantial impact on important public policies or private sector decisions." The Condition Reports are considered Influential Scientific Information, and for this reason, are subject to the review requirements of both the Information Quality Act and the OMB Bulletin guidelines. Therefore, following the completion of every condition report, they are reviewed by a minimum of three individuals who are considered to be experts in their field, were not involved in the development of the report, and are not Office of National Marine Sanctuaries employees. Comments from these peer reviews are incorporated into the final text of the report. Furthermore, OMB Bulletin guidelines require that reviewer comments, names, and affiliations be posted on the agency website: http://www.cio.noaa.gov/Policy_Programs/prplans/PRsummaries. html. Reviewer comments, however, are not attributed to specific individuals. Reviewer comments are posted at the same time as with the formatted final document. Following the External Peer Review, the comments and recommendations of the reviewers were considered by sanctuary staff and incorporated, as appropriate, into a final draft document. In some cases sanctuary staff reevaluated the status and trend ratings and when appropriate, the accompanying text in the document was edited to reflect the new ratings. The final interpretation, ratings, and text in the draft condition report were the responsibility of sanctuary staff, with final approval by the sanctuary manager. To emphasize this important point, authorship of the report is attributed to the sanctuary alone. Subject experts were not authors, though their efforts and affiliations are acknowledged in the report.

Notes

THE NATIONAL MARINE SANCTUARY SYSTEM

The Office of National Marine Sanctuaries, part of the National Oceanic and Atmospheric Administration, serves as the trustee for a system of 14 marine protected areas encompassing more than 150,000 square miles of ocean and Great Lakes waters. The 13 national marine sanctuaries and one marine national monument within the National Marine Sanctuary System represent areas of America's ocean and Great Lakes environment that are of special national significance. Within their waters, giant humpback whales breed and calve their young, coral colonies flourish, and shipwrecks tell stories of our maritime history. Habitats include beautiful coral reefs, lush kelp forests, whale migrations corridors, spectacular deep-sea canyons, and underwater archaeological sites. These special places also provide homes to thousands of unique or endangered species and are important to America's cultural heritage. Sites range in size from less than one to almost 140,000 square miles and serve as natural classrooms, cherished recreational spots, and are home to valuable commercial industries.

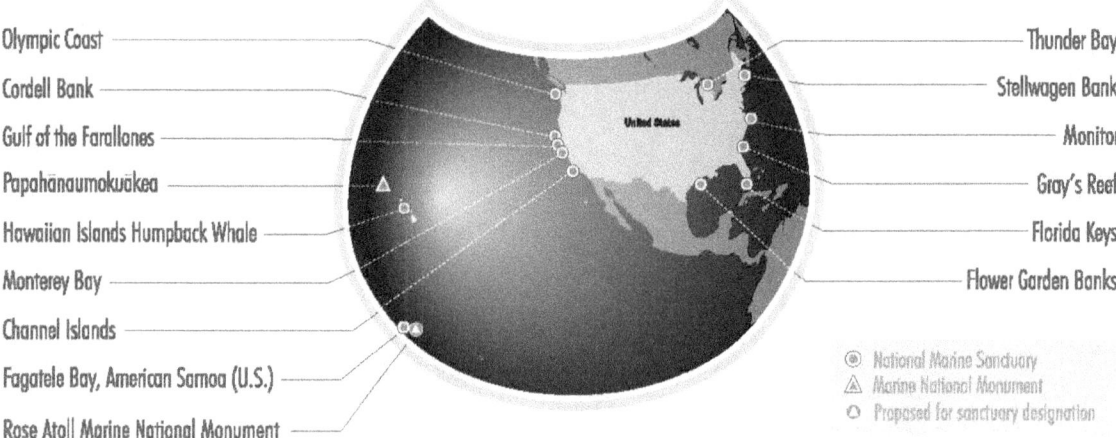

Olympic Coast — Thunder Bay
Cordell Bank — Stellwagen Bank
Gulf of the Farallones — Monitor
Papahānaumokuākea — Gray's Reef
Hawaiian Islands Humpback Whale — Florida Keys
Monterey Bay — Flower Garden Banks
Channel Islands
Fagatele Bay, American Samoa (U.S.)
Rose Atoll Marine National Monument

⦿ National Marine Sanctuary
△ Marine National Monument
○ Proposed for sanctuary designation

Scale varies in this perspective. Adapted from National Geographic Maps.

The Office of National Marine Sanctuaries is part of NOAA's National Ocean Service.

VISION – People value marine sanctuaries as treasured places protected for future generations.

MISSION – To serve as the trustee for the nation's system of marine protected areas to conserve, protect and enhance their biodiversity, ecological integrity and cultural legacy.

NATIONAL MARINE SANCTUARIES